Social Welfare in Pre-Industri

SOCIAL HISTORY IN PERSPECTIVE

Social History in Perspective
General Editor: Jeremy Black

Social History in Perspective is a series of in-depth studies of the many topics in social, cultural and religious history.

PUBLISHED

John Belchem *Popular Radicalism in Nineteenth-Century Britain*
Sue Bruley *Women in Britain Since 1900*
Anthony Brundage *The English Poor Laws, 1700–1930*
Simon Dentith *Society and Cultural Forms in Nineteenth-Century England*
Joyce M. Ellis *The Georgian Town, 1680–1840*
Paul A. Fideler *Social Welfare in Pre-Industrial England*
Peter Fleming *Family and Household in Medieval England*
Ian Gazeley *Poverty in Britain, 1900–1965*
Kathryn Gleadle *British Women in the Nineteenth Century*
Harry Goulbourne *Race Relations in Britain since 1945*
Anne Hardy *Health and Medicine in Britain since 1860*
Tim Hitchcock *English Sexualities, 1700–1800*
Sybil M. Jack *Towns in Tudor and Stuart Britain*
Helen M. Jewell *Education in Early Modern England*
Alan Kidd *State, Society and the Poor in Nineteenth-Century England*
Peter Kirby *Child Labour in Britain, 1750–1870*
Arthur J. McIvor *A History of Work in Britain, 1880–1950*
Hugh McLeod *Religion and Society in England, 1850–1914*
Donald M. MacRaild *Irish Migrants in Modern Britain, 1750–1922*
Donald M. MacRaild and David E. Martin *Labour in Britain, 1830–1914*
Christopher Marsh *Popular Religion in the Sixteenth Century*
Michael A. Mullett *Catholics in Britain and Ireland, 1558–1829*
Christine Peters *Women in Early Modern Britain, 1450–1640*
Richard Rex *The Lollards*
George Robb *British Culture and the First World War*
R. Malcolm Smuts *Culture and Power in England, 1585–1685*
John Spurr *English Puritanism, 1603–1689*
W. B. Stephens *Education in Britain, 1750–1914*
Heather Swanson *Medieval British Towns*
David Taylor *Crime, Policing and Punishment in England, 1750–1914*
N. L. Tranter *British Population in the Twentieth Century*
Ian D. Whyte *Migration and Society in Britain, 1550–1830*
Ian D. Whyte *Scotland's Society and Economy in Transition, c.1500–c.1760*
Andy Wood *Riot, Rebellion and Popular Politics in Early Modern England*

Please note that a sister series, *British History in Perspective*, is available, covering key topics in British political history.

Social Welfare in Pre-Industrial England

The Old Poor Law Tradition

PAUL A. FIDELER

For Liz

© Paul A. Fideler 2006

First published 2006 by
PALGRAVE MACMILLAN
Houndmills, Basingstoke, Hampshire RG21 6XS and
175 Fifth Avenue, New York, N.Y. 10010
Companies and representatives throughout the world

PALGRAVE MACMILLAN is the global academic imprint of the Palgrave Macmillan division of St. Martin's Press, LLC and of Palgrave Macmillan Ltd. Macmillan® is a registered trademark in the United States, United Kingdom and other countries. Palgrave is a registered trademark in the European Union and other countries.

ISBN-13: 978–0–333–68894–6 hardback
ISBN-10: 0–333–68894–5 hardback
ISBN-13: 978–0–333–68895–3 paperback
ISBN-10: 0–333–68895–3 paperback

This book is printed on paper suitable for recycling and made from fully managed and sustained forest sources.

A catalogue record for this book is available from the British Library.

A catalog record for this book is available from the Library of Congress.

10   9   8   7   6   5   4   3   2   1
15   14   13   12   11   10   09   08   07   06

Printed in China

Contents

Acknowledgments

This book found its own circuitous path to completion, and along the way I have benefited from the support of many persons and institutions. My brief expressions of gratitude here and the book itself are testimony to this. Different aspects of the wide-ranging perspectives I bring to the study of pre-industrial social welfare have been inspired and at times encouraged generously by Jeremy Black, Marjorie McIntosh, John Pocock, Joe Slavin, and Keith Wrightson. Of course, they bear no responsibility for what I may have done with their well-intended interest in my work.

My colleagues in the humanities faculty at Lesley University have taught me much, and Mary Dockray-Miller read and commented on a portion of the manuscript. The staff of the Ludcke Library here have helped immeasurably in furthering my teaching and scholarly interests. And in countless visits to the Houghton and Widener Libraries at Harvard University, the Kress Library and the Goldsmiths-Kress Collection at the Baker Library of the Harvard Business School, the Folger Shakespeare Library, and the Library of Congress responsive librarians and their skilled staffs have made my work easier.

Terka Acton and Sonya Barker reacted with flexibility and good will as the scope of the project grew and deadlines had to be renegotiated. The final manuscript preparation was moved forward ever so much by the resourcefulness and word-processing skills of Katie C. Donahue and the extraordinary copy-editing care of Penny Simmons. Finally, to my wife, Liz, my gratitude is almost beyond expressing. Her devotion, limitless patience, critical insights and reading, and encouragement through thick and thin, made the book's completion possible.

The author gratefully acknowledges permission from Taylor and Francis Publishers to use material previously published in: Paul A. Fideler, 'Poverty, Policy and Providence: The Tudors and the Poor', in Fideler and T. F. Mayer, eds, *Political Thought and the Tudor Commonweal* (London and New York, Routledge, 1992), ch. 7.

Note

With the exception of book titles, all materials quoted have been modernized in spelling and capitalization.

Introduction

Some may think this to be an overly ambitious study. It spans the development of local, parish-centered poverty or 'poor' relief and related undertakings from their emerging coherence in the four-teenth and fifteenth centuries through to their effective demise around 1800. Over the course of those 400 plus years the English people shaped a medieval social and commercial order infused with Christian purpose, calibrated themselves to the social changes and expanding government of the early modern years, and reacted with hope and trepidation to the myriad challenges of early industrializa-tion. Crossing boundaries to formulate a history of *longue durée* such as this surely will attract suspicion from period specialists. If, in addition, one seeks to integrate many themes into the narrative – in the spirit, if not the extraordinary level of accomplishment, of Miri Rubin's 'total history' approach to charity in medieval Cambridge[1] – the likelihood of raising the concerns of social, economic, demographic, intellectual, and cultural historians, among others, is heightened as well. In this regard, E. A. Wrigley and R. S. Schofield commented wisely about the 'constant tension between clarity and comprehension' they faced in reconstructing England's pre-industrial population history. It seemed that if one was 'to be obtained, the other must be sacrificed in some degree.'[2] While we might hope that clarity and comprehension are not mutually exclusive and achieving them both should be our goal, Wrigley and Schofield's candor on that likelihood stands as a caution. Why, then, attempt a chronologically long, conceptually broad, and critically vulnerable study of pre-modern social welfare? Because it is needed.

Since the first studies of English social welfare history were undertaken in the later eighteenth century (see Chapter 6), the genre often has been hostage to the concerns of historians about the quality of social welfare in their own time. For instance, Sir Frederic Eden and Thomas Ruggles in the 1790s used their histories of poverty and poor relief to support their differing views on whether the Elizabethan Poor Law should be abolished or reaffirmed. A bit more than 100 years later, in the first quarter of the twentieth century, pre-modern social welfare historiography and attention to the Poor Law were given an enormous boost in the works of E. M. Leonard, Sidney and Beatrice Webb, and R. H. Tawney, each of whom was committed to an expanded role for the government in Britain's social welfare.[3] The advent of the new social and anthropological history in the 1950s and social reform-oriented 1960s brought to the fore renewed attention to the poor and other 'silent' cohorts in the past. And, roughly two decades later, perceived threats to the welfare state in Prime Minister Margaret Thatcher's policies called forth yet another wave of interest in the lessons embedded in the history of social welfare.[4]

As vibrant as this corpus of work was and continues to be, it has been limited in different ways and degrees by several inclinations. One has been to focus too much on the development of the Poor Law to the detriment of charity, philanthropy, and hospitality. Another has been a reluctance to distinguish short-term policy ideas from deeper ideological currents that were shaping the social welfare agenda. Yet another has been the tendency to overlook the embedded nature of customary local relief predispositions and its irreconcilability with government policy mandates. And finally, periodization boundaries, although becoming much less of a problem generally, still limit our overall grasp of the abiding characteristics of pre-modern social welfare and the reasons for its endurance and eventual demise. Thus, it is time for an integrating study that will readjust our perspective on premodern social welfare chronologically, broaden it conceptually, and, perhaps, reduce the presentist cant in the historiography.

I have chosen to focus on the parish-centered character of pre-industrial social welfare and the array of influences that established its goals, its operations, and its degree of accomplishment for practitioners and recipients alike. This will require period boundary crossings from the later medieval to the early modern years and from the seventeenth to the long eighteenth century. The latter move is no longer particularly unusual, but the medieval–early modern one remains so. Peter Lake has made the important point on this matter. 'Early modernists,' he writes, 'are far too ignorant about the nature of late medieval society and politics'; and, this encourages them to proceed from a 'dimly perceived medieval background toward whatever aspect of modernity they [think] they were studying.'[5]

The chronological dimensions of the present study are shaped in part by an emerging consensus among economic historians that a pre-industrial, commercial and market economy took shape in England in the thirteenth and fourteenth centuries. And this economic footprint remained more or less recognizable until it was disrupted by the emerging industrial conditions of the later eighteenth century. Another historiographical shift, toward acknowledgement of a long Reformation, is also at play here. The 'three interrelated, but... distinct' objectives of the Reformation, 'de-Catholicization', 'Protestantization', and ultimately 'Christianization', span the sixteenth through the early nineteenth centuries. And, if Patrick Collinson is correct in suggesting that de-Catholicization began with Wyclif's pronouncements in the 1370s, the English Reformation was more than a five-centuries-long phenomenon.[6] From the vantage point of the parish in those years, the sectarian distinctions among, for example, Catholics, Lollards, Anglicans, Arminians, Puritans, Methodists, and Tractarians, which have tended to predominate in Reformation historiography, are often viewed now as more blurred and less mutually exclusive. Certainly there were differences and tensions, but, placed in a more encompassing perspective, we can appreciate the 'cycles of Reformation endeavor,' a succession of reformations, whose 'professed aims... were often strikingly similar.'[7]

I seek to demonstrate that parish-centered poor relief and its theological-ideological justification, which I identify initially as the medieval *societas christiana*, endured across the pre-industrial centuries. In the mid-fifteenth century they begin to vie with more secular theory and plans for government-mandated social welfare. Thus, in Chapter 1 I explore with some thoroughness the structure of the medieval economy; church-generated discussions of property, poverty, and charity; the emergence of parish-centered voluntary poor relief and health care; criticisms of the 'professional' poverty of monks, friars, and hardy vagrants; and the first stirrings of government social welfare policy. From these strands and others that emerge in subsequent chapters, I develop a 'plaited' narrative of pre-industrial social welfare. And throughout I will be assuming that 'late medieval,' 'early modern,' and the 'long-eighteenth-century' were phases or subperiods of 'pre-industrial or pre-modern England,' whose characteristics underpinned and bound all three.[8]

Parish-centered social welfare and pre-industrial institutions, thought, and commerce formed an interdependent whole that lasted for more than 400 years with, of course, many nuances along the way. The Elizabethan Poor Law (1598, 1601) did designate the parish as the civic poor relief agency of record. However, the uncomplicated arrangements that had emerged by the thirteenth and fourteenth centuries – funds generated by parish members' tithes and other contributions and then distributed to the local poor after some assessment to establish which of them were deserving and which not – proved to be formidable and long lasting. And it became clear early on that there were two cohorts of poor people. The 'afflicted poor' – known residents of a parish, town or locality who were unable to support themselves or their families because of old age, chronic mental or physical illness, fire or other calamities to their property, widow-hood, and, if children, the loss of parents – were cared for through the ministrations of the parish. The poverty 'problem,' on the other hand, most often had to do with those I will be calling the 'structural poor,' migrants or strangers unknown to the locals and apparently healthy but without gainful employment. They attracted far more suspicion and intended discipline than relief. In the ensuing chapters, I will assess the social, economic, and demographic changes as well as the episodic visitations of disease, dearth, economic collapse, social or political uprising, and price inflation that expanded or contracted the numbers of the structural poor. Equally important, I will explore the sequence of reauthorizations of the parish's responsibilities, beginning with the *societas christiana* mandates of the fourteenth and fifteenth centuries, through the humanist and Protestant reforms of the sixteenth century, the political arithmetic calculations of the seventeenth, and the contending philosophical and historical mandates of the eighteenth century.

A discomfort with narrative, particularly if it focuses on 'modernization' or the development of the state, is prominent in current historiography and is captured in the labels, 'center narrative' or 'Whiggish history,' which long since have become terms of opprobrium. This emerged from Foucauldian, post-colonial, and 'silent cohort' historians' chal-lenges to claims for the Enlightenment's hegemonic moral and intellec-tual importance and their endeavors to uncover the agency of its perceived victims. Applied to the study of pre-industrial England's social welfare, however, the Whig aversion has more to do with the exhaustion of government and reign-centered, top–down administrative history. The development of a new, more protean, pre-modern historiography has been under way for more than four decades. The point person in this, Peter Laslett, began in the late 1950s to fashion what has come to be known as the new social history or sociological history. Its goal was, and continues to be, to draw attention to the great number of English people, who by the lights of the old history 'stood in the background, in the penumbra of historical consciousness, while matters of significance were left to the consideration of a narrow circle of their betters'.[9]

The priorities of this new scholarship tend to place more emphasis on political culture, social levels, custom, and identity and less on national or macro-politics, government, law, and civil status. In a subtle and insightful formulation in 1996, Keith Wrightson pointed out that the new social history was not avoiding the political, however; the political already was embedded in the work. To appreciate this, we must broaden our definition of the political to embrace 'the social distribution and use of power' at all levels or simply 'the political dimensions of everyday life.' In the place of the old political history's penchant for narrative, the new social history favors 'process' or 'continuity and change.' And interpretive priorities are shifted from 'structures' and 'systems' to the more dynamic 'agency' and 'negotiation.'[10] This orientation offers many possibilities for approaching the history of poverty and poor relief in resourceful ways. It figures most prominently in Chapters 2, 3 and 4, in which I discuss the challenges that roiled rural and urban settings in the sixteenth and seventeenth centuries and the political processes involved in establishing one's eligibility for parish relief.

Nevertheless, along the way I will raise occasional questions about the nature and conclusions of sociological history. My intention is not to cast aspersions at what this insightful research has been teaching us about social welfare, much of which I am synthesizing in this study. It is rather to point out that sociological historiography, like any methodology, tends to be a self-contained discourse. Its assumptions inform a distinct conceptual vocabulary that shapes its stance toward the past. Much like Martin Rein's characterization of a 'perceptual frame', a historiography provides a 'way of inquiry, of *making* sense as well as *masking* sense of the world.' I hope to supplement what the new social history has been making sense about by focusing some attention on what is has been masking. For example, in the social welfare story national politics must continue to have an important place. Paul Slack has emphasized without apology that, however much it was 'embellished and adapted' subsequently by and to the localities, 'the Poor Law was a poor *law*' with national impact and significance.[11]

In addition, Slack, A. L. Beier, Margo Todd, Ole Peter Grell, and the present writer have argued that ideology and what pre-industrial people actually were thinking about poverty and the best responses to it must be put back into the history of social welfare's development.[12] Throughout this study I apply the term 'ideology' somewhat loosely and spend considerable time establishing the intellectual and ideological contexts that provided motives, goals, and performance standards for social welfare across significant periods of time. The medieval *societas christiana* was challenged by 'commonwealth' thought in the fifteenth and sixteenth centuries; by Christian humanism, Lutheranism, and Reformed Protestantism in the sixteenth and seventeenth; and political arithmetic in the seventeenth and eighteenth. Also a priority in the present study is to distinguish among the deep, gradual shifts in emphasis, the geological plates, so to speak, in social theory, world view, and ideology that were enlivening (and perplexing) the denizens of the pre-industrial years.

As suggested above in my remarks about Reformation historiography, the perspectives that Ronald Hutton and Eamon Duffy have brought to their work on late medieval Catholicism and its gradual transformation by, or reconciliation with, the government's Protestant policies are instructive for the study of poverty and social welfare because of their close association with customary, parish-centered religious belief and practice.[13] Hutton, in a similar vein to Rubin's explanation of change in medieval Cambridge, concludes that ideological promptings were more telling than social and economic ones in the long-term transformations he has been seeking to explain.[14] And, Duffy, also agreeing with Rubin, maintains that the distance between 'elite' and 'popular' religion in the late medieval and early modern centuries was much smaller than current scholarship seems willing to concede.[15]

Another important theme in this study is how social reform or renewal was to be accomplished, traditionally and voluntarily or innovatively and, perhaps, involuntarily. Or to put it another way, was the common weal to be restored or invented? A recurring issue in the book is the tension between what I call *societas*, née *societas christiana* (voluntary community embedded in shared custom and morality) and *civitas* (mandatory association bound by law and government policy).[16] The collision between the two was perhaps most blunt and costly in the Pilgrimage of Grace (1536–37), but it was never far beneath the surface throughout the pre-industrial centuries. Its manifestations ranged from the stubborn persistence of 'merry' England's customs, to the continuing importance of private and endowed charity in sustaining the poor, to the contrast between the 'commerce of benefits' (in published texts of Cicero and Seneca) and Puritan confrontational rhetoric and behavior toward the poor.

Finally, in Chapters 5 and 6 the end game of the parish as social welfare agency is examined. The emerging industrial order gradually, but inexorably overburdened the 15,000 parishes or 'little commonwealths.' Factories in the north attracted migrants to formerly small towns, which put great stress on their parishes' social welfare capabilities. In the south the decline of agricultural labor and cottage industry pushed many more people than usual, including a higher percentage of women, toward becoming 'chargeable' to their parishes. Wrigley and Schofield, in their reconstruction of England's population history from the sixteenth through the nineteenth century, find that by the later eighteenth century England was moving from primarily a rural and agricultural configuration toward becoming the first nation 'reshaped' by industrialization. And Wrigley conjectures that the pre-industrial demographic patterns could be shown to have prevailed in the later Middle Ages, were the data available.[17] The sense of exasperation with the Poor Law which had been building at least since the 1750s intensified during the severe dearth of 1795. Among the inquiries undertaken to assess its continuing viability were the first histories of poverty and poor relief, at least in England. And it is on them, particularly the ambitious efforts of Eden and Ruggles, that I dwell in Chapter 6. They, too, suggest a sense of impending *fin de l'époque*, in this instance for the Poor Law itself. And it is interesting to note in this context that the first eighteenth-century historians who sought to explain England's economic emergence into manufacturing and commerce, David Hume, Sir James Steuart, Adam Smith, and John Millar, viewed the sixteenth through the eighteenth centuries as a single period of profound importance.[18]

Chapter 1: The Medieval Societas Christiana (c.1350–1450)

In the thirteenth century most English men and women resided in agricultural settings or estates, enmeshed in hierarchical arrangements in which landlords and peasants or tenants lived closely, by custom. This 'manorial system' was not replicated precisely in the towns as they grew, but distinctly stratified relationships between urban merchants and artisans and laborers did emerge.[1] Medieval people were encouraged by sermon and statute to accept their social place and carry out its responsibilities with selfless commitment. The clergy, whether in rural or urban settings, were expected to infuse the prevailing order with Christian meaning and obligation; the king and his retinues guided and protected it. A tripartite social order of priests, knights, and peasants (prayers, warriors, and workers) was thought to be natural. Preachers often conjured metaphors to encourage cross-level cooperation. For instance, the great Dominican homilist of the fourteenth century, William Bromyard, compared the different classes to strings on a harp. For the making of 'good melody,' each must keep to his own duties – the lower orders 'in working and obeying, those who are called "ministers," the lawyers and churchmen, in consulting, praying and speaking, the rulers in ruling and protecting, whose office is like that of the harpist.'[2] And, lest it be assumed that social and status hierarchy implied spiritual inequality, Bromyard was quick to add that all 'are descended from the same first parents and all come from the same mud'; thus, 'thy boasting is excluded.' Others pictured the social order as the head, torso, and legs of a human being, with the interdependence of the three components vital to the health of the whole.

The plainspoken Master Ralph of Acton held that, while God could have made all men of equal strength and status, he had chosen not to do so. Rather, he willed 'these men to be strong and healthy, wise or rich', that they might save their souls by 'helping others through love of them'. Those others he made 'weak or foolish or in want' that they might save their souls by 'enduring hardship in patience'. Hence, according to Acton, 'God says – "The poor ye have always with you." '[3] If there was any sense of what modern Westerners casually refer to as 'social change' in medieval England, it was discussed primarily in this moral register. Until the turn of the fifteenth century, there was little sense among the social commentators that social and economic processes were anything other than the cumulative effects of human virtue or vice. The faithful either were trying to live up to their inherited roles and responsibilities, or they were not. And, if not, they risked squandering the temporal and eternal blessings of upright living and fostered injustice and societal disintegration. As Chaucer reminded in his *Parson's Tale*, the proper order was simple and uncomplicated: since the time of grace: 'God ordained that some folks should be more high in estate and in degree, and some folks more low, and that each should be served in their estate and in degree'.[4]

The Economy

Medieval preaching, social commentary, and local and national government activity were preoccupied with the distance between the ideal of a differentiated social hierarchy tempered by Christian love and the quotidian facts of life. And, it is no wonder. In recent years, we have begun to learn much about the bottom–up energy and complexity of the medieval economy, particularly the importance of agricultural sector productivity, the intricacies of marketing and distribution networks, and shifts in the distribution of wealth. Nevertheless, consensus among historians on a general overview of late medieval economic and social change remains elusive. What does seem beyond dispute, however, is that England experienced a surge of population growth in the twelfth and thirteenth centuries from about 2 million to perhaps 4.5–6 million by the turn of the fourteenth century. Then, for reasons that are still in dispute, the population contracted rapidly to about 2–3 million by the 1380s or so and did not begin to expand significantly again until the early sixteenth century.[5]

Also widely agreed upon is a significant shift in the geographical distribution of wealth in the later medieval centuries. If we think of England as a somewhat askew hour-glass, more bulbous in its bottom globe and cinched along a line extending diagonally from the Severn Estuary north and east to The Wash, the wealth in the upper globe was seeping steadily into the lower by the turn of the fourteenth century; and that flow continued well after the turn of the sixteenth century. A fundamental transformation in the overseas demand for English wool, from raw product in the twelfth and thirteenth centuries to cloth in the fourteenth and fifteenth, was the primary economic reason for this. R. S. Schofield calculated the assessable lay wealth per 1000 acres of land in each of the 34 counties for the fifteenth and tenth levies in 1334 and the Tudor subsidy of 1514–15 and demonstrated the vast economic changes that had been wrought by the rise of the cloth trade. The most startling increases were in Devon and Middlesex, both south of the hour-glass cinch; each was more than eight times wealthier in1515 than it had been in 1334. At the other extreme, Lancashire's wealth declined over the same time span; and the East Riding of Yorkshire grew only 0.16 percent or less than 3 L per 1000 acres.[6]

We will see in Chapter 5 that with the onset of the industrial revolution around 1770 national wealth generation will move northward again across the cinch line into Lancashire, the upper Midlands, and the northeast counties.

Accompanying the population explosion of the twelfth and thirteenth centuries was what we might call loosely urban growth. Towns or urban settings in medieval and early modern England, with the exception of London, were generally much smaller and less distinct from their surrounding countryside than the major cities of Italy, France, and Flanders. And just how a settlement was determined to be urban by contemporaries involved efforts both by the town's people themselves – seeking a royal charter of incorporation to gain particular legal and fiscal privileges or to pursue guild merchant status for special commercial advantages – or outside estimates of its level of commercial activity. One of the latter was the designation to send representatives to parliament. Sometimes this was accomplished by a royal summons sent directly to the towns; in other cases the local sheriff decided which towns in the county would be chosen. Estimates of town status occurred also when sheriffs and chief tax officers had to distinguish more highly taxed urban goods from rural products in their assessments (the records of this are the Nonae Rolls). Another was the calling of rural soldiers in 1316. In this instance, too, sheriffs were to decide which communities were towns, and thus spared the levy, and which were villages, hundreds, and wapentakes (these data are gathered in the *Nomina Villarum*). James Willard, who studied the taxation and parliamentary records, concluded that the sheriffs and chief tax officers based their urban designations most often on the degree of commercial activity they observed rather than on size or population.[7]

Historians have identified 51 of these designated towns that, by the fourteenth century, were the crucial links in a vibrant national economic network. The towns were swept up in the cloth-trade currents mentioned above, and many changes occurred in ranking according to assessed wealth. For instance, Colchester, Reading, and Exeter, three towns well below the cinch line, rose dramatically in ranking between 1334 and 1524: Colchester from fifty-third to thirteenth, Reading from fortieth to twelfth, and Exeter from twenty-eighth to sixth. In the north, York declined from third to eleventh in those same years. London was seemingly impervious to national trade and population trends, and continued throughout to enhance its standing as a credit, commercial, and merchandising center and would remain the only continental-like city in England until much later.[8]

Perhaps the most startling revision to emerge from recent research is that in the later Middle Ages the English economy was more market driven than previously had been assumed. According to Maryanne Kowaleski, by the later fifteenth century the 'crucial shifts' had been taken that 'moved western society towards a capitalist economy'. Essential to this view is the recognition of the interdependence of towns and countryside in the emerging economic grid and the crucial contributions of the smallholders, peasants, and lower and mid-level artisans, manufacturers, and retailers to its vitality. The impact of international trade connections and the role of large estate owners is not ignored in this recent work, but more emphasis than heretofore is placed on the vital interactions among urban and rural settings and the crucial bottom–up force of the domestic economy. Kowaleski's prosopographical method in studying late medieval Exeter has allowed her to profile ten groups of key late fourteenth-century players in the town's growing prosperity, ranging from merchant oligarchs and the 525 most prominent householders, through creditors and debtors and merchants from overseas, to dealers in fish and hides and skins. She brings to life the town's complicated economic activity and demonstrates that commerce in a prospering southwestern town was more subtle and sophisticated than historians had previously thought. The merchant oligarchs were very important in the economic mix, but their contributions were outweighed by the resourcefulness and energy of the 'legions of victuallers, artisans, and small-town traders' involved in the system. Perhaps more than anything the middle and lower orders of economic actors, including the smallholders and peasants in the countryside surrounding Exeter and dozens of other commercial centers like it, provided the crucial linkages between the towns and their immediate hinterlands that were the engines of regional prosperity.[9]

James Masschaele finds, for instance, that as towns grew and became more socially and economically complex, they developed needs for the surpluses from 'corn' and 'horn' agriculture nearby. The smallholders and peasants were just as interested to enter this trade. Thus, interactions among rural and emerging urban markets in particular localities in the thirteenth century formed 'integrated, hierarchical systems of exchange'. Gradually during the next century they intertwined laterally and vertically with other regional market arrangements and became part of a realm-wide commercial system.[10]

An indication of the importance of rural–urban exchanges in the developing economy was the thousands of attempts to establish royally chartered markets in the thirteenth and fourteenth centuries. They were needed for localized and efficient offerings of the surpluses of local agriculture and the consumables of urban manufacture. The 'Domesday Book' (1086) recorded only 60 such entities in the realm, but concomitant to the later surge in town growth as many as 1000 markets may have been established between 1200 and 1350. Much like determining which settlements were entitled to town or urban status, the acquisition of a market franchise required, often in capricious combinations, local initiative, a royal grant, and the sheriff's appraisal and oversight. The holder of a market grant was entitled to collect a variety of fees, tolls, and fines. Those who used markets strictly for 'household provisioning', the poorer participants ordinarily paid no tolls. There were toll returns to be made nevertheless from the many who used the market intentionally for profitable ventures, but even a royal charter could be obviated if the sheriff determined that a new market was damaging to existing ones.[11]

A recent estimate of the distribution of England's gross domestic product by social level in the early fourteenth century holds that no less than 66 percent of the total was accounted for by the peasantry, 18 percent by town dwellers, and the remaining 16 percent by gentle and clerical society.[12] While we might have expected that a much higher percentage would have come from the 'gentle' sector, it is becoming clear that cultivating the demesne portions of large estates for sellable produce was not a priority; preferred was cash income from a range of sources, such as rents (villeins increasingly converted them to cash), entry or court fines, milling perquisites, and market tolls. Consequently, the agricultural surpluses entering the market were coming from smaller estate holders and ordinary peasants.

At the turn of the fourteenth century there were 1000 to 1500 large estate holders in the realm, 'knights' whose annual incomes were 15 L or more. The lesser gentry, with incomes of 5 L–20 L and occupying about 100 acres of land comprised another 10 000 to 15 000 owners. Next were the upper echelons of the peasantry, a bit more than 222 000 households, distinguished by annual incomes of about 4 L and holdings of a vingate or 30 acres of land. These were the wealthiest one-quarter of the 5 million or so who lived off the land. Below them were those for whom distinguishing between subsistence and surplus was dependent on the overall vigor of the economy. A grid of skeletal market relations both regionally and nationally was taking shape which required demographic and economic vitality, a co-dependent and productive agricultural sector, and prosperous long-distance trade, some of it oversees.[13] A system of social welfare, centered in the parishes but enhanced by hospitals, almshouses, monasteries, guilds, and individual and endowed charitable activity, developed concomitantly to the emerging economic grid and market activities in the twelfth and thirteenth centuries. And the two systems endured symbiotically, although each in quite different iterations, until the fundamental disruptions presented by early industrialization and the appearance of classical economic theory in the late eighteenth century.[14]

Property, Poverty and Charity

Before we look at the social welfare arrangements that grew with the pre-industrial economy, however, we must examine the Christian theological, even ideological, views on poverty, property, and charity that shaped them. These ideas were parsed by theologians and propagated in compendiums like Gratian's *Decretum* (*c*.1140) and its *Glossa ordinaria*, the first and unrivaled compilation of canon law principles and authorities, and processed into plain speak in numerous sermon manuals.[15] Thus did the church attempt not only to give meaning to the temporal order of things but also to ensure that the faithful would engage diligently with it, resist greed, and relieve distress.

An abiding reverence for the poor and those who suffered permeated the New Testament. The key passages were Matthew's description of the exchange between Jesus and the wealthy young man who sought to be perfect and Luke's rendering of the Sermon on the Mount.[16] In its milder form, this reverence encouraged a suspicion of wealth or, at least, a search for its justification. Applied more doctrinairely, it led to the *imitatio Christi* and the accompanying voluntary renunciation of one's possessions. Equally prominent in the gospels was the duty of liberality.[17] In that spirit, Paul cautioned the Colossians that, above all, they must 'put on love, which binds everything together in perfect harmony' (3:12–14). And Matthew's parable of the sheep and the goats (25: 31–9) shaped Christian understanding of last things. In the process, he articulated six of the eventual seven corporal works of mercy (feed the hungry, give drink to the thirsty, welcome the stranger, clothe the naked, visit the sick, and visit the stranger; bury the dead was added to Matthew's six in the third century) and made performing them the most important criterion in Christ's judgment of one's eligibility for salvation.[18] The corporal works, along with the seven spiritual works of mercy (teach the ignorant, counsel the needy, chastise the sinful, comfort the sorrowful, forgive enemies, suffer tribulation, and pray fervently for all) and the seven virtues (faith, hope, charity, fortitude, temperance, justice, and prudence) became the heart of medieval Christianity's moral theology and the main counterpoises to the seven deadly sins (pride, envy, anger, avarice, sloth, gluttony, and lust).[19]

The iconography of medieval painting, sculpture, and architecture was a constant reminder of the contrast between the virtues and vices, but preaching was the vital conveyer of church doctrine to the faithful. *The Book of Vices and Virtues*, a popular late medieval English sermon guide, left no doubt about the efficacy of mercy. It reminded the faithful that at the Last Judgment God will thank those who were charitable for 'the deeds of mercy that they did here in the world, and thereto he will give them joy and life without end'.[20] Important theoretical and practical issues had to be addressed, however. Was relieving the poor an act of mercy (a beatitude, a voluntary and spiritually beneficial work) or justice (a moral or legal obligation)? Must charitable offerings be drawn from what is necessary to maintain one's social position or only from superfluities? Were all poor persons to be relieved regardless of their attitudes, behavior, or circumstances, or were some more worthy (deserving of assistance) than others? Was a donor under greater obligation to assist family and household members or strangers?

Thomas Aquinas, whose thinking on most matters of theological importance became synonymous with Christian orthodoxy by the early fourteenth century, claimed unequivocally that 'the perfection of the Christian life consists radically in charity'. Love of God and love of neighbor are the two commandments upon which the whole law rests. Almsgiving, which can be either spiritual or corporal, is a legitimate expression of charity if done 'formally... for God's sake, with delight and readiness, and altogether as one ought'. Although spiritual alms deeds normally outweighed the corporal, conditions might obviate that: a starving man had more need for food than philosophy. Even 'the excommunicated and the enemies of the commonweal', if they be in urgent need, must be given succor.[21] Humankind's Edenic communism exercised some claim on property's use, but the ubiquity of private property made for limitations on that claim. So, according to Joannes Teutonicus (*c*.1215 CE), the donor who gives from his superfluities is only returning to the poor man what is justly his (in the spirit of goods in common); but, the donor who gives from his own necessities is performing a merciful work as well. Thus, charity, depending on the circumstances, can be an act of justice or an act of mercy. The underlying assumption here was that the goods available to humankind are finite; consequently, the poor, barring mercy, have rights to a community's superfluities.

Furthermore, a person in extreme need might have to steal from another's abundance to acquire his just portion. Mirroring all this, Gratian's *Decretum* and its gloss proclaimed: 'Feed the poor. If you do not feed them, you kill them'; 'Our superfluities belong to the poor'; 'Whatever you have beyond what suffices for your needs belongs to others'; and 'A man who keeps for himself more than he needs is guilty of theft'.[22]

But, can or should judgments be made about one's obligation to the particular person in need? Is the donor's obligation first to strangers or to family? Is being indigent in some instances fortuitous and in others deserved? Aquinas insisted that a proper charitable attitude requires a man to love God, then himself, and then all mankind. Yet, he established a definite order of preference as to whom charity normally should be extended. The natural order of things disclosed that every agent 'pours forth its activity first and most of all on the things which are nearest to it.... Therefore, we ought to be most beneficent toward those who are most closely connected with us'. He resisted formulating any all-inclusive axiom on this matter, however. An individual's need, holiness, or usefulness to the community can outweigh his relationship to the donor in determining whether he deserves alms.

Among the earliest theologians, St John Chrysostom (d. 407) had called for unquestioned assistance to all persons in need, while St Ambrose and St Augustine distinguished between deserving and undeserving poor people. Augustine, for instance, held that the church 'ought not to provide for a man who is able to work... for strong men, sure of their food without work, often do neglect justice'. Teutonicus noted that Roman law condemned to slavery able-bodied persons who accepted public relief. Who, then, were the worthy or deserving poor? The canonists and theologians tended to give the nod to persons who were patient in their distress or had renounced goods purposely to imitate Christ. Nevertheless, the espousal of the spiritual nobility of poverty was a potentially disruptive idea in a social and institutional order inundated as it was with private property and wealth. Accordingly, the Dominican Aquinas and the Franciscan St Bonaventure, both of whom took a moderate position on the use of property by the mendicant orders, insisted that the *imitatio Christi* be confined to the voluntary, supererogatory poverty of the few, meaning the regular clergy who were busy 'about spiritual things for the betterment of others.' Beyond that, according to Aquinas, those 'who hold that our Lord forbade all solicitude in seeking one's bread, are guilty of an utterly unreasonable error.' Society is already burdened enough by those who 'by reason of poverty and sickness' must be supported from the 'bounty of others.' Furthermore, begging is not a satisfactory path to humility; to give is better than to receive and, in any case, it has 'the appearance of wrong.' Voluntary renunciation of goods was pointedly discouraged and the obligations to toil for one's sustenance, use one's excess goods charitably, and endure poverty with patience were emphasized.[23]

But how was one's place in the social order determined? Medieval *belles lettres*, influenced heavily by Boethius and classical mythology and *exempla*, made frequent mention of Fortune and Fate.[24] Dante, for example, Christianized Fortune in his lengthy discussion in Canto VII of 'The Inferno.' This 'high Dame, the Lady of Permutations' as he called her, was one of 'the Primordial Beings of God's joy.' Her work was to minister all the world's goods, but man's 'mortal reason cannot encompass her' (ll. 61–96). Dante's Lady Fortune, like Boethius's, was the putative cause or explanation of what remained inscrutable in God's governance of the world. On the other hand, John Gower ridiculed belief in Fortune in his Prologue to *Confessio Amantis*: 'That we fortune call so/Out of the man himself it grow' (ll. 548, 549).

Aquinas held that the distribution of men in various callings resulted on the first level of cause from providential decree and on the second from different inclinations in people which he described as gifts of grace. He embraced a social order based on private property and class distinctions and accepted the permanence of social dependency along with the promise that spiritual benefits accrued to both the patient poor person and the generous donor.[25] Human frailty being what it is, however, led him to conclude that the ranks of those who seek assistance always will include more than the deserving poor. These unworthy persons should not receive charity, but, even worse, they complicate the entire charitable process by providing some basis in fact for illiberal attitudes.[26] In the best charitable encounters, virtue prevailed in the giver and in the recipient.[27] To compensate for this potential restriction of voluntary charity, Aquinas advocated coercion in the gathering of alms. Because of the just claims of the deserving poor on the superfluous property of the rich, the government could force persons of means to provide for the poor over and above the demands of the tithe.[28] It is not robbery, according to Aquinas, if princes 'exact from their subjects that which is due to them for the safeguarding of the common good'. And, should all other means fail, the poor themselves, when faced with dire circumstances, are entitled to steal the goods they need to survive.[29] Pope John XXII put the church behind this moderate worldliness in a series of papal bulls issued around the time of Aquinas's canonization in 1323. For instance, *Cum inter nonnullos* declared heretical the idea that Christ and his apostles had not owned property; and, *Quia vir reprobus* maintained that the right to hold property resulted from God's intent at Creation, not from the Fall.[30]

Social Welfare

The application of this moral theology by and to real people in the vibrant and bruising medieval economy was always problematical. The most vulnerable of the able-bodied people were those at the economy's social base and on its local margins. They were drawn into the market in periods of its maximum centrifugal expansion or centripetal pull but participated only precariously. Their 'occasional bushels of wheat and pounds of wool, multiplied several hundreds of thousands of times over,' gained them entry into the market exchange for the goods of 'the petty retailers,' whose production too benefited from the availability of inexpensive labor in villages and towns.[31] It was episodically and indeterminately that they became actors in the economy of surpluses. And, just as unpredictably, they were thrust or fell away when the economy's dynamism abated, as it inevitably did. The most vulnerable, the least resourceful, the disingenuous, the criminal, as well as the eager and ambitious, were a part of the traffic flow to and from the market centers and towns in good times and bad. And all too often the migrating poor vied with their locally embedded counterparts for employment, exchange opportunities, or whatever charitable resources were available from local parishes, monasteries, hospitals, and benefactors. Social welfare historians refer to conditions that require poor people to combine institutional and self-support as an 'economy of makeshifts.'[32] Therein lay the medieval version of the ageless problem of 'structural poverty': when the economy expanded there was not enough employment capacity or other opportunities to provide subsistence for everyone who was seeking work. When the economy contracted, there was not enough institutional support and individual charitable predisposition to meet the swelling need for assistance. And, whether the economy was expanding or contracting, there was an irremediable cohort of people, the 'afflicted poor,' orphans and foundlings, the impotent elderly, the chronically ill, the insane or deranged, lepers, and abandoned mothers and pregnant women, whose situations called for a charitable response, the imperative for which was deeply imbedded in medieval Christian ideology.

As early as the thirteenth century, individual charity, vigorous as it may have been, was being eclipsed by institutional efforts.[33] According to canon law, the bishop in each diocese was charged with distributing a quarter portion of the ecclesiastical revenues for the relief of the poor. By the thirteenth century, however, as a practical matter the delivery of poor relief and most of the available funds were in the hands of parish priests or vicars, hospital masters, foundations, guilds, and monasteries. Parishes themselves rapidly were becoming independent economic units and, through the priest or vicar, dispensers of social welfare. Their revenues accrued from endowments, oblations or offerings of the parishioners for sacramental services, and the all-important tithes. Each parishioner able to do so was to give one-tenth of his goods or annual income as tithe to the parish fund, one-third of which was to be used to care for the local poor. Furthermore, the parishioner was expected to give again from the remaining nine-tenths of his possessions to collections independent of the parish fund for additional relief projects, such as the burial of deceased indigents.[34]

It seems likely that these canonical mandates were known to the local priests. For example, Canterbury I (1213–14), the first synodal statute addressing parish obligation to relieve the poor, read: 'Let priests be as hospitable to the poor as their resources allow, and not mean.' Similarly worded diocesan statutes emanated from Salisbury (1217 and 1219), Winchester (1224), Exeter (1225 and 1237), Worcester (1240), and Norwich (1240 and 1266). The Chichester legislation (1245 and 1252) decreed that priests 'be resident in their (parish) churches, tending to hospitality and other works of charity as far as their resources allow, unless they are absent for a while for a necessity and by license granted by us.'[35] Surviving diocesan registers and visitation records are not extensive enough to estimate with any precision the actual dimensions and effects of parish social welfare efforts. Nevertheless, the constant complaints that absenteeism, pluralities (priests occupying more than one church living), and inadequately endowed vicarages were causing insufficient care for the poor in victimized parishes suggest in an indirect way that some semblance of conformity to the canonical mandates was at least being attempted. And, depending on the locality, parish resources may have been complemented by local endowments for the poor, the charitable work of guilds, monastic doles, and the services of a hospital or almshouse.

Monasteries, although primarily focused on corporate liturgical worship, likely dispensed the not insignificant sum of 3 to 5 percent of their resources on charitable activities. Nevertheless, their most pronounced impact on the relief of poverty may have been unintentionally negative: the potential or actual diminishment of available relief funds in parishes whose incomes had been appropriated to monastic foundations. Certainly the perception that this was the case

was widespread. Not surprisingly, then, from the Third Lateran
Council (1179) onward monastic or other appropriators of a parish's
income were expected to provide a resident vicar with adequate
funding to carry out the parish's normal responsibilities, including
relief of the poor.[36] While the evidence is meager, it seems that in the
middle and late decades of the thirteenth century the English social
welfare achievement bore some semblance to the desired *societas
christiana* goals. So much so that the canonists eased their earlier insistence
that reluctant parishioners should be coerced into paying their tithes
through the *denunciata evangelica* process of the ecclesiastical courts.
Taking stock of this led Brian Tierney to assert that no subsequent
century was kinder to its poor until the twentieth.[37]

Hospitals

Medieval people assumed that religious practice and healing went
hand in hand, and this gave rise to the ideal of the physician as
priest and counselor. Theologians from St Augustine onward
described Christ as the heavenly physician, *Christus Medicus*, who
treated diseased souls and bodies.[38] Medical practice in the high
Middle Ages was typically a part-time undertaking, for pay, of a
widely representative swath of society, men and women, rich and poor,
serfs and free people, Christians and non-Christians, tradespeople
and university-trained physicians. There even was an alternative path
that emphasized the maintenance of a healthy life's regimen, a kind
of 'medical humanism,' inspired by the Roman Stoic, Pliny, and
promoted by Roger Bacon in the thirteenth century and Chaucer in
the fourteenth.[39]

The appellation 'hospital' applied to an array of medieval institutions. Some provided hospice or hotel-like provisions for overnight
respite or brief accommodations to poor and unwell people. More
typically, hospitals, *maisons dieu*, or almshouses provided residential
care for the chronically infirm, not all of whom were poor. Leper
hospitals or lazarhouses offered long-term, rather quarantined care in
mostly suburban settings. Furthermore, the differences among hospitals and religious houses were imprecise and would remain so
throughout the Middle Ages. In Anglo-Saxon times hospitals were
likely attached to monasteries and provided care primarily for ill
members of the religious communities. From the eleventh through the

thirteenth centuries, they tended to be physically separated from the monasteries and were more public in their clientele; yet their routines for staff and patients alike usually were organized around some version of a monastic 'order,' most often the Augustinian rule. By the four-teenth and fifteenth centuries, many hospitals were being transformed into general purpose religious houses, fraternities, colleges, or chantries with limited concern for the unaffiliated poor and infirm. At the same time, perhaps to compensate for that, a second wave of almshouses was being established.

The models for hospitals in the high Middle Ages were established by Lanfranc, archbishop of Canterbury (1070–89), one for long-term infirm patients (St Gregory) and the other a leper house (St Nicholas). The proliferation of like institutions was rapid: by the middle of the thirteenth century there were perhaps 390 hospitals and more than 540 on the eve of the Black Death. Patrons of these institutions were most often the crown, bishops like Lanfranc, monas-teries, noble families, or town councils. And the sites of the hospitals followed roughly the wealth and population distribution of the market economy's emerging national grid we discussed above: clustered in the lowland zone of the Midlands, East Anglia, and the South. Most hospitals were located on the outskirts of towns and were modest in their capacity: a master, assisted by several brothers or sisters, and perhaps a dozen inmates. There were exceptions, though, in both geographical location and size: the largest of the medieval hospitals, St Leonard York, could accommodate upwards of 200 inmates.[40]

Towns and market centers not only attracted migrants who were unable to take care of themselves during economic downturns. The higher morbidity and mortality rates in urban settings also yielded greater concentrations of orphans, indigent and infirm people, poor pregnant women, and elderly widows and widowers, among others, who required care no matter what the condition of the economy. There were enough families of means in the towns to provide patronage for local hospital foundations, which could also serve as local landlords, creditors, and general dispensers of poor relief. Some hospitals became quite complicated structurally: located in an expanded parish church within a town, a hospital might include a resi-dence for the clergy, a school, and an almshouse.[41] Rural people, too, the vast majority of the population, were affected by the economy and the vagaries of climate, and were as susceptible to leprosy and the array of human frailties and diseases, if less noticeably, as town dwellers. Powerful benefactors of many types, ranging from landed families, to bishops, to monasteries funded the hospitals that dotted the countryside by the thirteenth century.[42] These rural institutions were widely dispersed and usually smaller than the suburban or in-town establishments.

Although in principle medieval hospitals were committed to care for the poor and infirm, and some did admit all comers, it would be a mistake to assume that poor strangers or known malingers, ill as they might have been, were admitted for care easily. 'Open door' policies were most prevalent in the hospice and hotel-like institutions, which offered overnight shelter or short-term residence. Houses of this type in London and other port towns were open to visitors from all over the realm and from foreign countries. Nevertheless, admission to hospitals and almshouses, the institutions most known for long-term care, was usually restricted. Some almshouse charters specified local residents only; in others, patrons interfered to ensure preference for their friends; and there were institutions that sought only well-off inmates or corrodarians (those whose expenses were paid by patrons or by their estates). There seems to be no doubt that admissions were biased against those who appeared to be malingers or about whom little was known in the locality. As we will see in Chapter 4 below, in our discussion of the difficulties poor persons often encountered in gaining access to parish relief in the post-Elizabethan Poor Law decades, admission to a medieval hospital often involved negotiations around issues of residence, marital status, wealth, degree of illness, and social status.[43]

For the poor and infirm who survived the admissions process to a hospital or almshouse, medical treatment likely consisted of rest, clean bedding and clothing, baths, wholesome food, and regular prayer and confession. This practice of cleanliness and spiritual exercises, the *regimen sanitatis*, reflected the widely held assumption that physical and spiritual purity went hand in hand as did disease, putrifications of all sorts, and the soul's impairment.[44] Hospitals inspired by Christ, then, had to provide mutually beneficial care for the inmate's body and soul. And, of course, there were social and political dimensions to this. Both staff and inmates were expected to be obedient, patient, and charitable in their dealings and to participate in regular prayer rituals. Men and women were segregated and individual shortcomings were corrected in chapter meetings[45].

Plague, Policy, and Revolt

Part of the difficulty medieval people had with the labor market derived from their predisposition, driven by the moral priorities of the *societas christiana*, to distinguish the able-bodied poor who seemed to be willing to work from those who were not. And, as Tierney has pointed out, the canonists certainly had no sense of the 'structures' of employment and unemployment that historians routinely find.[46] An unemployed and able-bodied laborer in the fourteenth century was perceived to be one who refused to accept his responsibilities. It is ironic that an important contributing factor to the growing suspicions between the comfortable and the poor that developed quickly, even before the turn of the fourteenth century, was the tight quarters they shared in the economically maturing towns.[47] The haves and have nots observed one another at close range and with growing unease. An indication of the status distance becoming established in the towns was the social-level designations to be found in urban and royal chancery records beginning in the thirteenth century. Merchant elites were often *probi homines*, 'the worthy men,' or the 'greater and healthier (*sanior*)' ones, or the 'greater people.' The rest were the 'lesser people,' occasionally the *animales viles*, and frequently the 'lesser and weaker (*infirmior*)' part of the commune.[48] And, it was only a short step from assuming that dirty and befouled bodies housed corrupted souls to perhaps the most pervasive cause of several degrees of contempt for the poor, especially indigent aliens and stangers: their association with the spread of disease. For example, contemporaries often referred to the plague as the *morbus pauperum*.[49]

The step-up in preaching that had begun with the arrival of the Franciscans in 1224 was centered in the towns and market centers, and it tended to move the faithful's attention away from traditional concerns of how to achieve social *stability* and toward emerging issues of social *sensibility*. For example, rape and murder were spoken of less and charity more, as were gluttony, avarice, and sloth. And it was not only the comfortable who were encouraged to be charitable; artisans and peasants often were addressed *ad status* by skilled preachers and encouraged to their own charitable activities. The *pauperes verecundi*, formerly comfortable people who had fallen into poverty and were perhaps the most shamed of all, were singled out for particular care.[50] Nevertheless, they were only a small number of the structural poor, and it was unlikely that the ordinary town denizen identified all poor persons, known and unknown, with Christ in any case.

When times were hard and largesse for the poor in short supply, which of the poor were to be assisted? As we might have expected, the decision often rested on the perceived need and virtue of the person and his or her closeness to the donor.[51] In addition, revulsion with vagrants' filth, diseases, and assumed spiritual decay contributed significantly to an acknowledged inclination to favor the known and trusted poor in almsgiving and care, and likewise to keep strangers from settling. In the early fifteenth century the very devout Margery Kempe insisted to her confessor that greater spiritual merit was to be garnered from helping friends and neighbors whose rectitude could be known than strangers about whom one knew nothing. Although her maxim challenged Matthew 25 and the Church's teaching on the importance of giving to strangers, she spoke for most of her contemporaries.[52] Once rapid population decline and economic disruption became established in the middle of the fourteenth century, even more calculating attitudes and behaviors toward the structural poor became embedded in charitable practice; and, they would persist in one form or another through the pre-industrial years.

Around the turn of the fourteenth century the marginal-land areas that had been cultivated during the years of expanding population, sometimes a type of enclosure known as 'assarting,' were being abandoned because of poor yields. This, in turn, triggered food shortages and, not insignificantly, the onset of rapid population decline which was accelerated dramatically by famine in the 1310s and the plague outbreaks of the mid-century.[53] The cumulative effect of these changes in economic and demographic fortunes on the lower strata of society was far from all bad, however. Dramatic population losses meant a shortage of urban and rural workers, and even priests. The more opportunistic of the surviving servants and laborers often were emboldened to be less loyal to their current employers and more calculating in committing to employment. Agricultural laborers were not only less compliant with their traditional obligations and wage scales, they also began to hit the road seeking better arrangements. Village by-laws often were formulated to keep potentially delinquent laborers in place. The larger context of decreasing land values, the shrinkage of estates under cultivation, and the beginnings of enclosure only contributed further to a sense of disruption within the *societas christiana*.[54]

These patterns alarmed not only village magistrates, but great and small employers, parliament, and the crown. In 1349, the government began its own attempts to shore up the manorial labor system: Edward III's council issued the Ordinance of Laborers. Here medieval social theory was articulated as enforceable social policy, not moral exhortation. All persons under 60 years, free or unfree, male or female, who were incapable of self-support must serve 'whomever' required their labor. Lords had first claim on their own wayward villeins or servants, but could retain only as many as they needed. Fines were to be levied for those who paid or received wage levels in excess of their customary local rates in or around 1346 and to victuallers whose prices exceeded 'reasonable' levels. Imprisonment was promised to anyone in service who left it before term.[55] However, the lack of guidelines for acceptable wage rates and sparse capability for legal enforcement combined to render the Ordinance ineffective. Two years later, in the wake of the Black Death, parliament passed the Statute of Laborers (1351), which was more than a reiteration of the Ordinance, although it was committed to the same goals. It established maximum wage rates for specific types of labor and compelled that servants be sworn to their service twice yearly by lords, constables, bailiffs, or stewards. Enforcement was urged on Justices of the Peace under commissions, and in 1368 another statute authorized the Justices to attend to all labor legislation.[56]

Attempts to achieve wage regulation persisted but in more flexible ways. Legislation of Richard II in 1388 and 1389 specified annual wages for servants of husbandry and empowered Justices of the Peace to set daily wages for other laborers, adjusted to fluctuations in food prices. In 1427, Henry VI authorized Justices of the Peace and the Mayor of London temporarily to establish all wage rates, but later legislated specific wages and suitable clothing expenses for all servants, artificers, and laborers. A proclamation issued by the City of London in 1359 had noted the numerous able-bodied vagrants who had come to the city to beg and, in the process, diverted 'diverse alms, which would otherwise be given to many poor folks, such as lepers, blind, halt, and persons oppressed with old age and divers other maladies.'[57] The 1351 statute pronounced that, due to the scarcity of labor, many ploughmen and laborers 'will not serve unless they may receive excessive wages, and [are] rather willing to beg in idleness, than by labor to get their living.' And, lest there be any doubt that said disregard for provisions of service and inappropriate wage demands damaged the 'great men' of the realm and impoverished those of moderate means, exactly that was proclaimed two years later by 'Petition of the Commonalty' (25 Edw III, st. 2).[58] The petition notwithstanding, concern with recalcitrant laborers was present across all levels of employers. For example, well before the government began to legislate against labor mobility the localities had been acting. Smallholders and village employers, *probiores homines ville*, felt even more immediately threatened with economic ruin by unstable employment practices. They became involved in the enforcement of the statute as sub-collectors, identifying offending laborers and setting their fines. And some of these same individuals must have been instrumental in the construction of the aforementioned local 'bylaws.'

This activity was but a further indication of what is becoming indisputable thanks to work by Marjorie McIntosh and others: 'controlling misbehavior' was indigenous to fourteenth-century village and local life and thus well-established by the time Puritan communes took it up in somewhat different form around the turn of the seventeenth century.[59] In McIntosh's protean study of 267 leet courts in 255 localities, spanning the years 1370 to 1600, we learn that these local courts acted independently of the government, and their presentment juries were gatherings of modestly prominent denizens of market towns, villages, and hundreds, the same types of people who acted as sub-collectors in enforcing the Statute of Laborers and much later would be the implementers of the Elizabethan Poor Law in their parishes. The jurists had on their minds limiting behaviors that were thought to be disruptive, specifically those that clustered around 'disharmony', 'disorder', and 'poverty'. The transgressions associated most often with poverty were hedgebreaking, feeding or sheltering vagabonds, refusal to work, and harboring subtenants. McIntosh found that the number of courts reporting poverty-related concerns increased from 2–3 percent early on (*c*.1370–99) to 46 percent by the later sixteenth century.[60]

As was their want, canonists and preachers in the decades after the mid-fourteenth-century plague outbreaks and labor legislation exhorted the faithful to meet their parish tithing obligations. So strong was the pleading that the ongoing conundrum of whether one could be coerced into tithing came in for particular attention. In the mid-thirteenth century, Innocent IV, reversing earlier doctrine, had maintained that coercion was valid only in situations of the most egregious parsimony. The canonist Hostiensis (d. 1261) saw no possible role for coercion in a matter so binding in conscience as caring for the poor.[61] In the fourteenth century the church's position had moved back partially to the ante-Innocent IV position: lay people could not be held accountable legally for their tithes, but clerics could, for their responsibilities as collectors and dispensers of alms. Parliament helped the parish-alms cause inadvertently, but frequently in its statutes that reinforced the theologically 'unworthy' status of persons who were vagrant, unemployed, and able-bodied. And the statute of 1391 went even further in shoring up parish policies by insisting that sufficient poor relief funds must be provided by appropriators (monasteries or other foundations that used a parish's income) to the affected parishes to ensure the services of a vicar and aid for the poor.

The French commentator, Jean Froissart, writing in the wake of the Peasants' Revolt (1381), thought that in England the nobility in Kent, Essex, Sussex, and Bedford bound the commonalty particularly harshly 'by law and custom,' to plant, harvest, store, thrash, and winnow the grain and to harvest the hay. He attributed the uprising nevertheless to 'evil-disposed' commoners who complained unfairly of being oppressed.[62] A century earlier most peasants still were villeins, some descendents of slaves, others customary tenants; there also was a substantial mixture of free tenants. The ranks of the free expanded in the more occupationally fluid fourteenth century as rural industrialization attracted outsiders of free status. The bargaining and income advantages of these workers and the free tenants could not have been lost on the unfree, especially in the context of landlords' escalating labor and rent expectations. The 1381 rising itself and its most important demand, that serfdom be abolished, were brazen repudiations of *societas christiana* doctrine and indicate the degree to which the labor tensions of the mid-fourteenth century had strained the voluntary cooperative bonds among the social degrees.

The violence manifested itself suddenly, without planning, in the most urbanized counties where the labor force was mobile: Middlesex, Surrey, Herefordshire, Suffolk, Norfolk, and Cambridge, in addition to those mentioned by Froissart. Rodney Hilton suggests that the rising was more a 'plebeian' movement than strictly speaking a peasant one. The rebel ranks were predominantly middle- and lower-strata people from the countryside, smaller towns, and London; and there was a sprinkling of rich peasants and freeholders, and even mercantile bourgeoisie. John Ball, a cleric who had been preaching against the ecclesiastical and social hierarchies since the 1360s, was the revolt's leader and main theorist.[63] And, the motivation and behavior of the participating cohorts illustrated well what historians now call 'political culture.' Their 'experience, interests, sense of the past, and perceived differences from the "other,"' in this case the great lords, drew them into the maelstrom.[64]

In his *Mirour de l'Homme*, written shortly after the rising, John Gower stated baldly that three things, 'all of the same sort are merciless when they get the upper hand': 'a water flood, a wasting fire, and the common multitude of small folk'.[65] A confession manual of the period urged that the poor be queried as to whether they have withheld tithes or personal labor or failed in reverence to their lords. Furthermore, common sins were said to prevail equally among peasants, serfs, and artisans: 'they will labor fervently before a man's face, but feebly and remissly behind his back.' If they be rebuked for this, 'they murmur or withdraw from the work or labor all the worse.'[66] The poor were taken to task for assuming that their condition alone made them more worthy than others. And the taste for fine clothes, practicing false flattery to win favor, and cheating in matters of coin were declared to be typical of the poor. Of course, there was some basis in fact for these aspersions. It is indisputable, for example, that in the wake of the plague's acceleration of the already declining population, surviving peasants and laborers could and did command higher than usual wages. Yet, to avoid prosecution under the Statute of Laborers, employers often under-reported wages or supplemented them with goods in kind. The related perception that the working poor were actually far from helpless and in historians' parlance practiced 'agency' in the employment marketplace contributed to a hardening attitude toward the able-bodied poor.[67]

Estates theory, of course, allowed for equal opportunity carping. Preachers and social commentators had much to say in defense of the poor and vilifying the rich. In *The Book of Vices and Virtues* under the 'boughs' of usury and extortion, an aspect of usury is to deceive poor laborers by taking 'three pennies worth of work for one penny.' Included in extortion is oppressive lordship by those 'that pile on the pore folks' with exorbitant loans, evil customs, making them pay 'great amends for little trespass.' Still another cohort of extortionists were the bailiffs, reeves, sheriffs, constables, and beadles who pillage and perpetrate great wrongs 'all upon poor men and poor widows and children, that can not help themselves.'[68] The sins of pride, avarice, and cupidity came in for particular attention in addressing the behavior of the non-poor. Avarice excluded the poor from many goods of the world that they needed; cupidity deceived the poor into surrendering what little they had; pride equated the worth of the soul with one's rank and possessions. These vices undermined the conventional way of bridging the gap between theological equality and social inequality, the insistence that social relations be tempered with justice, giving each his due.

William Langland in his *The Vision of Piers Plowman* (1360s) sought to rehabilitate the reputation of 'poor' laborers. He reinforced the traditional view that they were necessary to the harmonious social order and that their calling was as valuable as any. The laborers' peculiar task was to work patiently and, as was required of all, to practice Christian love. To the degree that they did this they would share in Piers's pardon. On the other hand, 'Bidders and beggars have no place in this pardon / Unless an honest impulse induced them to begging.' Langland took careful aim at the upper two orders of society, the clerics, lords, and legislators, but was most harsh on the merchants and local officials who had frequent and immediate contact with the poor. Their vice had not so much to do with perverted or insufficient almsgiving as with their active exploitation of the poor. To all he intoned that 'faith without works is vain and idle, /And as dead as a door-sill unless deeds follow.' Love, the performing of charitable acts, is 'the wicket gate that goes to heaven'.[69]

The Robin Hood ballads, which circulated in the fourteenth century, provide a glimpse at the social attitudes of unlettered poor people.[70] Robin's values were conventional. It was not privilege *per se* that he objected to; it was its abuse that riled him. He was always loyal to the king, and predisposed to be courteous to the rich. He could lend 400 L to Sir Richard atte Lee, an honest knight fallen upon hard times, without a second thought. It was the grasping sheriff of Nottingham and similar unprincipled officers who were the quintessential villains for their perversion of the meaning and administration of the law.[71] They made it impossible for the law to guarantee justice and harmony within the social order itself. Robin's brief, then, was not with the order of things, it was with the personal vices that weakened it and turned it toward oppressing those on the bottom.

Calls for Reform and Disendowment

From the 1370s through the 1420s notice was taken inside and outside of government of shortcomings in parish poor relief and the diminishing attention that hospitals were giving to the poor and infirm. Both developments likely were affected by the general coarsening of attitudes toward the poor. Adding to the sense of instability were the crown's expanding financial needs that accompanied the ongoing war with France. Several times beginning in 1371 church disendowment ideas were floated in and around parliament; they would have allowed the government to make fungible some church properties to supplement insufficient tax revenues. Church property, so the argument went with some reinforcement from Gratian's *Decretum*, had been donated to the church by the crown and landed lords solely to be put to God's service and care for the poor in times of great duress. There was in this the implication that the church's ongoing right to these properties was contingent on performing its obligations well.[72] Failing that, the granted properties could be repossessed for cause by their rightful owners.

These ideas became more pointed in the hands of neo-Augustinian revisionists of the church's conventional views on property, poverty, charity, and by the Pelagian notion that salvation was earned or squandered through one's works. Such were the Austin friar Gregory of Rimini, Archbishop Richard Fitzralph (*c*.1360) of Armagh, and the Oxonians, Thomas Bradwardine and John Wyclif. Most important was their attraction to Augustine's doctrine that only those in a state of grace could claim dominion over worldly goods; all else was mere possession. Fitzralph had made just that argument in his *De Pauperie Salvatoris* (1356) and in a notorious sermon against the mendicants delivered at Paul's Cross London in 1357.[73] Although Wyclif was considered at Oxford more a 'Thomist' than a 'Scotist,' he became captivated by Augustine's thought and eventually embraced predestination. Further, an early fascination with Franciscan views on poverty led him to embrace the idea of a poor, Christ-like church.[74] Wyclif's *De Ecclesia* described the church as one predestinate body in which the reprobate had no part to play. From this conceptual ground, it was only a further step to the claim that a churchman's authority was contingent on his holiness. Ironically, given his original interest in the Franciscans, it was the mendicants whom Wyclif and his followers, the Lollards, viewed with the most opprobrium for their hypocrisy and worldliness. They begged like so many 'Caims', namesakes of Cain, who presented sullied gifts to God and was banished for his subsequent fratricide to life as 'a fugitive and vagrant in the earth.' And, invoking a kind of zero-sum understanding of alms, the Wyclifites taught that the offerings the mendicants attracted were really purloined from alms intended for the needy poor. All the more damning was that they lived in such opulent lodgings, 'Caim's castles.'[75] Here was more than a hint that disendowment might be necessary in exceedingly difficult times for the crown; it was a full-blown, theology-based demand, although a heretical one when all was said and done.

Among the 24 heresies with which Wyclif was confronted at the Blackfriars Council in 1382 were 'that temporal lords may at will take away temporal goods from habitually offending churchmen' and that, since tithes are essentially alms for the poor, 'parishioners may, on account of the sins of their curates, withhold them and freely confer them on others.' In 1393, the bishop of Buckingham accused Anne Palmer and six other Lollards of denying the holiness of Caim's castles and, thus, doing all their praying at home or in nature's fields. And, perhaps even more important, Anne and her associates held that 'it is vain to give alms to any beggar' other than the truly needy.[76] In their own way, the Lollards distilled all ambiguity from the ever-more difficult distinction between the worthy and the unworthy poor. Their defining language was drawn from Luke 14: 13–14: 'But when you give a feast, invite the poor, the crippled, the lame, the blind; and blessed shall you be, because they have nothing to repay you with; for you shall be repaid at the resurrection of the just.' In effect, the Lollards urged a piety that combined voluntary poverty with simple and virtuous living and challenged the church's professional mendicancy so prominently displayed by the friars. However, their stance also lent support to the view that any able-bodied person was undeserving of assistance. Wyclif had elaborated on three types of begging: innuitive (Christ's symbolic poverty); insinuative (showing and asking to relieve need only), and declamatory (loud begging; lawful when calling attention to one's extreme need; unlawful when done repeatedly and willfully by strong men not in need, for example, typical mendicants).

There is evidence that a bold Lollard-like tract that challenged the evolving institutional care for the poor was circulating in the 1390s. 'Twelve Conclusions,' which appeared in 1395 for parliament's attention, was a set of church, hospital, and parish reform ideas. Central to it was that the government should disendow the most Caim castle-like religious houses and use the funds to create additional nobles and parish priests and to establish 15 universities and 100 almshouses (*domus eleemosynarias*). According to the petition, the lives of the church's mendicants and possessioners deprived the worthy poor of their due; and, funds used to ensure prayers for the dead were acts of simony, not charity and efficacious almsgiving. As to proper poor relief, the 100 almshouses established throughout the realm by the government would be the best way to care for the realm's poor. The *Petition to Parliament* in 1410 was very much in this same spirit. Disendowment was to operate on two levels: the government would extract funds from the bishoprics, monasteries, and colleges and establish the 100 almshouses; ordinary parishioners could circumvent the parish and deliver their alms directly to the worthy poor persons.[77]

The demographic and economic downturns of the fourteenth century had intense and transformative consequences for the inclination and capability of hospitals to attend to the poor and infirm. One might have expected that the population losses would have reduced staff and inmates equally, resulting in smaller establishments but not fewer of them. In reality the dynamics were much more complicated. Fewer parishioners meant diminished tithe incomes, and thus reduced funds to be appropriated to hospital foundations. In spite of the growing reputation in these years of London's St Mary of Bethlehem, 'Bedlam,' or its care for the insane, in general the hospitals were losing their fabric, their luster, and their independence. Perhaps as many as 100 foundations, 20 percent of the realm's hospitals, had declined into insolvency and closed by the turn of the fifteenth century. Still others were annexed to religious houses, sometimes academic colleges, which had little or no commitment to caring for poor people. For example, Oriel College absorbed St Bartholomew, Oxford, in 1343, while in Cambridge St Margaret Huntington was absorbed by Trinity Hall in 1461. Half a century later St John's hospital was turned into an academic college by Lady Margaret Beaufort.[78] But, even the substantial hospitals that were going to survive faced a mission-altering choice between keeping priests on their staffs or continuing to care as well as possible for the poor and ill. More and more hospital patrons began to choose the clergy for their essential role in leading masses and prayers for the dead, a growing preoccupation among wealthier parishioners. So deep was this movement away from their primary mission to care for the poor and sick that the House of Commons in 1414 had to remind the king, and particularly the hospitals, why they had been founded. That was no less than to sustain 'impotent men and women, lazars, men and women out of their wits and minds, and poor women with child.'[79]

Hardening attitudes toward laborers and the working poor did not mean that charity for the deserving poor had lost its priority (nor the attention of potential donors to their spiritual health). Special bequests to receive and feed the poor on certain days continued unabated. And the weakening commitment of established hospitals to the poor and infirm was offset at least partially after 1350 by a new proliferation of almshouses or *maisons dieu* ('masendewes' in Yorkshire), some founded by guilds, some by individuals, often men of aldermanic rank. On balance these almshouses were smaller and less elaborately staffed and run than hospitals, sensitive to perceived need, and not as often monuments to the memory and generosity of their founders. Some were located in neighborhoods of considerable privation, and the most leanly endowed of them might be no more than a section of the founder's home. In any case, hardly any of the houses were intended to be perpetual institutions. They cared mainly for the deserving poor, those unable to work because of health or age. And the frequent aldermanic connections meant that upon the death of the founder, oversight of the almshouse often passed into the hands of the corporation if it was not taken up by surviving heirs. Here we have an early example of the private-to-public crossover in philanthropic responsibilities that will be more pronounced and significant in the seventeenth century and beyond. Yet another crossover potential was the transformation from almshouse to chantry (an endowment for singing or saying masses for the soul of the endower). This possibility resulted partly from the fact that chantry chaplains often ran the almshouses on a daily basis.[80]

Early Social Welfare Policy?

There were other currents in these same years that challenged the church's traditional, morality-based, hortatory approach to good order and care for the poor. For example, Sarah Rees Jones has discerned in London as far back as the later thirteenth century evidence of a pre-humanist, classical discourse which emphasized the cultivation of the secular and civic attitudes required to achieve social concord or harmony in a potentially volatile urban setting. Jones argues that in describing *Utopia*'s (1516) protagonist, Hythlodaeus, as a Senecan philosopher, Thomas More was revealing his own familiarity with this long-standing tradition of urban thought in London.[81] Another sign was the rebels' exchange during the Peasants' Revolt: 'With whom hold you? With King Richard and the true commons.' The subtext suggested that government (the king) and society (the true commons) were separate entities who allied voluntarily and willfully to preserve order and justice. The willingness of some early and mid-fifteenth-century commentators to separate the unmalleable, natural, or providentially settled features of experience from those that might be responsive to human intervention and adjustment was noted many decades ago by Arthur B. Ferguson. He found a 'new realism' beginning to show around the turn of the fifteenth century that achieved some level of insight in *The Libelle of Englyshe Polycye* (1436–38). The pamphlet's anonymous author, probably a spokesman for the merchant Staplers, probed the economic changes under way in the realm and hinted at the government's capability to guide them.[82]

David Starkey has maintained that the government-society alliance to secure justice may have crystallized conceptually under the new banner, 'commonwealth,' in these very years, as a by-product of the Lancastrian–Yorkist rivalry and Cade's Rebellion (1449–50). Sir John Fortescue, loyal Lancastrian for most of his career, likely drafted *The Governance of England* (1471) in the 1440s. At the time, freshly appointed chief justice and member of Henry VI's council, he meant *Governance* to be the framework for a three-pronged Lancastrian program to restore the proper relationship between the government and the commons: resumption of the king's lands; reform of the council; and a parliament more responsive to the commons' complaints about taxation and civil disorder. These goals rested on Fortescue's distinction between the king and the commonalty (*regnum politicum et regale*), which bound the two in mutual cooperation and respect. The loss of Normandy to the French in 1450 triggered the impeachment of Henry VI's favorite, the duke of Suffolk, for traitorous behavior that compromised the 'common weal' of the realm. At the same time, angered by the government's malfeasance and the ongoing depredations of the war and the European-wide deflation, rebels in Kent, Sussex, and Wiltshire rose for the 'commonwealth of England.' Subsequently 'commonwealth' and Fortescue's reform program itself were taken up by both the Yorkists and Lancastrians. It would seem that a deep and coherent expectation for competent government and 'policy' was taking shape that supplemented or challenged the reach and effectiveness of the voluntary *societas christiana*. These developments, too, were symptomatic of the gradual erosion of chivalric ideals and style by more educated, civically involved courtiers.[83]

An inchoate social policy was being devised and implemented as early as the middle and later fourteenth century. For example, in 1388 the Cambridge Statute (12 Rich II, c. 3) along with the statute of 1391, already mentioned, might very well be considered the first Poor Law legislation. The 1388 statute reaffirmed all former acts still in force that dealt with artificers, laborers, servants, and victuallers, and established a criterion for legitimate unemployment. It held that all servants going from place to place must carry 'a letter Patent containing the cause of his going, and the Time of his Return, if he ought to return, under the King's seal'. It prescribed the wages to be paid for all types of labor and restricted putting to apprenticeship any child who had done agricultural labor to 12 years of age. Further, it distinguished between the treatment to be afforded to able-bodied and impotent beggars. A man able to work was to be placed in stocks until he can gain surety to return to his original place of service. On the other hand, those too impotent to serve will abide in the towns where they are at the time of proclamation of the statute. However, 'if the people of cities or other towns will not or may not suffice to find them', the worthy beggars 'shall draw them to other towns within the hundreds...or to towns where they were born...and there shall continually abide during their lives.' Three years later, in order to ensure that parish alms (which had become the backbone of church-sponsored poor relief a century earlier) were not abandoned in the face of the swarms of able-bodied beggars, the 1391 statute mandated that the parishes continue to distribute alms.[84]

Furthermore, a convincing case has been made by Chris Given-Wilson that the government from the 1360s to the 1440s, with great intensity, was constructing a national labor policy to keep the working poor in their jobs. More than one-third of the 77 parliaments called between 1351 and 1430 passed labor-related legislation. And in 1376, 1377, 1385, 1391, and 1402 petitions to parliament sought legislation to hold villeins to their terms of labor. The 1391 petition revealed the exasperation of wealthy landlords with their urban counterparts, the burgesses, who 'were obstructing...attempts to reclaim their villeins.'[85] The petitions and legislation were much influenced by the broad goals of the labour ordinance and statute of the mid-fourteenth century, but branched out to address three related questions: Should labor rates be set locally or nationally? Should employers or employees pay for violations? And should the national government or local institutions benefit from the fines? Legislation for a national wage scale was passed in 1351, 1446, and 1495, while the Act of 1390 introduced almost a half-century of Justices of the Peace determining local wages. Later, the 1495 Act not only set wages nationally but also working hours for summer (5 a.m. to 7–8 p.m.) and winter (dawn to dusk). As to whom should be fined for violations, there was much legislative waffling until by 1427 it was settled that employers would not be fined. The disposal of the fines at first was up to the local collectors and sub-collectors, who occasionally used the accrued fines to reduce the tax levy in their village or hundred. By the fifteenth century a practice emerged that allowed both the crown and the local accusers to benefit.[86]

Conclusion

Several trends were converging by the middle of the fifteenth century that intensified the importance of the poor in the parishes. We have seen the central role that charity played in the moral theology of the medieval church. Attitudes toward the structural poor had grown more jaundiced in the wake of the economic downturn of the fourteenth century and the resulting labor tenure and wage matters addressed by the Statute of Laborers and subsequent legislation. Lollard calls for reform of poor relief and hospital management were not the only challenges to the traditional order of things, however. We noted that the foundations of a 'commonwealth' and policy alternative to the *societas christiana* were evident in the fifteenth century. Nevertheless, for other reasons that are not altogether clear, by the later decades of the fifteenth century and extending into the first years of the Reformation, the English were more infatuated than previously with the doctrine of purgatory. And, the prayers of the spiritually reliable poor became ever more central to parish rituals.

Chapter 2: From God's Poor to Man's (c.1450–1540)

As we shift our attention to the last half of the fifteenth century through the 1530s, a number of contrasts, rural and urban, local and regional, will come into sharper focus. Laborers, whether in the countryside or towns, continued to benefit from the constricted population and steady prices until both began to rise dramatically, prices in the 1520s and population in the 1540s. Much land was changing hands owing only partially to enclosure and, at that, with regional variations. Outwork on cloth manufacturing was moving to the economically depressed countryside, thus shrinking the employment base in most towns. The dynamic element in the economy, the export of wool cloth, peaked in the mid-sixteenth century. At about the same time a significant price inflation began which was induced in part by the great debasement of the coinage (1542–51). The biggest gainers from these transitions were the lower gentry and entrepreneurial yeomen, merchants, and lawyers. Those further diminished in livelihood and status were the smallest holders, the dispossessed, and the landless. When we look more closely at the the countryside and the towns, we are left to choose whether the economic glass was half full or half empty.

Countryside and Towns

The energy of the agricultural and urban market exchanges notwithstanding, the countryside was hardly a stable and predictable economic setting in the late fifteenth and early sixteenth centuries. The most unsettling changes in agriculture across the pre-industrial centuries were those emanating from enclosure. As we have seen, the earliest practice, 'assarting' or transforming waste into arable tracts, was a response to rural population pressure in the twelveth and thirteenth centuries and was often undertaken with cooperation across status divisions. It had already reached its bourne and was pulling back before the Black Death. The most unpopular and vehemently resisted was the enclosure of common fields, which displaced tenants and often changed the land use from arable cultivation to grazing. This practice was widespread by the fifteenth century and probably peaked in the 1520s, when the profitability of wool relative to grain prices began to narrow. It continued nevertheless over the next two centuries with the government's tacit, and then active, approval until by the last half of the eighteenth century upwards of one-half of England's cultivatable land had been enclosed. Depopulation and dissertion of villages was real, and anti-enclosure riots (and occasional risings) frequent. Sermons and tracts deploring the greed of the perpetrators and enclosure's 'poor-making' conseqencues were prominent in fifteenth- and sixteenth-century social commentary. The government reacted with its inititial anti-enclosure Act in 1489, and Cardinal Thomas Wolsey called the first enclosure commission in 1517. Nevertheless the successsion of monarchical administrations was generally ineffective in protecting smallholding cottagers from the worst effects of enclosure, the ultimate extinction of the family farm. Even the anti-enclosure Act of 1536 insisted that some enclosing was necessary.

The historian reflecting on these developments notes that grain production had become excessive in some regions and the reutilization of abandoned arable tracts for enclosed grazing proved to be necessary and economically beneficial in the long run. To those on the ground in the fifteenth century, however, the prospect of surviving through agriculture must have seemed problematic at best; certainly it propelled thousands of under- or unemployed laborers and tenants onto the roads and into new villages or the towns. And, once there, all too often they acquired the visages of unwanted strangers and vagrants. This was particularly so in the Midlands counties; Northamptonshire, Leicestershire, Warwickshire, Buckinghamshire, Bedfordshire, and Lincolnshire, where open-field farming was most inflexible.[1] We must not forget, however, that developments like these still were perceived mostly through the *societas christiana* moral prism. John Rous, for example, was much concerned about enclosures in his county of

Warwickshire. He petitioned the Coventry parliament about it in 1459 and in 1480 drew up a list of 60 deserted villages. The displaced peasants, he said, were victims of 'destroyers and mutilators,' who enclosed fields and made parks to satisfy their greed regardless of the deleterious consequences. 'An Act Against Pulling Down of Towns' (4 Henry VII, c. 9), passed in 1489, reflected much the same frame of mind and declared that enclosure not only had 'greatly decayed' husbandry but in 'some towns' reduced workforces of several hundred to 'two or three herdsmen and the residue fall into idleness.' And that was not all: churches were 'destroyed, the service of God withdrawn, the bodies there buried not prayed for,' and the defense of the realm weakened, all to the displeasure of God and the 'subversion of the policy and good rule of this land.'[2]

Closer inspection of enclosures reveals that few were abrupt. Warwickshire's data brought to the government's first Enclosure Commission in 1517 reveals that only five presentments involved more than ten households.[3] Most villages that eventually would be deserted were the smaller and second-tier settlements in their localities populated largely by villeins. And the evictions after 1450 were not sudden but tended to occur at the end point of long periods of disintegration and depopulation. For instance, the tithe-corn farm at Upper Ditchford in Gloucestershire shrank to one-half its value between 1384 and 1419, and only ceased all productivity around 1475 when it was leased for enclosure. It seems also that landlords on the whole sought to sustain their villages. They called for the return of villeins who had fled, repaired buildings, and reduced rents to discourage additional departures. Nevertheless, migration was steady and not only to the towns. Most rural migrants were heading for woodland terrain where 'corn and horn' agriculture was possible. Margaret Spufford in her ingenious study of the disappearing small farmers of Cambridgeshire found that these rural transitions in the early sixteenth century and beyond were most beneficial in general to yeomen and less so to small farmers and laborers. But proportionally more small farmers persevered in the fens regions than in the more custom-bound chalk and clay villages. We should not be startled to learn that over a typical 50-year period, in most villages 75 percent of the families were new arrivals.[4] Rural England was on the move, voluntarily and involuntarily.

Overseas trade in these years continued to be the economic elixir for the most dynamic towns. After two severe depressions in 1403–21 and

1449–1470s that bracketed a brief upsurge, cloth exports expanded dramatically between the 1470s and the 1550s. Some of the towns that had benefited from the business recovery in the decades right after the Black Death, for example, Coventry, Colchester, York, Yarmouth, Bristol, and Gloucester, did not recover quickly from the fifteenth-century downturns and were still languishing in the early 1500s. An explanation for this, town by town, was the degree to which its overseas exchange activity began to be rerouted through London during the periods of downturn. Thus, once boom conditions returned in the 1470s the most prominent participants were London and a range of smaller towns: Crediton and Tiverton in Devon; Stroud and Minchin-hampton in Gloucestershire; Westbury and Trowbridge in Wiltshire; and Wakefield and Leeds in Yorkshire, to name a few.[5] This reversal of fortunes is one reason for the urban crisis theory, but there were other contributing factors to the uneven performance of town economies in the sixteenth century. Recession-related unemployment narrowed the work opportunities for migrants in cloth manufacture. Nevertheless, the generally higher standard of living in the towns compared to the countryside required specialized or apprenticeship training for workers in building trades, pottery, metal working, and food and drink preparation.

On a daily incremental basis the traditional expectation of rightly ordered societal harmony in which, according to Edmund Dudley, writing in 1510, every man is 'content to do his duty in the office, home, or condition that he is set in' was being challenged by the ferment of economic change.[6] The multiplication of crafts and skills in the towns alone rendered the venerable 'human organism' simile of the social theorists all but irrelevant. Tudor Norwich boasted 80 occupations, London probably double that number.[7] And some towns were gaining reputations for their unique products, all of which required still more well-prepared workers, thus: Colchester russets, Salisbury rays, and Norwich worsteds, and the like. Desperate and untrained migrant laborers would likely not have made easy entry into town labor forces, except in times of economic expansion.[8] Add to this expansion of occupations the affectation of higher status and the increasing hold of fashion in apparel, especially among men, and the visible social structure itself became less instructive of place and order. Thus the clothing statute of 1533 rued 'the sumptuos and costly array and apparel customarily worn in this realm' which subverts 'knowledge and distinction of people according to their estates, preeminences, dignities, and degrees.'[9] Here is a continuing manifestation of the long-standing literature of estates, a formulation of the *societas christiana* ideal, which had been shared by Langland and Froissart, Wyclif and Gower.[10]

Nevertheless, we must not accept too easily the notion that the towns – because of their oligarchic hierarchies, relatively high standards of living, specialized crafts, and their guilds' control of the most envied employment – were completely inhospitable and their prosperity inaccessible to all newcomers. In the fifteenth and sixteenth centuries there was a lively turnover among the burgesses in most small and modest-sized towns. The rising burgesses typically emigrated from small boroughs and carried with them experience in artisanal and commercial work. They might have traveled from great distances in good times, but mostly had moved less than 15 or 16 miles when the economy had turned down. In London, where both the challenges and economic rewards were significant, most of the wealthiest oligarchs had arrived with little or no inherited property. Aspiring burgesses, beyond demonstrating a skill and some measure of social acceptability, had to buy their way into a trade by paying an entry fine or accepting a seven-year apprenticeship. Admission records of trading companies in late fifteenth-century London reveal that one-third to one-half of the new apprentices were small-town youths. Once having entered the burgess 'caste,' however, permanent status was hardly guaranteed. Fertility rates at this social level were low and sons did not always follow in their fathers' professions; it was unusual for a burgess family to span even three generations.[11]

These were stirring times for some, embittering for many more, and baffling to most. The residue of rancor left by these differing fortunes pervaded the anti-enclosure literature, the satires of John Skelton, and popular ballads of the period, such as *The Booke in Meeter of Robin Conscience* and *Vox populi*.[12] Sir John Fortescue had seen into the dangers of the weakening economy early on, in the 1440s, when he advised Henry VI that his greatest honor and security lay in helping his realm become rich 'in every estate.' Nothing will encourage the people to rise more than a lack of goods which they will attibute to a lack of justice.[13] The not-infrequent tax rebellions (1489, 1497, 1525), the numerous anti-enclosure actions of the early Tudor years, and in a somewhat different way the Pilgrimage of Grace in 1536–37 made amply clear to the crown and government that they could ignore Fortescue's caution only at great peril.

Sermons in the *societas christiana* tradition warned travelers to London and towns of the vices and temptations in store. 'What abominations should he find in them?' Nothing less, came the answer, than 'lecherous beds, adulterous chambers, fleshly concupiscences, surfeitings, drunkeness, gluttonous living', and more.[14] Similar attention to urban vices dominated the works of the translator Alexander Barclay. In *The Ship of Fools* pride and sloth were given prominent place, and the sumptuous values of the budding commercial environment were impugned as Wyclif or Langland might have done. The lesson was clear: no longer can riches by attained by virtue. Instead, one must deceive, bribe, and despoil innocent persons. 'Thus the poor only for their symplicity / Are tread under foot by such as have might.' In the 'golden age,' however, poverty had been the 'inventor' of all laws and the confounder of vice. It actually inspired the great virtues of the earliest Romans and Greeks. The protagonists in the eclogue, *The Cytezen and Uplondyshman*, Faustus and Amyntas, concede the rough and unbridled behavior of ploughmen, the descendents of Cain. And, once they have agreed that it is the meek and humble shepherds, heirs of Abel, who bring dignity to rural life, the assault on the cities takes over. Man is alienated from man, the rich divided from the poor; and, rape, guile, fraud, perjury, oppression, and usury set the tone. In the midst of this ruthless pursuit of 'coin', the poor are dying from 'pure cold and hunger' at the doors of the rich.[15]

This impugning of rapacious city values from the vantage point of an idealized rural society kept alive the 'vices and virtues' explanation of social change or, perhaps better said, social stasis, for that was the goal. It was taken up in the mid-1530s by a successful merchant, Clement Armstrong. His conventional indictment of urban economic actors included the small town *arrivistes* we have just mentioned, who were making their way into burgess status. Merchants, whether buyers or sellers, declared Armstrong, are 'commonly poor men's sons natural born to labor for their living.' Once they have abandoned husbandry and come to the city and served their apprenticeships, however, they devote their energy exclusively 'to nothing else but only to get riches, which knowith no common weal.'[16]

These warnings (or enticements) notwithstanding, the flow of migrants to the towns had become ominous enough to local officials and to parliament by the turn of the sixteenth century that earlier initiatives to control it were brought up to date. The goals were either to keep laborers and artificers in their current employment by setting

limits on wages or, failing that, to discourage migration with the threat
of severe punishment at the end of one's trek. As we have seen, in a
1495 statute Henry VII revived Henry VI's wage rates from 1444–45
with slight gains for bailiffs, master masons, and carpenters, and
established working hours for summer (5 a.m. to 7–8 p.m.) and winter
(dawn to dusk). Yet another statute enacted in 1495 stipulated that
sheriffs, mayors, bailiffs, and petty and high constables search out
hardy vagrants and place them in stocks for three days. And eight years
later, in 1503–04, a statute of Henry VII encouraged justices of the
shire and even the chancellor of the realm to examine local officials on
their commitment to the anti-vagrancy policies. Meanwhile, all wage
rates had been abandoned precipitously in 1496 only to be resurrected
in 1514–15 at their 1495 levels.

London officials sought to stem the in-migration tide by adding
proactive capabilities to the established guidelines: punishment for
being healthy and unemployed and providing alms for the aged and
unemployable. Their concern is suggested by the appointment of the
'Master and chief avoider and keeper out of this city...of all mighty
vagabonds and beggars' sometime around 1520. City ordinances of the
1520s and later called for searching out and punishing hardy vagrants
and the licensing of the serving poor to beg. In 1533, the City
authorized the Aldermen to appoint collectors who were to solicit alms
from the parishes and distribute them weekly to the poor.[17] The
vagrancy statute of 1531 noted the increase of vagabonds and beggars
that contributed to 'the marvelous disturbance of the common weal of
this Realm.' Its conventional operating principles distinguished
between the impotent and the healthy poor, authorized licensed
begging for the former, and ordered that healthy vagabonds be
arrested, publicly whipped, and sent to their residences of three years
earlier or their birthplaces.[18]

Re-enchantment of the Parish

In spite of these developments, or perhaps because of them, an attempt
to re-enchant local life was evident in these same late fifteenth- and
early sixteenth-century decades and shows in the parish and municipal
records that began to accrue. They reveal that a shift was under way
in the setting for customary celebrations from the manor to the town
and parish. By the middle of the fifteenth century, too, a more

purgatory-infatuated faith was emerging, based on 'communion, intercession, and penance (in this world and the next), all provided through increasingly elaborate, and very popular, structures of ritual.' Robin Hood plays, May games, and parish ales were becoming a regular part of life in the localities. A more 'merry England' in tone was emerging at the grass roots, and it fostered closer interaction and cooperation among clergy, lords, and laborers.[19] A rekindling of the *societas christiana* in some form was taking place, while the continuing favorable ratio of laborers to available employment contributed to a less bleak experience of the quotidian economic realities in these years.

Accompanying the increased focus on the parish was a more intense involvement with the doctrine of purgatory.[20] Historians have noticed an increase in wills that called for the distribution of doles for the poor at the testators' funerals. The offerings ranged from money, to clothing, bread, and beer and, more and more, carried the implication of a *quid pro quo*. Some sort of exchange, of course, is the classic meaning of philanthropy.[21] Expected in these circumstances were the poor recipients' prayers for the departed that they might spend as little time as possible in purgatory. Christ's identification with the poor suggested that the prayers of poor people, as long as they were disposed properly in humility, love, and charity, would be particularly efficacious. Distributions to groups of five (Christ's wounds), 12, and 13 (Christ and his apostles) were frequent. This led to the emergence of a specialized category of poor persons. We might think of them as a new elite among the poor 'in charity,' the holy ones, 'poor prayers' who served the liminal aspirations of parish rituals, perhaps in their own way even replacing the discredited mendicant clergy as intercessors. Likely this honor and responsibility was thought not to be appropriate for strangers or itinerant people, but confined to local poor persons with known reputations for piety and genuine need. And, presumably, only the poor of the highest reputation would have been selected by the royal almoner, when the king on his birthday washed the feet of the number of poor persons equal to his age or when archbishops, bishops, abbots, and priors did the same. And, following the annual Good Friday 'creepings to the cross' by the monarch, high churchmen, and nobility, ordinary lay persons typically made offerings of money followed by the representative poor bearing apples or eggs in kind.[22]

The late medieval profession of poor or professional prayer likely reached its zenith in the lives of the bedesmen at institutions like the almshouse at Ewelme, founded in the 1440s. Here, literally, 'the living served the dead', and the 13 bedesmen, chosen for their poverty, presentableness, respectableness, and literacy were regarded as secular Carthusians by their overseer, Alice Chaucer, who regulated them with a brace of statutes of no fewer than 89 clauses. Just how poor were the bedesmen? They probably were mostly *pauperes verecundi*. Most importantly, they were known and respected, not strangers invited in off the street. Much of their days at Ewelme were spent praying. Awakened before 6 a.m. each morning for the first of their several private praying routines in their cells, the bedesmen participated in five public praying sessions in the church (matins, mass, midday prayers, evensong, and a final praying session at 6 p.m.), and other special gatherings. They were expected to keep in mind King Henry VI and the duke and duchess of Suffolk while offering 'thirty-nine Pater Nosteres, 177 Aves and seven Creeds.'[23] Here was a 'prayer factory' whose selection policy indicated the degree to which the 'worthiness' distinction was veering against the more roughly hewn structurally poor people. Marjorie McIntosh has shown that choosing the 'elite' poor for admission to almshouses was practiced widely in these years.[24]

Concomitant to the transformation of many almshouses into chantries 'employing' carefully selected poor prayers, local leet courts throughout the realm were reacting more frequently to the offenses against order peculiar to poorer residents of the locality – hedge-breaking, providing hospitality to vagabonds, refusing to work if one was able, and renting to subtenants. Across the realm in the 1460s and 1470s such offenses became more numerous, amounting to about 14 percent of all leet court proceedings. An indication that accusations of vagrancy may have been bandied about loosely, however, were the appeals for trial and release that began to arrive at Chancery in these years from persons claiming to have been falsely accused. The leet jurists also were willing to act to prevent what they considered ill-advised charity by their neighbors to unknown strangers; yet, in those same communities the poor considered to be worthy were treated with diligent concern.[25] These cross-currents were not as anomalous as they appear at first glance. They are consistent with the well-established traditions of concern for the disabled or impotent poor, the formerly well-off *pauperes verecundi*, and suspicion of strangers, especially if they appeared healthy but idle.

Since the mass was the essential portal for the parishes' liminality, we should not be surprised that a boomlet in the demand for priestly services paralleled the growing infatuation with purgatory. Ordination rates expanded in the dioceses of Coventry and Lichfield, Lincoln, York, London, and Winchester in the late fifteenth and early sixteenth centuries; and an ever-increasing number of them were recruited from the countryside. The upsurge of vocations abated only in the 1520s from the cumulative disincentives of the increasing tax burden on priests and the imposition of higher standards for acceptance.[26] Another factor no doubt was the rise in anticlerical sentiment, beginning around the turn of the sixteenth century, that ranged beyond the lingering pockets of Lollardy.[27] Defenders of the poor played an important role in the campaign. Their barbs ranged from the old Lollard call for the church's disendowment to disillusion with the clergy's apparent unconcern for the suffering poor commons. The contemporary sermon guide, *Dives and Pauper*, indicted the clergy in general for their parsimony toward the poor, but was particularly harsh on the mendicants for feigning poverty while 'they maintain their pride and their avarice, and occupy greater lordships, than do many dukes earls and barons.'[28]

The activities of the parish in these years were becoming more varied and complicated. Coordinating the various chantry activites was not all; there was the church fabric to maintain and responses to the ordinary poor. To address these time-consuming and sometimes onerous tasks, each parish typically elected two churchwardens from among its most prominent townsmen.[29] Funds were accumulating from bequests and gifts, church lands and rental properties, the Easter and Christmas collections, and the expanding number of ritual and celebratory functions. Obits, suffrage, and chantry functions were given much attention.[30] And, because of the largely voluntary nature of the parish relief measures and the general reluctance to provide for strangers, only a small percentage of the actual 'parish fabric' was directed to social welfare purposes.[31] Nevertheless, the parishes continued their traditional voluntary care for the needy and experimented with new undertakings. These included loan making as appropriate, designating the poor who would be allowed to beg, and setting up parish and chantry almshouses. Religious fraternities or guilds were widely subscribed in these years and they distributed funds to their own poor, and to others as well. For example, in 1518–19 the Blessed Virgin Mary guild in Boston, Lincolnshire, dispensed more than 20 L in weekly payments to 13 paupers and contributed to the upkeep of six almshouses.[32]

Christian Humanism

A number of profound conceptual transitions were under way in these years that contributed to opposing senses of loss and hope. For instance, suzerainty, power resting in personal obligations and contracts, was being challenged by sovereignty, public authority and coercion resting in the king. *Dominium* was challenged by possession, custom and morality by law and policy, vassal by subject and citizen, knight by gentleman, kinship by kingship, community by family, the sacred by the secular, pope by monarch, dogma by bible, and providence and fortune by history and reason.[33] Stephen Greenblatt has suggested that the worst insecurities in these years of changing authorities were often experienced by the 'new' men, the socially, economicially, intellectually, and geographically mobile, post-chivalric gentlemen.[34] Greenblatt focused on Thomas More, William Tyndale, and Sir Thomas Smith, but one easily could add Cardinal Wolsey, Thomas Cromwell, Thomas Starkey, Richard Morison, Hugh Latimer, John Cheke, and others. The discontent of their own spirits resonated with the ominous societal disintegration they perceived around them, always most graphically witnessed in the suffering or surliness of the poor.

What or who motivated and sustained the energy for reform that historians agree was obvious in the 1510s through the 1540s? Beyond Christian humanist and Protestant ideologies, several sixteenth-century individuals have been proposed, including, More, Wolsey, Cromwell, and Christopher St German.[35] The historiography of this has been complicated, but by the early 1990s the matter seemingly had been resolved in favor of Christian humanism's importance or at least the crucial importance of thought and ideology in explaining social policy innovation.[36] Since then the exclusive claims of Christian humanism have been questioned by proponents of the overlooked role of Lutheran Protestantism.[37]

Most recently Paul Slack has moved these issues forward by doing what he does so well: distinguishing among clusters of reform or policy ideas. He finds that, beginning in the 1460s, disgust with 'decay and ... great poverty' and 'desolation ... [and] ruin ... without a refor-mation' in both towns and countryside was becoming more prominent in social commentary. By 1510, Dudley could lament that for many years the whole common weal had been in 'sore decay.' Within a decade of Dudley's assessment, a variety of cleansing and renewal efforts were under way. Few now would disagree with Slack's assessment that Wolsey was the most effective early advocate for 'cleansing the common weal from top to bottom.' From his proclamations of the common weal (1514–16), through his enclosure commission (1517) and initiatives to control the plague (1518), to his commissions for finding grain and controlling its sale in dearth times (1527), the cardinal set the realm on the pursuit of national social policy, nothing less than a determined expansion of *civitas*'s domain. And his commitments to address vagrancy and public health at the local level were evident not only in his episcopal sees, York and Lincoln, but in London, Coventry, Norwich, and Kings Lynn as well. Furthermore, Slack points out, the term, 'common weal,' had begun to appear in statutes and the local ordinances of the Glovers, Bakers, and Goldsmiths, beginning in the 1470s, often times without the qualifiers 'of the realm' or 'city.' Thus, the term in many of its earliest uses did not connote a broad program or an ideological manifesto; it was more a 'rhetorical slogan.'[38] Perhaps something akin to the much overused 'community' in our day, the term conferred legitimacy on a variety of aspirations and undertakings.

If there was a new tone in the discussion of indigence in the early sixteenth century, it was impatience with the waste that was poverty, its needless stifling of one's full humanity. Slack now holds that it is fruitless to try to distinguish between the humanist and Protestant roots of this emerging outlook.[39] The practical goals of both camps were similar: the discouragement of begging; punishment and make-work for the healthy unemployed; locally funded and supervised relief outdoors for the deserving poor; hospitals for the sick poor; and efforts to minimize the spread of disease.[40] Nevertheless, the intentions behind, and the relations among, the reform undertakings and the shifting tectonics of world view and ideology they represented remain important for understanding pre-industrial social welfare.

In the early decades of the sixteenth century, the growing distress with vagrancy in the localities and the refinement of Christian humanist discourses of social criticism and governance sparked concern about man's poor and government's role as a meliorative presence. Desiderius Erasmus, 'the leading northern spokesman for a Christian humanism,' was enamored with Cicero's thought and convinced that it should be applied resolutely to contemporary social issues and governance.[41] Erasmus was a close friend of Thomas More and worked closely with Juan Luis Vives. Cicero's emphasis on civil concord in *De officiis* convinced them and other humanists that contemporary poverty was a manifestation of lost fellowship. Cicero had insisted that thoughtful people can discover that societies are bound together by justice and that the most natural of all human activities is liberality. Consequently, those who cultivate *sapientia*, strength of mind for good fellowship, citizenship, and counsel, make a better preparation for service to the commonwealth than those who build up their bodies for war. In the best commonwealths 'war [will] give place to policy and triumph to eloquence.'[42]

The *Institutio Principis Christiani* was Erasmus's elaboration of very general principles of statecraft that, if widely acted upon, could yield a society of justice and liberality. Erasmus's work and More's *Utopia* were both written in 1515, and More likely saw the *Institutio* in draft.[43] According to Erasmus, the well-educated prince, unlike sixteenth-century monarchs, would not pursue extravagance or war. The uncomplicated laws in his state would make clear the folly of idleness and greed, and yet be humane enough to eschew harsh punishment for theft. Erasmus's most singular contribution to the humanist policy commitment was the claim he made for the role of reason in the kingly office. The prince, imitating God's 'supreme judgment' in his rule of the universe, should 'cast aside all personal motives, and use only reason and judgment.'[44] In effect, the Christian humanists amplified the most pretentious aspiration of the medieval tradition, at least from the subsequent Protestant viewpoint: the human capability of self-improvement.

It was one thing to be sanguine about the essential goodness of human nature; it was quite another to hold, as the humanists did, that intelligence was distributed only narrowly in society. Thomas Elyot put the matter succinctly: 'The disposition of reason be not in every man equal, therefore God ordained a diversity or pre-eminence in degree to be among men for the necessary direction and preservation of them in conformitie of living.'[45] Calling or vocation was, therefore, an important issue to the humanists. Their infatuation with human will and their hope to circumvent the old order of estates – persons born to high station were not necessarily intellectually gifted – put the humanists more in Gower's tradition of self-selection than in Aquinas's obedience to providential decree or Dante's acceptance of Dame Fortune's mysterious decisions. They were attracted to Galen's humoric explanations of character type and, most of all, to Cicero's discussion of character and calling in Chapters 31 and 32 of *De officiis*. There he urged each person to scrutinize carefully his or her own talents, inclinations, virtues, and vices in order to better fit conduct to character. In effect, personal fulfillment and service to society can only be achieved when conduct or vocation is in keeping with character. Occasionally we may be driven 'by necessity' to do what is against our essential character or 'time and chance' will impinge on us. He had in mind here high or low social position at birth and the insecurities inherent in royal, civil, or military power. Nevertheless, he concluded, 'The role we choose in life...depends entirely on our own wishes.'[46]

In 1510, More had been appointed under-sheriff of London and in that capacity was responsible for deciding which matters of law were within the sheriff's jurisdiction. One statute that must have been prominent in his work was 11 Henry VII, c. 2 (1495–96), which mandated that the sheriff, along with other local and parish officials, was to implement the laws applying to vagabonds and beggars.[47] Erasmus reported that More worked harder than necessary in his post, often remitted the fees of plaintiffs and defendants alike, and was noted in the city for his generosity. We shouldn't be surprised, then, that the question 'Couldn't things be better?' is irrepressible throughout the discussions of the poor, the economic system, the maxims of statecraft, and the church in Book 1 of *Utopia*.

More brought reason and the humanist policy impulse to bear on poverty and generated three challenges to traditional analyses. First, he moved the standard of assessment from medieval self-denial and poverty of the spirit to the neo-Stoic cultivation of intellect and modest physical pleasure. Second, he identified the source of most structural poverty: wrong-headed statecraft (for instance, the legalization of enclosure) which institutionalized greed on the one hand and vagrancy and crime on the other. Here More insisted that poverty was largely a creation of man, not a divine visitation. And this man-made calamity had a withering effect on human personality: in the thrall of systematic poverty an individual was a kind of fallen being, impervious to the blandishments of the *studia humanitatis* and thus prevented from possessing his or her full humanity. And third, More stimulated confidence that government policy, conceived in the spirit of Cicero's *sapientia* and Erasmus's wise prince, can remediate poverty and other shortcomings of the common weal. Altogether More's analysis of structural poverty within a context of classical values controverted the usual wisdom. The ignorance, idleness, surliness, and debauchery, on which popular attitudes (and vagrancy legislation) rested, were symptomatic of the poor's deprived and untutored humanity, not their inherent depravity.

The implication for any 'state' worthy of the name was clear: a more profound solution to the poverty problem must be undertaken than merely to punish vagrants and encourage patience in the working poor and impotent. But what was to be done? The Utopians, for their part, as he pointed out in Book 2, had designed a counter-society to that of contemporary England and Europe. They eschewed private property, avoided greed, and achieved a peaceful and modestly prosperous commonwealth, ruled benignly by their *intelligentsia*.[48]

Being at one and the same time the elusive, ironic, and didactic work that it was, *Utopia*, as Goerge Logan has shown, confounded its readers from the outset. It continues to bedevil the critic and the historian alike. Surely Logan and Quentin Skinner are correct when they assert that in *Utopia*, More was challenging from the inside the pieties of the humanists themselves, for example, their continuing commitment to social hierarchy and their reliance on *sententiae* and exhortation rather than social analysis.[49] And surely Logan, Skinner, J. H. Hexter, Brendan Bradshaw, and Dermot Fenlon are correct in their general agreement that *Utopia* was More's view of a desirable polity, either a truly Christian one or, in Skinner's designation, '*de optimo reipublicae statu*.' However, the interpreters cannot agree on whether More intended that contemporary Europeans should try to replicate Utopia's institutions.[50]

Vives, resident in the English humanist circle in the 1520s, prepared his *De Subventione Paupeum* (1526) for the city officials of Bruges and presented it to them a year after a reform plan had already been established there. Similarly, magistrates in Lyons, Leisnig, Rouen, Geneva, Padua, London, Norwich, among other cities in England and on the continent, were exploring city-wide reforms to poverty relief.[51] In seeming agreement with More, Vives maintained the total naturalness of men acting with concern for one another. Vives's plan adopted what has come to be identified as the Christian humanist 'discourse,' which we will see identified by subsequent commenators. It incorported four principles: human perfectibility; *mediocritas* in goods; the transforming value of education; and reason's crucial role in guiding the commonwealth. Vives held that natural and man-made calamities, as well as individual errors, meant that indeed 'the poor ye always have with you.' Nevertheless, even though his plan 'will not prevent a man from becoming a pauper,' it will remove him quickly from that condition and restore him to usefulness, virtue, and active participation in civil concord.[52]

Early Protestantism

It now appears that Vives and other urban reformers may have been affected as much by Luther's thinking and example as by the humanists' eloquence. Lutheran doctrine was circulating throughout Northern Europe in these same years, challenging the core assumptions of humanism. The Protestants, too, viewed with alarm the greed and illiberality of the rich, the surliness of many of the poor, the apparent spread of idleness, and the generally contentious tenor of the times. Lutheran social welfare discourse can easily be overlooked, however, because its short-term goals were indistinguishable from those of the humanists: reaffirmation of social hierarchy and avoidance of rebellion; greater liberality to the deserving poor and the elimination of vagrancy; and the achievement of common weal.

Lutheran-informed practice may have been the more compelling force in moving care for the poor from the voluntary commitment of the medieval *societas christiana* to the *civitas* mandates of the commonweal. Luther's disillusionment with traditional, good-works-centered charity had been broadcast widely in his tract, *To the Christian Nobility of the German Nation* (1520), and in 1523 he had drafted a poor relief scheme for the city of Leisnig. Begging was to be prohibited, alms collected and distributed centrally, the poor surveyed periodically by elected overseers to ascertain need, hospital care provided to the impotent, and education or apprenticeship provided to poor boys and dowries to girls.[53] Luther's collaborator in showing the way to improved urban social welfare was Johannes Bugenhagen, who drew up numerous local and regional orders for, among other jurisdictions, Hamburg (1529), Lubeck (1531), Denmark (1537–39), and Schleswig-Holstein (1542). Luther had mentioned, and Brugenhagen insisted, that proper health-care facilities had to be included in any reform of a city's social welfare. Brugenhagen even reached out to England through his *Epistola ad Anglos* (1525), which was put into English in 1536 and responded to in print by Thomas More himself.[54]

The premises that informed Luther's and Bugenhagen's plans were quite different from the 'humanitas–policy–concord' register of Vives's. Luther stressed the practical goal that Christian love 'may be led into channels of truth and works of kindly benevolence.' Parishioners were required to give money or in kind to the parish fund, the Common Chest; the distribution of relief was the responsibility of ten overseers elected annually in the parish. This was to ensure that the possibility of unchristain impulses in private acts of charity would be eliminated. As Luther put it, the overseers were to distribute from the fund 'for the sake of God and the common good, with a clear Christian conscience, laying aside all considerations of fear, favor, malice, profit or other likely motive.'[55]

Luther had revealed his deep disagreement with Erasmus about human nature in *The Freedom of a Christian* (1520), emphasizing that the flesh is unregenerate and does not affect the 'inward self.' It makes no matter if the body is free, active and healthy or imprisoned, ill and weak. 'This sort of thing never touches the soul a little bit, nor makes it free or captive, religious or sinful.'[56] Luther scorned the possibility for spiritual conditioning implicit in the 'works' of medieval Christianity as well as in humanism's commitment to the restorative powers of education. All institutions in the world were, to Luther, factories of pride; yet, he did concede that intelligent men were able to found kingdoms and commonwealths, to govern them with good counsel, and to design many positive supports for social cohesion.[57] Nevertheless, he did not expect government to be an agent of social or economic transformation; at best it could prevent evil. Luther was drawn to the quiet, bucolic atmosphere of the medieval social ideal far more than to the dynamic urban one that was gathering momentum around him.

A person's position in the world was passed on from the hand of God through other men, and accepting one's calling was essential. It was the structure through which God demanded obedience, and the practice of one's calling within existing social institutions was the best expression of social love.[58] Nevertheless, Luther regretted that many merchants, laborers and citizens of all degrees did not live fully Christian lives. Without strong and harsh oversight by the state, commerce would become corrupted and society anarchic. Thus, Charles Trinkaus was probably accurate in his estimation that Luther's ethical position was 'sentimental': it allowed an experience of inner righteousness while the intractable outer world was treated with wary shrewdness.[59]

William Tyndale, the principal colporteur of Lutheran doctrine in England, imparted a particular tone to his formulation of Lutheranism that gave it a much livelier cast than the original. For Tyndale, a proper faith should make individual and social life better. This commitment stemmed from the importance he placed in the divine compact. If men seek to bind themselves to God, to accept the general contract proffered, 'then God hath bound himself unto us, to keep and make good all the mercies promised in Christ throughout the scripture.'[60] In his elabortion of the famous 'lillies of the field' passages (Matthew 6: 28), which had so attracted Francis of Assisi and other medieval practitioners of the *imitatio Christi*, Tyndale gave the 'compact idea' a utilitarian significance with regard to worldly prosperity that was important. Christ promised the faithful man, according to Tyndale, 'an hundren fold, even in this life, of all that thou leavest for his sake.'[61]

As Luther had been, Tyndale was very concerned to clarify the significance of works. He made explicit often the Lollard and Lutheran formula that proper works follow *from* faith. They were, in effect, the outward signs of one's inner rectitude. Real, achievable 'apostolic poverty,' according to Tyndale, was nothing more, or less, than to be 'content with a competent living,' whether it be acquired through inheritance or with one's own labor. The goal was to be 'doing service to the commonwealth,' so that 'my neighbor may have a living by me as well as I.' And, 'as riches do not exclude thee from the blessing, so does not poverty certify thee.' Only 'trust in the living God' can do that.[62]

The immediate impact of Lutheranism *per se*, separate from official anti-Romish doctrine in the 1530s and 1540s, is difficult to ascertain, aside from whatever interest Luther's and Bugenhagen's city plans may have ignited in those interested in reforming social welfare. The matter-of-fact tenor of Lutheran social thought and reform plans made them philosophically a formidable rival to Christian humanist reform thinking, especially the latter's infatuation with government policy. And it represented a fundamental corrective to *societas christiana's* deepening complicity with supererogatory poverty, works, and the diversion of alms to chantries. Luther's 'priesthood of all believers' not only deprived priests of their spriritual authority; it transformed parish values. Instead of celibacy, the model of probity became marriage and family life. And, practical relationships with one's brother and sister Christians implied caring for them if they were in need. The emphasis was on charity's vital, this-worldly role in improving the parish and locality, and not in its private grace-earning possibilities. Thus, Tyndale's formulation of Luther's ideas likely served more as a beginning reorientation of English social thought that will blossom later under the influence of Calvinism. Doctrinally more appealing at court were Melancthon's moderate views on human will and reason and his emphasis on obedience to authority. His 'middle way' on reason was written into the official Henrician *King's Book* (1543) and Forty-Two Articles (IX) and the Thirty-Nine Articles (X) of Elizabeth in 1563.

Reform and the Pilgrimage of Grace

The humanist–Protestant differences were but one complicating factor as local officials and the government assessed the vagrancy and poverty problem. An additional difficulty was the widespread contempt for the poor commons and near or marginally poor. Even the seemingly idealistic Christian humanists were uncomfortable with the menacing lower orders. It has been said of Erasmus that in theory he was a democrat, by inclination an aristocrat, and in the face of reality a monarchist.[63] More thought it unwise to put the translated scriptures into the hands of any but the educated and refined and, by publishing *Utopia* in Latin, kept his most provocative work inaccessible to the commons. And no wonder: the government was kept in constant fear by rumors and prophecies of impending rebellions and assassinations that circulated among the commons.[64] Thus, when commonwealth thinkers discussed the artisans, laborers, and ploughmen as the hands and feet of the social organism, they oversimplified and euphemized a more troubled perception. In truth they saw an incipient behemoth, separate from themselves, capable of both indiscriminate rage and bovine torpor, a menacing, unpredictable creature of appetite and superstition. Starkey's *Dialogue between Pole and Lupset* was not published until the nineteenth century, but it provides a sounding of a thoughtful mind at court in the 1530s. Starkey was interested in the high proportion of beggars, the work habits of laborers, the uses being made of the realm's natural resources, and the variety and degree of imports. These were the kinds of issues that would be taken up by Sir Thomas Smith at mid-century and Sir Fancis Bacon at its end. Starkey was particularly concerned with what he perceived to be the excessive worldliness and lack of common purpose among the various degrees of society. As bleak as this may have appeared to him, Starkey was convinced that government could restore the common weal by enforcing labor and vagrancy laws, developing a plan for the realm's economy, and instituting municipal responsibility for poor relief. In short, what was needed was that 'the good order and policy by good laws established and set' be put into effect so that the political body will be ruled by 'reason' and achieve health, prosperity, proper worship and brotherly love.[65]

Starkey was aware, however, that intellectual cant might impair policy: in the *Dialogue* Lupset (Thomas Lupset) cautions Pole (Reginald Pole) that Plato's (and More's?) 'vain imagination' not be allowed to interfere with a careful and accurate understanding of conditions in England, lest the resulting policies be formulaic and ineffective. And, as T. F. Mayer has shown, Starkey's understanding of what policy actually was had changed during the six years or so he had tried to gain influence at court. Early in the *Dialogue*, for instance, he was convinced that reason and nature were independent from God; but further on he decided that the soul contained a 'sparkle of the godly and eternal reason.' In 'What is policy', his response to Cromwell's request for a treatise on Aristotle's understanding of policy, Starkey's attention ranged from human nature, to the origins of civil society, to consitutional forms. He concluded that policy in the hands of wise men was the instrument that transforms the multitude into a Christian polity. And, in his *Exhortation*, Starkey declared that 'faithful love and charitable faith' allowed a person to live 'like a christ, like a god, like reason it self.' Whether Starkey's faith was Italian Evangelical as Mayer maintains or Protestant as Cromwell thought, he saw policy's civil dimension as a means to its religious ends and was forging a polyvalent, humanist and providential language of reason and policy.[66]

Richard Morison in *A Remedy for Sedition* (1536) had confronted what he called the 'evil education' of the commons that was a deeper source of rebellious inclinations than their alleged poverty. Lusts and appetites must be conquered and all such statutes 'as reason and honesty shall think worthy to be enacted' must be obeyed.[67] Furthermore, the commonwealth policy strategists of the mid-1530s were willing to concede only the most general promise of prosperity to the commons and had little sympathy for upward status mobility (save for Morison's well-known defense of ascent for intellectuals).[68] Their priorities were elsewhere: to enforce obedience to the moderate Henrician religious reform and thus prevent anabaptist and sectarian dissension. Curiously, the fifteenth-century sermon guide *Dives and Pauper* was published by the crown in 1534. It made mention of apostolic poverty, the 'poor for God's sake and by way of virtue,' as a worthy state; but, there is no reinforcement of this concept in the avowedly Protestant homiletic and doctrinal literature that began to appear. And, as we recall, the Christian humanists several decades earlier, although individually of ascetic temperament, had affirmed *mediocritas* in goods as a necessary prerequisite for the cultivation of reason and higher culture.[69]

The Christian humanists had been exceedingly temperate on the property issue, and that posture seemed to be carried forward in the policy thinking of the mid-1530s. For example, Reginald Pole in Starkey's *Dialogue* intoned that 'it may not be doubted...that the most prosperous state of man standeth in the virtues of the mind coupled with worldly prosperity.' At the same time he lamented the excessive worldliness that had come to permeate the realm. His remedy was firm and resourceful policy, including enforcement of sumptuary, labor, and vagrancy statutes and planning of the realm's economy, all under the direction of a courageous, intelligent king.[70] Morison maintained that the commonwealth was strongest that paid the highest honor to qualities of mind, second to qualities of body, and only third to riches and rank. Furthermore, a commonwealth is worthy of the name only when 'every one is content with his degree' and willing to do that which may be contrary to his interest, yet beneficial to the whole.[71]

After the traditional anti-vagrancy statute of 1531, Thomas Cromwell, Henry VIII's chief minister, wished to propose a significant new poor relief bill. He likely turned for a proposal to William Marshall, one of his thinkers and writers and most notably translator of the Ypres poor relief plan. Marshall was close to Anne Boleyn, soon to be queen and a dedicated Christian humanist, known for her commitment to innovations in poor relief and religion who 'greatly strengthened' the reformers at court. In 1528, the exiled Simon Fish had sent to Anne his *A Supplication for the Beggars*, hoping that she would defend it with the king, to whom the tract was dedicated. And Marshall dedicated his 1535 translation of the Ypres poor relief plan to Boleyn. It is interesting to note in that regard that both Anne and Marshall were willing to concede that alien and indigent people baffled and endangered all the citizens. Anne, sounding a bit like Margery Kempe a century earlier, urged her household to favor known poor people in their relief efforts on her behalf.[72]

Fish's *Supplication* had linked the greediness of the clergy directly to needless suffering by the worthy poor in a manner that ranged beyond the usual Lollard agitation with the Caim-like monks and friars. As he saw the matter, alms needed by the impotent poor were all the time being siphoned away to the malingering 'bishops, abbots, priors, deacons, archdeacons, suffragans, priests, monks, canons, friars, pardoners, and summoners.' If this were not bad enough, lasciviousness, the other major vice of the clergy, corrupted many a maiden and demoralized the poor commons in general. Fish's advice to the king, which Stephen Greenblatt suggests had Protestant roots and intentions, was that Henry should punish the errant churchmen severely and publicly. Their ubiquitous example of idleness would be confronted, the King become more popular, and the realm more prosperous.[73]

Thomas More himself answered Fish. More's *A Supplycacion of Soulys* is a curious performance for the author of *Utopia* in that it reveals More the partisan for Catholicism rather than the partisan for justice. He disposed of Fish, whom he characterized as ignorant and possessing a 'malicious mind,' in less than two dozen pages at the beginning of the lengthy tract. He denied the claim that the number of suffering poor was increasing, that many were dying for lack of alms, and that the clergy were a perverse influence on the realm. The much weightier portion of the piece was its defense of the orthodox teaching on purgatory. More understood that the mutual exchange (philanthropic?) between suffragans and their deceased benefactors confirmed the liminal nature of the church body: through it the living and the dead formed a bond as vital as the earthly ones encouraged by the *societas christiana* ideal. Parenthetically, the suffragans stood to receive much more than the alms that supported them, since the prayers of the dead in purgatory were the most efficacious of all intercessions with God. Sensing that 'Luther's teachings' and 'Tyndale's testament' against purgatory were disguised in Fish's rant against the churchmen and the professional prayers, More gave voice to the pleas of the departed souls that they not be forgotten and abandoned to their suffering.[74]

Marshall drafted a remarkable bill, Christian humanist in its operating values, that would rescue the realm's poor by means of government policy. It acknowledged many causes of poverty beyond the 'visitation of God' and the pauper's 'own default' and committed 'to help and succor' all the different types of poor and 'to prevent that other shall not hereafter fall into like misery.' A national 'council to avoid vagabonds' would provide wages, food, and medical care for the able-bodied unemployed who would be put to work renovating ports, building roads, and dredging and cleansing waterways. These national endeavors, financed by the king's benevolence and yearly levies on church dignitaries and wealthier laymen, were to continue to 1540. At the local level, parishes were to appoint overseers who would supervise a voluntary fund of money and in-kind contributions to provide relief and hospital care for the poor. Each bishop was to provide a sermon for Sundays and holy days that praised charity and impugned sloth.[75]

With Cromwell's urging Henry brought the proposal to the Lower House himself on 11 March 1536, reminding the members not to pass it just because he 'giveth in the bill...[but only] if it be for a common weal to his subjects.'[76] The bill evidently shocked the Commons, was withdrawn almost immediately, and a substitute, 27 Henry VIII, c. 25, was introduced quickly by the government and passed. The statute announced more conventionally that it would clarify and extend the mandate of the 1531 statute. Local officials and householders were urged to receive the poor and vagrant 'most charitably.' And the clergy were to exhort church members to contribute voluntary donations to their parish's fund, from which the impotent would be relieved and the able-bodied put to work. Most, but not all, corporate and private almsgiving was prohibited, although some begging was allowed to continue; and idle children were to be apprenticed.[77] These 1530s anti-vagrancy and poverty initiatives had an unusual half-life. Only the 1531 vagrancy statute was mentioned in the continuance bill of 1536, nor was 27 Henry VIII, c. 25 formally renewed in 1539. There is some hint, though, that by the latter date Cromwell was contemplating another effort in parliament for Marshall's draft. And, a proclamation in 1538 had called for the enforcement of the *statutes* against vagrancy (1531 *and* 1536?). The Draconian anti-vagrancy Act of 1547 discontinued all previous legislation without mentioning specific statutes, but, when it too was repealed in 1549, only the 1531 statute was revived. Finally, in 1624, in the midst of the puritan 'civic moment', the 1531 statute was repealed.[78]

The 1536 statute's metamorphosis of the traditional canon law and episcopal requirement that parishes's care for their poor into a civil law and government policy mandate brought to the surface a deep tension in the social welfare dynamic that had been brewing since the mid-fourteenth-century labour legislation and never disappeared completely. Several centuries of living the 'medieval Poor Law' had allowed its tithe and charity obligations to become habitual and customary. Most medieval English people lived uncontestedly or unconsciously within the moral compass of the *societas christiana* and no doubt thought of themselves as voluntary agents or deserving recipients of its charity. During the 70 years or so prior to the Cromwell initiatives, the advance of merry England with its further sacralization of parish communities could only have intensified their voluntary bonds. Ironically, it was the concomitant dissolution of the monasteries and chantries by the government that precipitated the archtypical *societas–civitas* confrontation, the Pilgrimage of Grace.

As we saw in Chapter 1, the long-standing dissolution idea had its roots in the 'Twelve Conclusions' of the 1390s (which called for the government to use the funds realized from disendowment to create additional nobles and parish priests and to establish 15 universities and 100 almshouses) and Fortescue's and others' calls for the re-endowment of the monarchy's depleted estate. Cromwell had authorized the *Valor ecclesiasticus* in 1535 to assess clerical incomes in general and, particularly, to establish the worth of the monastic houses in anticipation of absorbing them. The statute of March 1536 dissolved the smaller religious houses, whose annual worth was under 200L, totaling slightly more than 370 institutions across the realm. By 1540, the remaining 200 or so wealthiest houses had surrendered voluntarily. Here was a provocative, frontal assualt by the government on two cornerstones of the *societas christiana* charitable apparatus, the mendicant regular clergy and their alms-dispensing religious houses. By early October 1536, insurrection was sweeping across Lincolnshire and had enveloped Yorkshire, Durham, and Northumberland by year's end. Henry's disingenuous offer of an amnesty set off a new wave of troubles in Cumberland, Westmorland, Lancashire, and Cheshire which were quelled in February 1537. Altogether this was a major rising involving upwards of 20 000 insurgents across the northern and lake counties, and at its end the punishments were swift but fair: 178 executions, along with 37 acquittals, 108 pardons, 16 reprieves, and 13 convictions overturned.

There were economic issues that grated particularly on the poor commons in the north. The harvests in 1535 and 1536 had been bad, and complaints about the recently passed fifteenth, re-established fuedal fees (Act of Uses, 1536), and unchecked enclosure were prominent in the insurrectionists' articles.[79] The rebels in the northernmost regions campaigned under the banners of Captains Poverty, Charity, Faith, and Piety, prompting R. W. Hoyle to see in that some attachment to the 'mystical world view' of Piers Plowman.[80] The men of the north implored the king to consider the consequences of his policies. Were not his taxes making them poorer and his new religion depriving them of their spiritual contentment and needed monastic alms? Common purpose in Penrith, for example, was promoted with a daily mass during which four 'Captains of Poverty' entered the church with swords drawn and led the recitation of five aves, five paternosters, and the creed. Scott M. Harrison finds the lake counties' actions generally to constitute a 'reactionary rebellion.' Whether one looks to its religious, economic, or political dimensions, the pilgrims 'wanted to reestablish the traditions and practices their fathers had known.'[81] Henry alternated between being hurt that his subjects in the north did not appreciate his care in keeping them so long in peace and prosperity and expressing outrage that his 'lewd,' 'common and inferior subjects' in Lincolnshire would fain any opinion about his rule.[82]

But the Pilgrimage attracted more than poor adherents. There were gentry and burgesses' entreaties for reform in parliamentary elections and requests to have the body meet in more convenient locations for the northern members.[83] Early on, the risings' leaders were commoners, but gentry and nobles, like Robert Aske and Lord Darcy, soon took primary control. What the northern commoners and gentry shared more than anything was their revulsion with the blunt instruments of Reformation policy that were emanating from court, particularly the dissolution of the monasteries and the substitution of heretical for traditional theology. The rebels attributed these errors to the men 'of low birth and small reputation' at court, specifically Cromwell and Sir Richard Rich, the Chancellor for Augmentations. In their positions of influence close to the king, they were despoiling the church and the commonwealth. Aske noted explicitly (and no doubt with the prompting of local priests) in the first of the Pontefract Articles the heretical teachings of Luther, Wyclif, Hus, Melancthon, Oecolampadius, Bucer, the Augsburg confession, as well as Tyndale, Barnes, Marshall, Rastallo, St German, and the Anabaptists, who must be 'annulled and destroyed.'[84] Thus, of particular importance in the pilgrims' oath was 'the love that ye do bear unto almighty God, his faith, and to holy church militant [and for] the maintenance thereof....' Throughout their printed materials the pilgrims sought to 'restore' earlier laws, monks' and friars' privileges, the tenure of pre-Reformation bishops, and long-standing church rites and practices, and to do these things by 'act of parliament.'[85]

The Pilgrimage of Grace was not the first collision between local custom (*societas* or *communitas*) and government mandated behavior (*civitas*), and it would not be the last. It was a particularly blunt one, however, and revealed vividly the opposing impulses that can be glossed over when historians speak of 'continuity and change' or, more specifically, a slow versus a rapid Reformation. C. S. L. Davies assesses the subtleties involved in the Pilgrimage quite well. The pilgrims were motivated by more than the typical grievances of rural poor commoners goaded on by superstitious or magical faith. Running beneath the surface of the risings was the rebels' sense that their local communities, most intensely represented by voluntary participation in the social and spiritual life and fabric of their parishes, were being threatened by an insensitive, out-of-control government in London. The 'communal property set against destructive spoilization' in the unique context of the government's religious agenda could lead only to the pilgrims defending 'traditional and...."catholic" values against innovation.'[86] The perceptions and discourses available to the rebels and to the government permitted nothing else. The stability of *societas* was being threatened in the near term by 'an aggressive state' and in the longer term by 'evangelical Protestantism'. The sense of beleaguerment in the localities of the north could only have been deepened by the half-century or more of re-enchantment of parish life that preceded the Dissolution.

Dissolving and Reconstituting Hospitals

Yet another unforeseen and unsettling consequence of the government's move against the religious houses was its impact on the realm's hospitals and almshouses. In his deathbed will, Henry VII opined that 'there be few or none such common hospitals within this our realm and...for lack of them infinite number of poor needy people miserably daily die, no man putting hand or help or remedy.' Noting that he had begun the construction of a new hospital at the Savoy Palace, he left 10,000 L to complete the project. A suitable number of priests, servants, and nuns to care for 100 poor people nightly were to be supported by a yearly income of 500 marks, and the king's executors were urged to complete the Savoy and establish two similar institutions in the suburbs of York and Coventry.[87] Henry's inspiration for the Savoy in both design and medical practice was the Santa Maria Nuova in Florence, the banner institution of the wave of new urban hospitals on the continent. Thomas More, too, had been much affected by the Santa Maria in his thinking about the four extramural hospitals in Utopia. Completed in 1519, the Savoy was a large building in cruciform design with two chapels within and outbuildings for the staff's living quarters and the kitchen. Initially it followed the traditional *regimen sanitatis* in caring for its 100 nightly inmates. Baths, washing and delousing of clothing, fresh beds, and, surely, spiritual counseling awaited those admitted. The 'sisters' who provided that care were nuns and a variety of elderly women, some wage-earners, some working for their corrodies, some occupying the corrodies of their husbands, some the beneficiaries of those whom they had treated. The sisters, along with servants and bedesmen, also benefitted from general distributions on special feast days or when suplus revenues were distributed.[88]

Given the new hospital's prohibitive size and overhead, the utilization of regular clergy for administration, and the medieval theological assumptions and traditional care at its core, the Savoy did not prove to be a model for the renewal of the realm's beleaguered and ignored hospitals. The moment for that type of institution was passing. Far more than the Savoy, it was the advance of Protestant-driven dissolution ideas in the early 1520s that brought renewed attention to the hospitals, none of it particularly edifying. While not a central issue in the build up to the dissolution statute of 1536, the hospitals were, in time, affected significantly by the legislation. Since the administration and much of the care was in the hands of regular clergy and the numbers of indigent people that they actually served had declined noticeably, the hospitals easily could be lumped together with religious houses more generally as cesspools of pluralism, corruption, concupiscence, and superstition. Both Tyndale's *Obedience of a Christian Man* (1528) and Fish's *Supplication for Beggars* (1528) had noted that the religious houses held their estates from the king and nobility in trust for the performance of merciful works. But, the authors challenged also the works theology and purgatory doctrine which underpinned so much of parish routine and the financing and aura of the religious houses. In essence, the Lollard charges of old had found new energy: the houses had to close because of their vices and diverting of funds better applied more directly to aid the poor and because their entire *raison d'etre*, the pursuit of works theology, was discredited.

William Marshall's proposal in 1535 for a national, voluntarily funded plan to provide medical attention to the poor, which he included in his famous draft Poor Law, spoke to other humanist-minded commonwealth advocates. And Henry Brinkelow's suggestion seven years later that the government direct its profits from the Dissolution to stipends for physicians, surgeons, and provisions for sickhouses in all cities, towns, and hundreds certainly must have attracted support. Beyond Protestantism's impugning of Catholic notions of God's or 'hands on' cures, there was little to distinguish sixteenth-century from earlier views on the theological significance of disease or the importance of responding medically to it. Matthew's seven corporal works of mercy, including caring for the sick, remained a constant of moral theology. And the notion of Christ the physician, healer of the soul and body, continued to be touted much as it had been in the fourteenth-century *Fasciculus Morum*. As to whether illness signaled one's unlikely chances for salvation, Thomas Becon thought not: more often the most sinful were not struck by illness while it was visited on others for their spiritual profit. Illness was a warning or a chastisement to the wayward faithful person, and its cure involved spiritual and physical recovery.[89]

Robert Copland's *Hyeway to the Spyttal House* (1535–36) appeared just on the cusp of the dissolution and added no lustre to the already tattered reputation of hospitals. Copland (a person of Thomas Starkey-like curiosity about the origins of poverty and the conviction that better law enforcement would reduce the numbers of the poor) offered a discussion between himself and the porter of a hospital. The porter related that, while hospitals are intended to care for the sick poor, undeserving people have perfected techniques to be admitted. Copland lamented that vagrancy laws are not enforced and cautions those who think they are in no need of a hospital's care that they, too, with only a slight change in their fortunes could be on the 'hyeway to the spyttal house.' In the process, the author provided a broad view of the types of people who, through folly or vice, were falling into poverty or hell on earth. He chronicled the ranks of hard-working, modestly comfortable artisans, small merchants, wayward priests and clerks; smallholders who have lived beyond their means; bailiffs and stewards who were negligent in collecting their lords' dues; merchants and artisans who charged too much and squandered too much; servants who did not serve properly; lecherous persons; and borrowers who did not repay. Certainly, Copland concludes, 'Their end is fairest/If that with poverty they be suppressed.'[90]

Henry VIII, unlike his father, demonstrated no sustained interest in hospitals, nor were they part of his general indictment of the church. Once the dissolutions of the religious houses got under way, however, the hospitals were swept into the fray. Thus, in 1534 the Act of Supremacy required that hospital clergy, like all other beneficed religious, swear obedience to the king and become liable to the new clerical tax, 'first fruits and tenths.' The *Valor ecclesiasticus* inspectors examined the hospitals only selectively: the larger ones, which resembled most typically the religious houses, and the smaller ones, which had been taking on chantry-like functions with one or two priests. Most almshouses were ignored. Hospitals were not mentioned specifically in the Dissolution Act of 1536, but several larger establishments passed into the king's hands in its immediate aftermath and during the voluntary submission period to1540: St Mary within Cripplegate, St Mary without Bishopsgate, and St Thomas Acon, all in London; the redoubtable St Leonard York; St John Exeter; St Mark Bristol; Godshouse Southampton; and St Giles Norwich, among others. From what we know about several of these transactions, each must have been accompanied by active, sometimes desperate, negotiations. Hospital senior staff could be attracted to pension offers, and royal agents or well-connected locals often were anxious to conclude the surrender quickly and become involved in the disposition of the lucrative properties involved. These mostly *ad hoc* negotiations were legitimized by a 1539 statute that included under the dissolution umbrella not only monasteries, friars' houses, convents, and colleges, but hospitals as well.[91]

A second, more heuristic statute from the vantage point of the hospitals was passed later in the same year. It authorized the king to make 'better use' of religious property for a variety of purposes that impinged on hospital and almshouse functions. Was this a pale shadow of the medieval Lollard reform plan for 100 new almshouses or the provision for national care of the sick poor in Marshall's draft? After much discussion among the king's advisors, it was decided that each new or restored foundation would have a chapter of clergy, a school, an almshouse for old soldiers and former royal servants, and the capability to distribute alms to poor householders. The maintenance costs for each establishment was estimated at about 680 L, and beyond that 590 L was to be distributed as alms. By 1542, 18 renewed monasteries and monastic cathedrals had been authorized, with a paltry total almshouse capacity of 124 souls. The passage of the Chantry Act (1545) and the king's remarks to Lords subsequently further advanced the suggestion that he intended to put the remaining chantries, religious guilds, collegiate churches, and hospitals to better uses. Among other things, the legislation authorized the first survey of chantries, which was carried out by county in the spring of 1546. It found many more, if not all the hospitals in the realm, but before any coherent plan to act on these data could be developed, Henry died and the statute lapsed.[92] Overall, Henry VIII temporized on the fate of the hospitals. For their clerical excesses they warrented dissolution. But, as for how they and related institutions could be reformulated or renewed for 'better use,' his rhetoric far exceeded any practical accomplishment. And, in the process, when we add monasteries to the hospitals, hundreds of institutions that, in theory at least, served the poor had been closed.

Nevertheless, during these same years and on into the later sixteenth century, local officials throughout the realm took up cudgels for the poor. None were more resourceful than the men and women of Norwich. St Giles, the city's venerable medieval hospital that, like others, had become more involved with corrodarians than sick poor people by the early sixteenth century, had surrendered to the king sometime between 1538 and 1540. But, unlike the formerly mighty St Leonard York, which closed within two years of its submission, St Giles found new life as the Norwich Goddes Howse after 1546.[93] As we will see below, it was a part of the city's post-dissolution attempt to establish new and more effective responses to all varieties of poor people, local and known as well as alien and threatening.

Conclusion

In these years, migration from the countryside to the towns and London became a constant factor in the maturing economy. Enclosure and land shortages in particular localities almost required that some of the young and dispossessed seek their subsistence elsewhere, sometimes in more promising rural areas, sometimes in towns. There was also a cohort of ambitious or skilled artisans who sought better opportunities. And from these streams of 'subsistence' and 'betterment' migrants developed both the vagrancy problem which so perplexed parish and local officials and patterns of social mobility among urban burgesses.

Two quite different outlooks were vying for attention in the later fifteenth and early sixteenth centuries. 'Commonwealth' or 'common weal' thinking appraised these unsettling social and economic developments as matters that required, and could be ameliorated to some extent by, human intervention that went beyond the traditional, voluntry *societas* undertakings of personal and local charity. The new *civitas* ideas were predicated on the assumption that social problems, like the alarming and seemingly endless structural poverty in the towns and metropolis, were being caused primarily by human failures and would have to be remedied by man's planning and interventions. Here were the roots of the infatuation with 'policies' at the local and central government levels. The other response was a resurgence of the *societas christiana*, centered around the re-enchantment of the parishes. Forms of local ritual were shifting from the manor to the parish in the 1470s and 1480s and encouraging a 'merrier' England. At the same time, the renewed embrace of the church's purgatory doctrine led to much preoccupation with praying for departed souls, done mostly by 'professional' paupers. Also prominent were a swarm of traditional condemnations of the evils of urban life.

Christian humanist and Lutheran Protestant commitments began to intrude into these dynamic but anomalous conditions shortly after the turn of the sixteenth century. Each offered a perspective on the human condition generally and the effective ways it could be brought to its fullest potential. And both held that human character needed cultivation from both the scriptures and classical authors. The humanists, however, infatuated with the 'concord' promised in Cicero's *De officiis*, put their emphasis on human reason as the tool for designing a more just and fulfilling social order. The Protestants stressed the need for humans to be more available to the promptings of divine providence and God's 'inner commonwealth.' Ironically, Henry VIII's humanist inspired court in the 1530s attempted to impose a Protestant conformity on the realm. In the short run the consequences of these policies were quite damaging to the realm's existing social welfare capabilities.

Chapter 3: Parish, Town, and Poor Law (c.1540–1610)

Conditions that would lead to an increase in structural poverty for the next 100 years came to the fore around 1540. The favorable ratio of population to employment that had underpinned the relatively 'good' times for rural laborers since the late fourteenth century began to turn. E. A. Wrigley and R. S. Schofield have shown that between 1540 and 1640 England's population doubled and prices for consumables tripled. Agricultural productivity was unable to meet the demands of the rapidly expanding population. The resulting upward pressure on prices was made all the more punishing by a decline in real wages over at least a 40-year period beginning in the early 1570s.[1] These dynamics combined with the onset of dearth conditions in the mid-1580s and mid-1590s yielded a major crisis in poverty and relief. From this came the Elizabethan Poor Law (1598, 1601), which would be central to the realm's social welfare until the early nineteenth century

Social and demographic historians have been hard pressed to distinguish the structural poor from parish-assisted poor persons and to estimate their proportion in the realm's population in the sixteenth and seventeenth centuries. The national data base is exceedingly narrow: the assessment of 1522, the lay subsidies of 1524–25, and the hearth tax returns of the 1660s and 1670s. A *nil* assessment income level on these levies seems to have been a kind of *de facto* 'poverty line.' The bleakest estimate to emerge from these materials is that in the early Tudor years perhaps 60 percent of the rural population and two-thirds of the town dwellers lived with incomes near or below this designation. Later in Charles II's reign one-third to one-half of the populace were in dire need. More sanguine projections suggest that between 10 percent and 20 percent of the population actually had incomes at or below nil assessment in the 1520s and 15 percent to 25 percent in the 1670s. A. L. Beier cautions, however, that both projections must be corrected for life-cycle dependence, gender, geography, fluidity among population groups, and long-term economic shifts.[2]

Social Structure and Urban Migration

The fourteenth-century footprint of social and economic arrangements that we discussed in Chapter 1 persisted through the early modern years and beyond: thousands of differentiated rural hamlets and villages dotted the realm, each bound loosely into a local commercial network with a market or regional town as its focus. London, growing at a very rapid pace, remained *sui generis* for its sheer size and commercial magnetism that reverberated throughtout the economy. But the Malthus factor, held mostly at bay since the plague calamity of 1349, reared its ugly head again with a vengeance. England's population, which hovered at about two million souls when Henry VIII succeeded to the throne in 1509, would top five million in the years of the Civil War and Interregnum. As the numbers increased so did the population's distribution, mostly from the countryside toward the towns but also within the countryside. Towns, as they had been earlier, were distinguished more by their social structures and degree of commercial and administrative activities than by their size. Sixteenth-century England had about 600 entities that could be considered towns. They ranged from market settlements as small as 600 people to regional towns of 7000 or more (the likes of York, Bristol, Norwich, Exeter, or Coventry) to London with its 60,000 in 1520. By that measure, the cumulative 'urbanization' of the population under way in the sixteenth and seventeenth centuries was significant: from 10 percent to 12 percent in the 1520s to 20 to 25 percent at the Restoration in the 1660s.[3]

This internal migration was a shaping characteristic of sixteenth- and early seventeenth-century society. To some degree London and the larger towns were population black holes; their very unhealthiness contributed to high mortality rates and the need to sustain a steady influx of migrants. More generally, though, the incentives for those who hit the road continued to be the need for subsistence or the attraction

of moving up to better circumstances, thus 'push' for some and 'pull'
for others. And, at a very basic level, it had to have been jarring for the
denizens of otherwise coherent and complacent settlements to lose
neighbors and replace them with unkown 'foreigners,' just as it must
have been frightening for migrants to leave familiar confines and set
out for the uncertain and unknown. The latter is certainly the most
ubiquitous example of 'agency' among the poor that we have. Although
a strong sense of community did prevail in the villages and urban
neighborhoods, it was tested constantly by the transient nature of the
local population, particularly at the lower levels of the social scale.[4]

As we have seen, in some places the rate of turn-over could reach
one-half to two-thirds of the residents in a little more than a decade or
two.[5] Young people with limited opportunities in their birth locale
often left home to seek employment or apprenticeship and might pass
through several placements before attaining some modicum of enonomic
security. On the road they mixed with seasonal, displaced, and discontented workers forming the mobile, bounding cohort that had been
frightening local residents and officials since the Black Death. Young
seekers of greener and more accessible pastures in the early seventeenth
century were drawn to fens and forest areas where common fields
remained accessible. For example, parishes like Williamham in the
fenlands of northern Cambridgeshire and the Isle of Axholme in the
Lincolnshire fens held the possiblity for a smallholder or landless
peasant to graze animals, to pursue fishing and fowling, or perhaps to
seek employment in a local cottage industry. They ineluctably drew
souls away from settlements like Orwell in Cambridgeshire, where no
commons were available and younger sons faced landless futures.
Countless numbers of new cottages were built in the fens' growth
regions, as well as in woodland areas in Northamptonshire, Dorset, and
Wiltshire, where pasturing cattle and wood harvesting opportunities
prevailed.[6]

Local farming arrangements, field systems, and seignurial power
were embedded in the idiosyncracies of soil, climate, custom and law.
And these were shaped further by regional specializations in crop
selection, stock breeding, and patterns of land use, which marked the
differences among fielden, fens, and upland villages or the mixed
industrial-agricultural employment that prevailed in many regions. In
the mid-sixteenth century, the great magnates and peers (which before
the Reformation included bishops and mitered abbotts), knights, and
baronets or esquires, numbered 200–500 individuals. Their estates

exeeded 5000 acres each and totalled perhaps one-fifth to one-fourth of the realm's land. Below them were the 8000–10 000 gentry households who owned 30 percent of the cultivated land. For the rest, the median farm size in the sixteenth and early seventeenth centuries was 30 to 60 acres. Freehold and copyhold status continued to multiply at the expense of manorial oversight as possession became indentified more closely with property ownership, and less with mere occupancy and use.

A boom in land sales took off in the 1540s triggered by the government's moves to confiscate church properties. Ironically the crown lands, as well as the church's, began to diminish as the result of these transfers. They had constituted roughly 5 percent of the realm in the fifteenth century but would become negligible again by the the Civil War years. Beyond the gentry and comfortable yeomen, it was the lawyers, merchants, burgesses, and office-holders who benefitted the most from the land transfer business. The losers were those with insufficient means to participate in the buying spree or to protect their holdings: the lesser yeomanry, minor husbandmen, and small copyholders. It is estimated that by 1600 two-thirds of the realm's land was classifed as freehold, much of it large 'rentier' estates.[7] As we have seen, enclosure of common fields and the consequent displacement of tenants probably had peaked in the 1520s. Depopulation and desertion of villages, although exaggerated by preachers and commentators, was real nevertheless; and, anti-enclosure riots (and occasional risings) persisted into the seventeenth century.

Depopulation continued in villages from Devon to Northumberland. Contributing to this, was another long-standing practice with its roots deep in the Middle Ages: the land aggrandizing of upwardly mobile yeomen. This polarized the non-gentry rural population into its own wealthy and poor cohorts. And, to ward off the ambitious, land-grabbing yeoman, larger owners often felt the need to consolidate their holdings. Nevertheless, Maurice Beresford has shown that by the early seventeenth century the distinction between 'improvement' and anti-social enclosure was being made widely; and, the Tudor cliches, 'sheep eat men' and 'horn and thorn shall make England forlorn' were losing their punch.[8]

The smallholders – because of enclosure, foreclosure, or simply the inability to live off their land any longer – became part of the stream of migrants that steadily redistributed substantial numbers of poor people across the realm. The larger towns and London served as endpoints for perhaps half of them. York and Exeter each grew by 50 percent in the early modern years, and Worcester's population doubled between the 1560s and the 1640s. The metropolis continued its startling expansion, from 60 000 in the 1520s, to 200 000 in 1600, and 400 000 by 1650.[9] Just how these influxes affected urban life and what economic opportunities or social welfare were available to migrants is far from clear. For the last three decades, the study of early modern towns and London has been particularly vibrant, but disagreements run deeply among historians.

The larger cohort of urban historians find sixteenth- and seventeenth-century urban life, including conditions in London, to have been a time of jarring and unrelenting crises. This view, articulated first by Paul Slack and Peter Clark in the 1970s, holds that the towns exhibited the complicated continuity-and-change dynamic that Keith Wrightson and others have found in rural society.[10] This is rooted in the sociological history, or new social history, that Peter Laslett and E. A. Wrigley initiated in the 1950s; it maintains that early modern social welfare should be studied from local contexts outward and upward, and not from the top down. It is informed further by two assumptions: social processes close to the ground were shaped by social-structural time, not by decades or reigns; and poverty and the responses it engendered can be understood most fully in appropriate settings, such as, counties, hundreds, cities, towns, or villages. Thus, when sociological historians address 'national' matters, they refer less to monarchs, reigns, and policy initiatives flowing outward from the center and more to ubiquitous demographic, social, economic, intellectual, linguistic, and political forces throughout the realm. These impinged on urban and rural settings alike and produced numberless local crises of 'continuity and change'.[11]

Clark and Slack's volume signaled the reinvigoration of urban history after more than a generation of relative quiet. Their work and the urban history 'template' it inspired argues for a profound transition in the early modern towns and cities, from 'traditional, relatively closed, and semi-autonomous' corporate entities at the end of the fifteenth century to 'more modern, open and integrated,' but oligarchic, urban locales by 1700. In essence, the roughly 20 percent of the realm's population who lived in the cities and towns, but particularly those in the 120 or so moderate-sized municipalities, experienced a 'major collision of continuity and change.' The urban landscape was filled with obstacles to well-being, including de-industrialization, the constant influx of subsistence migrants, periodic ourbreaks of the plague, devastating fires, wage deflation, food price inflation, a growing distance between rich and poor, a dramatic reduction of church alms and other social services because of the Dissolution, and the weakening of local government's autonomy by the intrusion of government and county obligations.[12]

The cumulative effect of these difficulties was to induce 'urban decay' and a sense of 'crisis' in the towns. And, by 1600, poverty had become a ubiquitous calamity in the towns, despite the successes of many local magistrates in devising censuses of the poor, reviving post-Dissolution social services, and imposing a compulsory poor rate. Compared to the relative harmony that prevailed in those same corporations in the later fifteenth century, urban life had become narrow, oligarchic, 'short-sighted and inward looking.'[13] England's urban social order was becoming polarized between 'an increasingly pampered, narrow elite' and swarms of 'destitute poor tramping the streets.' The 'better sort' did become more skilled in managing the worst effects of poverty. For example, they appropriated more funds for outdoor relief, gave firmer direction to parish officers as the Poor Law began to be implemented, and saw to the founding of almshouses and hospitals. And, by 1700, corporations for the poor had been established in London, Bristol, Exeter, Norwich, and Hull. Nevertheless, these very undertakings and their calming effect on overt social tensions served more than anything to demonstrate the profound estrangement that had developed between the urban rich and poor.[14]

Ian Archer concentrates on politics and government, particularly two challenges that London's leaders had to face in the later sixteenth century. First, they had to remain on good terms with the crown without being perceived to be giving in to royal patronage and financial pressures. Second, even though most of the City's aldermanic elite were first-generation betterment migrants from modest provincial circumstances, if they were to be accepted from below as an 'aristocratic' not an 'oligarchic' regime, they had to establish by whom and how consent to their policies would be sought. Elizabeth's importunings to the City were never very strong, and the leadership managed them effectively for the most part. And at the parliamentary level, London was the most effective corporation in lobbying for its interests. The City's MPs were backed by 'an experienced, wealthy and well-organized lobby,' the Aldermen, who 'regularly paid fees and gifts to officials and retained the most well-known and effective lawyers.'[15] The consent matter was more complicated, however. Archer holds that the 'elite walked on the crust of a volcano' that coated over seething resentments between wholesalers and artisans, householders and servants, and freemen and foreigners, among others. Structural adjustments were made that widened and regularized participation in elections and deliberations, and, most important, the aldermen, mayor, and other officials determined to agree on their objectives as much as possible and to discourage factions. This commitment was boosted considerably beginning in the 1580s when Puritan theology enveloped the City government. The preachers expounded constantly on the theme that the Aldermen held their wealth as stewards and would be held accountable for their care of the City's poor. Archer's London elite attended much to the smoke and mirrors of image projection to sustain among their subalterns and lesser sorts the conviction that they indeed did care about them and the maintenance of the commonwealth.[16]

Other historians see the towns in the early modern centuries rising from their economic nadir in the later fifteenth century to bigger and better possibilities. The towns benefitted from the vitality and ingenuity of the newcomers, unwelcome as they may have been initially, and achieved an expanding prosperity. This narrative of urban progress acknowledges the vast number of urban poor, perhaps 40 percent of any town's population. The unemployed migrants tended to congregate in the suburbs, constituting literally 'another world' where indigency and crime required special attention. Yet, in spite of these difficulties, the urban setting overall was a dynamic one into which displaced poor people could enter and many of them prosper.[17] For example, Valerie Pearl has maintained that London's government, far from resting exclusively in the hands of an aldermanic elite, was unique in all of Europe for the proportion of its free population who were elected to office, perhaps 3000 at the ward level alone. There were further thousands of officials responsible for coordinating the implementation of the Poor Law, who cooperated with wardens and yeomen from the livery companies, guild officers, and hospital governors, virtually all of whom were elected to their positions, collecting and allocating resources for relief of the poor. Vestries, wardmotes and quarter sessions provided the opportunity for all but the most dependent poor to share opinions and aspirations.[18]

Steve Rappaport finds that the city corporation in the mid-sixteenth-century was a relatively open and flexible administrative unit, frequently collaborating with the liveries and guilds to address the

City's numerous immigration and poverty-related problems.[19] Limited by paltry funds and an insufficient bureaucracy at their immediate disposal, London's Aldermen developed a central government that, more than anything, was an 'integrative superstructure which coordinated the activites of smaller administrative units.' It was essentially a decentralized system dependent on the energy and efficiency of wards, precincts, parishes, and particularly companies to discipline the economy, raise taxes, administer the courts, and provide social services. These small organizations toward the middle and bottom of this interwoven system provided the vital energy and skills that allowed it to work. And they were the entry points into freedom and social mobility for a high percentage of the 'foreigners' (English migrants) and 'aliens' and 'strangers' (immigrants from overseas) who were propelling the city's rapid population growth. Claire Schen, using London churchwardens' accounts, Court of Alderman Records, and other relevant certificates and briefs, has shown the willingness of parish officials to act independently on the issue of an alien's right to casual relief. They evaluated each case on its own merits whether the petitioner appeared from the Barbary Coast, the Ottoman frontier, or the battlefields of the Thirty Years War.[20]

Rappaport pursues a career reconstitution effort to follow the paths to citizen's status of 530 men and 73 women apprentices in the 1550s. While it was quite rare for a woman to achieve free status, he found that fully 96 percent of the men he followed became freemen. Nevertheless, Rappaport does not claim that all was well all the time in sixteenth-century London. Available records are insufficient to conclude definitively about the City's economy; and, the dearth, inflation, and falling wages of the 1590s brought terrible hardships and much resentment against aliens and strangers. He does insist, though, that the resourceful, cooperative relationships between Guildhall and the companies, combined with the bottom–up energy and mobility within the system, made it possible for the City to cope with its challenges.

These patterns not withstanding, religious social criticism of the capital persisted from several quarters through the 1540s and 1550s. Thomas Lever and Hugh Latimer, for example, fanned the flames of urban phobia, attributing the suffering of the realm's poor to the habits of London's pagan and rapacious rich.[21] And, well before the uprisings of 1549, Henry Brinkelow had thrown down the gauntlet for the 'oppressed and overyoked' commons, declaring the government's efforts deficient in both curbing clerical abuses and orchestrating a more just and prosperous commonwealth. Very much in the spirit of later medieval social commentary, Brinkelow saw the poor commons as victims of 'wicked' laws, their related oppressions and the fornicating, covetous, and idolatrous population of London. The cause of all this, he declared, was the still-thwarted reformation of religion. Since the unregenerate episcopate persisted in forcing a Catholic-like religion on the realm, the continuing obfuscation of God's word prevented the realization of just social relations.[22] Robert Crowley, who became a fully committed Puritan after the Marian exile, sustained the medieval populist social analysis with *The Vision of William concerning Piers Plowman* (1550) and a series of pamphlets defending the rights of the poor. In his remedy for sedition, *The Way to Wealth* (1550), Crowley accused gentlemen, merchants and lawyers of oppressing the poor in a variety of ways, from raising rents to enclosing arable land. These excesses far outweighed the poor's lack of respect for the law and their social superiors. Yet, even if the king, 'God's minister to revenge the wrongs done unto the innocent,' had failed in his job, rebellion was not permissible. Oppression and evil rule are visited on a realm by God; the only justifiable remedy is for each man to examine his conscience, acknowledge that evil times follow from sin, and reform his life. Crowley concluded with a line worthy of Langland or Wyclif himself but which also captured the deepening providentialism of mid-sixteenth-century Protestant discourse: 'let thy desire be that God's will be fulfilled in thee.'[23]

Complementing this provocative rhetoric in these years was a constant undertow of status resentment and economic grievance that kept the poor commons susceptible to recruitment into insurrections regardless of the immediate causes. And the 'discourse of confrontation' of Kett's Rebellion (1549) suggests that the initiative for reform was shifting from the government (as in the mid-1530s) more to the grass roots, although not without the government's encouragement in this instance. One set of instigators were aggrieved primarily at local officials who seemed to thwart the government's own encouragement of the desire for social and economic mobility at or near the bottom of society. Other participants, however, were aggrieved with the government itself, offended by the Prayer Book of 1549 and the Somerset regime's determined efforts to stifle local rituals. The rising began as an ordinary riot of tenants against unloved landlords and, in succeeding transformations, developed first into a great demonstration about injustice and the Reformation, and finally into a bloody insurrection of national significance.[24] The duke of Somerset's measures from June 1548 to June 1549 against enclosure, and pardoning those who had thrown enclosure open, seemed to signal that the Lord Protector sided with the ambitious small farmers and businessmen against the large landlords, their lawyers, and the control they maintained over the courts and markets.[25]

In effect, the aspirations of the poor commons had been whetted by central government policy and blunted at the local and county level by conservative interests. John Cheke, the court's propagandist, reminded Robert Kett and his followers of the irony in seeking social advancement through rebellion: insurrection breaks down social distinctions. It is not that Cheke would ridicule the desire for mobility, however, just the means. The rebels were guaranteeing that the children of the poor would no longer move up in society and provide succor to their families. Even more interesting was Cheke's identification of the instrument of mobility in the first place; it was providence, not reason or state policy. Thus the ultimate presumption of the rebels was that they would put their faint wisdom in the place of God's plan to advance whom he chooses.[26] The relentless Protestant edge of Somerset's policies and propaganda was not without its detractors, however. In 1552, Dr John Caius, taking the measure of the realm religiously, was spurred to characterize the pre-Reformation years as 'the old world, when the country was called Merry England.'[27]

Calvinism on the Rise

We have seen that Luther's estimate of human nature differed dramatically from that of the Christian humanists. Both Luther and Calvin stressed the impairment that resulted from original sin; humans in their post-fall, historical state were corrupted vessels dependent on God's mercy. Thomas Becon, writing in the early 1540s, had conveyed bluntly this Protestant anthropology to his fellow Englishmen. We are 'born of the seed of Adam,' intoned Becon, 'very flesh, unpure, uhallowed, abominable before God.' Our just desserts merit no more than God's 'fierce wrath' and 'grievous judgment...sin, death, hell [and] desperation.' Yet, only if we acknowledge our utterly sorry state will we be disposed to fall down 'most humbly' before God, 'confess that our destruction cometh of ourselves,' and acknowledge that 'all our help cometh of God only.'[28] If the human situation without faith was hopeless, Calvinism at least offered many buttresses to the 'saints,' once they had put themselves wisely into God's providential hands. For instance, one's place in society was no longer fortuitous or meaningless; it was purposive, and the elect were to be found at all levels in the social order. It followed that the cumulative inner light of a locality's or congregation's saints would cause it figuratively to glow spiritually from top to bottom. Like other Protestant theologians, Calvin had no use for asceticism; he taught nevertheless that limits and moderation must accompany the pursuit of comfort. Appropriate 'riches and honors' followed from placing trust in God's blessing, not the practice of 'wicked arts.' And, even though 'unregenerate' traders, craftsmen, and merchants sullied commerce, pursuing a living by means of commercial calculations and actions was without inherent fault. More to the point, commerce illustrated God's intention that people should depend on one another; and, if carried out in the proper spirit of Christian duty, great benefits would accrue to a community.[29]

The transition to Calvinism in England had begun in earnest under Edward VI and, after the Marian Catholic hiatus, achieved full bloom in the Elizabethan and early Stuart years. Calvin's *Institutes of the Christian Religion* was translated into English in 1561, and many Marian exiles returned as committed reformers. More than Lutheranism had, Calvinism engaged the world with confidence in its ability to shape a biblically Christian commonwealth. The fact that God justified or planted the seeds of faith in the elect caused them 'to pass over from death to life.' But, since perfection eluded even the saved, they must attempt to imitate Christ within their 'puny capacity' and make whatever 'progress in the way of the Lord' that they can. As we might expect, Calvin's slant on the 'king as God' Scriptural passages was quite different from that of Erasmus and the humanists. It was the 'providence and holy ordinance of God' that brought authority to kings and earthly governors of all types. God is 'present, and ... presides among them, in making laws and in executing equitable judgments.'[30] While Calvin made less of the monarch's reason and independent judgment in law making and distributing justice, he elevated the prince's status. He was the essential conduit through which God's intentions for the realm were transmitted. It is interesting to recall that Thomas Starkey was inclined to conflate reason of state and providence as well.

Calvinism had a distinct conceptual vocabulary to bring to bear on understanding poverty and other social problems. It combined the consequences of justification, the utility of commerce and material aspirations, and the mutual workings of calling, human will, and divine providence in achieving Christian community. Calvinists were guided by three scriptural passages as they sought to explain and respond to poverty. 'But there will be no poor among you' (Deuteronomy 15:4) inspired the Reformed to attain a degree of liberality in their communities that would make begging unnecessary. 'Blessed is he that considereth of the poor, the Lord will deliver him in the time of trouble' (Psalm 41) encouraged confidence in a worldly reward for charity. And, 'If anyone will not work let him not eat' (2 Thessalonians 3:10) led Calvinsts to be suspicious of the healthy unemployed who they assumed deprived the deserving poor of their alms. This played out in an unsentimental appraisal of the poor, especially aimless and cunning strangers, a commitment to enhance the congregation as a charitable institution, an interest in medical care to keep the poor less menacing and more productive, and the inspiration for ministry-magistracy alliances at the local level to institutionalize Reformed societal aspirations.[31] Capturing this spirit at the turn of the seventeenth century, William Perkins wrote that begging 'doth proclaim to the world, in the ears of all men, the shame either of the magistrate, who restrains it not, having authority: or of the wealthy and able, that they have no mercy or compassion.'[32]

This close-to-the-ground approach to social welfare had been given a strong boost in 1557, with the publication of a pamphlet on poor relief by the deceased Calvinist Martin Bucer, former Regius Professor of Divinity. Drawing on the Acts of the Apostles, Bucer made a compelling justification for congregation-centered poor relief and cautioned against the 'uncertain sophistry' of those who use 'Utopia' as a model. Deacons, men above reproach in the parish, should be given the responsibility to visit the poor, distinguish genuine need from bogus, and supervise, distribute, and account for poor relief funds. Blunt in his approach to vagrancy, Bucer held that all sturdy vagabonds should be expelled from the congregation. On the other hand, sounding almost like Vives, he pleaded that every congregation bring up its youth virtuously, trained in 'good arts', so that each can 'declare himself to others a true, and profitable member of Christ.'[33]

A Mid-Tudor Social Welfare Crisis?

The challenges faced by local magistrates, parliament, court, and council were far more complicated than controlling vagrancy and cooling down anti-enclosure sentiments. As we have noted, population growth, lagging agricultural productivity, inflation, and diminishing real wages were beginning to weaken the economy. And a myriad of factors provided the immediate context for those general dynamics. Inflation was intensified by the coinage debasement that lasted from 1542 to 1551 and a run of poor harvests in 1545, 1549–51 and 1555–56. Plague outbreaks in 1543, 1544–46 and 1549–51, the Scottish war and rebellions in 1549 and 1554, depression in the cloth manufacturing trades beginning in 1551, and the Dissolution-caused closing of approximately half of the realm's more than 500 endowed alms-dispensing institutions added to the general woe.[34] Slack has described these years as a '*tabula rasa*' moment for social welfare leaders in London. They had to decide what could be salvaged from traditional responses to vagrancy and poverty, define 'their most urgent priorities and rethink their charitable and civic priorities.'[35] Certainly that char-acterization could be applied more broadly throughout the realm. As much as anything the government 'commonweal idea' of the mid-1530s had run its course by this time; a sense of this pervades the first vagancy and poor relief statutes of Edward VI. In its stead a variety of corporate bodies from towns and boroughs to hospitals and almshouses, perhaps by default, became the energy sources of its 'evening glow.' Until 1572, when the government reclaimed the social welfare initiative with its first definitive Poor Law since 1536, the policy *tabula rasa* gave rise to hundreds of 'little commonwealths.'[36]

Robert Tittler has concluded that the Dissolution produced nothing less than a 'dramatic and destructive impact on the traditional culture and institutions of English local society'. This very calamity, however, provided the opportunity for ambitious and opportunistic town corporations, the likes of Exeter, Norwich, Bristol, Leicester, and Gloucester, among others, to act on their own behalf. And, as they moved to assume control over the formerly church-supervised social welfare institutions, they enhanced their 'civic consciousness' and 'civil competence.' This has led Tittler to insist that a suitable historiography of late sixteenth-century towns must combine political culture, social and economic developments, and attention to a 'Protestant civics' that attracted middling and oligarchic leaders. His position rests subtly between the 1970s Clark and Slack urban history template with its emphases on poverty crises and rising oligarchy and Patrick Collinson's more recent proposal that after 1570 Puritan doctrine provided an ideology of urban rule that promoted discipline, morality, and deference.[37]

Officials in the metropolis and numerous localities had been endeav-
oring to cope with what seemed to them to be unusual numbers of
vagrants for at least two decades prior to the first wave of the Dissolution
in 1536–37. Suddenly they faced a drastic shrinkage in charitable
institutions. Their responses included cajoling renewed outputs of
voluntary charity, gifts, and bequests; initiating censuses of the poor;
imposing a poor rate; and re-establishing almshouses in some form.
These undertakings seem to have been motivated more by pragmatic
common sense than by either Christian humanism or Calvinist ideas.[38]

By the onset of Edward VI's reign, supervised procedures to allow
begging while discouraging indiscriminate almsgiving had been
devised in numerous locales, including, Norwich, Southampton,
Cambridge, Chester, Lincoln, Hull, Beverly, York, and King's Lynn.
Censuses of the poor were up and running in Chester (1539), Coventry
(1547), and Ipswich (1551); and, by 1557 compulsory poor rates were
being attempted in London, Norwich, York, Colchester, Cambridge,
Ipswich, and the Suffolk village of Cratfield.[39] But surely the most
ambitious of local, post-Dissolution efforts was the the establishment of
the five hospitals in London. In 1538, the City had petitioned the king
to restore St Bartholomew's and St Thomas's to gather in and care for
'the miserable people lying in every street, offending every clean
person passing by...with their filthy and nasty savours.' Henry
responded by 1546 with grants of St Bartholomew's, the Greyfriars,
and additional church property, stipulating only that the buildings and
proceeds be used for merciful care 'according to the primitive pattern.'
Soon thereafter Edward VI transmitted Bridewell Palace and the
Savoy's landed endowments to the City.

After much internal debate, five hospitals were launched between
1544 and 1557. St Bartholomew's was to care for the sick poor, and
Christ's hospital in the Greyfriars would raise and educate foundlings
and orphans. The old and feeble would be taken in at St Thomas's and
the mentally deficient at Bethlehem ('Bedlam'). The idle, but hardy
poor were to be put to work in Bridewell. Christ's was designated the
central repository and distribution point for relief funds raised in the
city's 100 or so parishes; it was hoped, unwisely as it turned out, that
each hospital would establish its own sustaining endowment.[40]
Bridewell's mission to redirect the idle and indigent to 'sciences profitable to the commonweal' was imitated widely across the realm and
made mandatory in 1576 (18 Eliz., *c*.8). And, after the establishment of
Amsterdam's 'house of discipline' in 1596, Bridewell-like institutions

proliferated on the continent. Slack considers the workhouse to be England's first and most original contribution to social welfare practice Europewide, eclipsing even the mandatory poor rate (1572).[41]

Rather than the 'war on poverty' approach of the Cromwellian humanists in the 1530s, the duke of Somerset in the first years of the boy king Edward VI's reign (1547–53) focused the government's policy's on a 'war on the poor makers.' Somerset's endeavor to diminish enclosure by taxes on sheep and reviving Wolsey's anti-enclosure commissions were the most obvious examples. But more than 40 percent of the statutes passed in the two parliaments of Edward VI addressed social and economic issues.[42] On a broad front the government was seeking to restore the economic decorum of the common weal, and thus prevent further 'poor making.' The comple-ment to this was to hold the line against further expansion in the numbers of unemployed migrants: thus the harsh anti-vagrancy tone of the 1547 statute, which mirrored conceptually and rhetorically the vagrancy statute of 1531. The 1547 Act's draconian possibilities were heightened by the contrast it drew between the 'foolish piety and mercy' of earlier legislations' enforcers and the 'perverse nature and long accustomed idleness' of vagrants.

The indictment of idleness as the 'mother and root' of the realm's crime and vice was central, and that claim persisted throughout the pre-industrial centuries. Thus able-bodied persons observed to be idle up to three days, or who had refused to work, or had broken their terms of service, 'being unprofitable members or rather enemies of the common wealth,' could have the letter 'V' burned into them and be made slaves of their accusers for two years. Those who fled these arrangements could be subject to being branded with the letter 'S' and returned to their place of origin to serve as public-works slaves. Idle children, too, were subject to discipline. Those between ages 5 and 14 could be taken as apprentices or servants without their parents' consent, if the prospective guardian promised before a Justice of the Peace or a parish constable and two witnesses to bring up the child in a trade. Mayors, sheriffs, and bailiffs were charged to break up gather-ings of beggars and inspect monthly the 'maimed and otherwise lame sore aged and impotent persons' among them. As many as possible were to be relocated to their places of birth or previous three-year place of residence. The rest would be housed in cottages at the locality's expense and 'relieved and cured by the devotion of the good people of said cities [and] towns.' Special alms were to be made available to persons that have had 'their houses or barns burned, or such losses.'

Of particualar interest here is the basic encouragement the statute gave to the traditional, *societas*-like charity among the local faithful. Toward that goal, after the gospel reading each Sunday and holy day, the parish curate was to offer a 'godly and brief exhortation' reminding the faithful 'to remember the poor people and the duty of Christian charity' to their 'brethren in Christ born in the same parish and needing their help.'[43] Two years later, a similar perspective and buttressing language from 1531 informed the vagrancy statute of 1549. It noted still more ineffectiveness in the government's anti-vagrancy campaign, this time attributing the failure to 'the extremity of some [statutes] whereof have been occasion that they have not been put in use.' Not surprisingly, it drew back from the branding and slavery authorised in the 1547 statute and repealed all acts dealing with vagabonds, slaves, aged, and impotent persons except the present one and the statute of 1531. This meant that punishment for idleness or unauthorized begging reverted to whipping, time in stocks, and resettlment. Still, idle youth were to be subject to guardians' supervision, the feeble poor housed by the local jurisdiction and cared for by 'the devotion of the good people,' and the parish poor relieved from charity encouraged by the curate's preaching.[44]

In 1552, an Act 'For the Provision and Relief of the Poor' (5 & 6 Edw. VI, c. 2) confirmed the vagrancy acts of 1531 and 1549 and their intent to both stem idle unemployment and provide relief for the deserving 'poor in very deed.' Now, however, the apparatus of compulsory giving began to be shaped. Two gatherers and collectors of alms for each parish, town, or city were to be elected annually and, if they refused, suffer a 20s. fine. In conjunction with the encouragement of charitable giving from the pulpit they will 'gently ask and demand of every man and woman' what they agreed to give weekly, record those donations, and report quarterly their accounts to city officials. Those refusing to give to the poor fund shall be 'gently' exhorted to do so by vicars, curates, parsons, and even the bishop if needed. And the expanding number and importance of charitable foundations is noted in the provision that bishops will examine them for proper functioning.[45]

Philip and Mary's government (1553–58) seemed only passively Catholic on these social welfare matters. The queen refounded her grandfather's Savoy hospital to provide care and a night's lodging to any poor person who showed up.[46] But the five London hospitals were not established fully until 1557, no doubt because Mary would have preferred their oversight by the church. On the other hand, both Cardinal Reginald Pole and Bishop Edmund Bonner favored large municipal hospitals on the scale of the Italian cities. In 1555, Thomas Paynel translated 12 sermons of St Augustine and dedicated the collection to the queen. Mocking the Protestant infatuation with the pulpit, Paynel rued that never had there been 'so much preaching and so little following, so much persuasion to succor and aid the poor, and such great poverty, so much good counsel given to ensure virtue, and so little apprehended and used.' The seventh sermon, 'Of Alms Deeds,' revived the *societas christiana* staple embedded in Matthew 25 that Christ will reward those who have provided even a 'cup of water' to his stand-ins on earth, the poor. With that in mind, Augustine wonders why or how one possibly could decide, 'I am a poor man, and not able to do any alms deeds.' Sermon 10 explored the tithing discourse.[47] While there was a noticeable upsurge in medieval parish rituals during Philip and Mary's reign, the government did not seem to be encouraging them; and, pre-Reformation levels were not approached. The curtailing of all begging and indiscriminate charity, called for in the Ypres and other urban reform plans and the Henrician and Edwardian legislation, caused the Marian government the most doctrinal discomfort.

Mary's contribution to the sequence of poor relief legislation (2 & 3 P. and M., c. 5 (1555)) also confirmed the 1531 and 1549 statutes and repeated the intent to stifle idleness and provide relief to the deserving. The responsibilities of the collectors, parsons, and bishops were carried forward. In a provision specifically directed at London, Christ's hospital was named the distributing agency for poor funds there. Two provisions were new: one a (Catholic?) suggestion that some poor may have to be licensed to beg elsewhere when available charity was insufficient to the need; and the other instructed wealthy parishes 'to contribute somewhat according to their ability' to the poor funds of the less affluent parishes. All of this, including the provision for licensing beggars, was continued in the first poor relief statute of Elizabeth (5 Eliz., c. 3 (1563)), although the penalties for refusing to be a collector were raised steeply and prison awaited delinquent collectors and the most obstinate givers.[48]

By reaching back to the commonplace statute of 1531 for their standard and passing over the more innovative legislation of 1535 and 1536, the Edwardian and Marian parliaments seemed to restore a less nuanced two-category definition of the poor: able-bodied unemployed who were to be punished; and the authentically needy to be given charity. The vocabulary of these statutes only slightly disguised the structural poor (strangers and vagrants) versus known poor (needy or sickly neighbors) distinction which, since the thirteenth and fourteenth centuries, reinforced the almsgivers' predispositions toward those they knew and trusted. In these *tabula rasa* years, parliament was conceding some of the governments initiative and appeared to acknowledge that at the grass roots, the emerging social welfare challenge would have to be met by corporate innovation and the re-energizing of traditional charity, both overseen locally.

In addition to the spate of poor relief and anti-vagrancy legislation since 1531 and the continuing efforts of the council on several fronts, the government embellished several lines of urban policy that extended back to the fifteenth century. These included redistribution of a portion of tenths and fifteenths to poorer communities, defense of monopolistic privileges in certain towns to sustain their economic livelihood, and obliging owners to restore land to tillage and rebuild decayed housing.[49]

Humanist and Protestant ideas about human nature, society, and the polity informed social commentary and policy debates throughout these decades. At the same time, the need to cope practically with dearth, plague, able-bodied migrants, and sick and impotent poor people did lessen the likelihood that ideas would be applied in a doctrinaire manner. Recall Lupset's advice to Pole in Thomas Starkey's *Dialogue* about the seductiveness of Plato's 'visions.'[50] Perhaps the most thoughtful of the sixteenth-century commentators and policymen was Sir Thomas Smith. Regius professor of civil law at Cambridge and vice-chancellor of the University, principal secretary to both Edward VI and Elizabeth, member of parliament, privy councilor, emissary and ambassador, as well as mentor to William Cecil, Smith was a man of learning and much practical experience. Through his responsibilities and personal connections at court from the 1530s to the 1570s he was a crucial bridge from the Cromwellian policy-making environment to that of William Cecil. Equally important, though, was his place between Starkey and Francis Bacon as a policy thinker. Unfortunately, an abrasive temperament and lack of political skills diminished the impact of his brilliance.[51]

In his ingenious dialogue, *Discourse of the Commonweal*, written in 1549 and published in 1581, Smith recast policy discourse on the poverty problem even more fundamentally than Starkey had, without focusing on poverty *per se*. Smith was actually crafting a kind of broad background perspective on the realm's social and economic challenges and how to deal with them that utilized his instincts for political economy. To him poverty, clearly structural poverty, was less a problem in and of itself and more a consequence of dearth, dwindling national wealth, enclosure, and the decay of towns and villages. Smith examined these problems deftly and independently, and offered proposals that, if acted upon, would have changed England, not attempted to restore it to an order already lost. For example, he refused to condemn all enclosure outright, although it was mostly an evil; and the decay of towns and villages and a damaging increase in imports were related to changing consumer fashions which English craftsmen were ignoring. Consequently, the economic culture of the towns must change: new crafts would have to be instituted, perhaps by attracting foreign craftsmen into England. Smith was convinced also that the devaluation of currency was the prime cause of the intractable dearth so complained about, and he urged a restoration of former currency names and values. Only in a country like 'Utopia,' he chided, which had no contact with other nations, could the delusion persist that precious metal and currency values could be changed dramatically without devastating effects.[52]

The ideological assumptions that Smith brought to the purposes, mechanics, and efficacy of policy make an interesting contrast with those of the policy formulators of two decades earlier, with the exception of Starkey. Poverty's waxing and waning was dependent on a complex set of forces, some resting in human nature, some in the quality of statesmanship, some in unfolding economic trends and forces. Prefiguring the political arithmaticians of a century later, Smith also was convinced of the need to keep servingmen and yeomen exercised and fit for war and realized that craftsmen actually created revenue for the realm.[53]

Smith had no doubt that experience, indispensable as it was, required supplementation by formal learning and that in any kind of governance, family, city or commonwealth, the most learned properly are chosen to govern.[54] Nevertheless, policy, even in the hands of the wise where it belongs, had its limits. 'All things that should be done in a commonwealth be not to be forced,' wrote Smith, 'but some so and some other by allurement and rewards rather.'[55] Smith regarded human nature as irremediably covetous; thus, in what may be yet another allusion to *Utopia*, he maintained that this covetousness could no more be purged from human inclination than could ire, fear, or gladness.[56] In the *Discourse*, Smith, as had Starkey earlier, used a polyvalent, humanist and Protestant language of social analysis and policy; and he did it with insight and sophistication. Smith was humane and hopeful, yet reconciled to the shadow of cupidity that fell across the human soul; he was an advocate of policy, yet aware of its limits in the face of worldly allure and profit. More than any of his predecessors or contemporaries, he secularized the idea of poverty and refocused the reform expectation from the quest for the familiar and static, to the contingency and meliorative possibilities of historical development. It was in this form that the Burghleys and the Bacons would take it up.

In these same years, expanding 'statism' was drawing the locus of political power and attention away from the 'country' estates and households where traditional hospitality had held sway through the era of chivalry. London was becoming the stage on which to affect one's presence and importance. Becoming ever-more fashionable there were Italianate civility and *politesse* in the style of Castiglione's *The Courtier*, which was translated into English in 1561 (the same year as Calvin's *Institutes*). In this new light traditional country hospitality stood in rustic and painful contrast to the new urban refinement, and in its legislation and policy since the 1530s the government had been seeking to funnel both rural and urban charity through the parishes. Local magistrates and parish overseers were encouraged to apportion assistance or punishment based on their judgment of the petitioners' worthiness. And, in these mid- and later sixteenth-century years, Felicity Heal finds a similar transition in hospitality patterns away from 'mutual amity' toward the modern meaning of 'charity' or, better said, 'welfare,' the narrower focus of giving something 'in monetary terms' to 'the needy and the deserving.'

Accompanying this transition was the distancing of recipient from donor or an emphasis on the 'otherness' and the 'alien' status of the receiver. Hospitality did not disappear, but a two-track system of caring for others was taking shape: hospitality among peers, charity to the needy.[57] The expansion of Tudor poverty legislation affirmed the 'separateness' between the poor and the household, 'the former being seen as a subgroup to be disciplined and/or relieved by public arrangements.'[58] Heal's observations are in keeping with the general suspicion of strangers and aliens in dispensing hospital beds and alms we have established in Chapters 1 and 2. Nevertheless, the sense that a purer form of hospitality was threatened and being diminished by the new civility was fueled by lingering attachments to humanist concord and Stoic integrity. Contemporaries concluded that hospitality was more likely to be found in the country than the city and in the past than the present.[59]

However, when we turn to philanthropy, private giving to establish charitable foundations, we find ourselves in a much different universe of giving. In his prodigious study of this phenomenon conveyed in extant wills, W. K. Jordan insisted that the Tudor Poor Laws were hardly a concession to the inevitability of publicly financed care for the poor.[60] Rather, they were meant to be prudent precautions in times of emergency. He held that ordinarily voluntary giving was expected to, and could, fund 'social relief' and 'social betterment.' The poor, after all, were the responsibility of 'the whole body politic,' not merely the government. And it was none other than the *nouveaux riches*, the commercially ambitious merchants and gentry, the very people Heal sees as lacking both refinement and an appreciation of traditional hospitality, whom Jordan finds to have carried the brunt of the charitable giving.[61] It has been easy to detract from Jordan's work because of his failure to compensate fully for inflation in making his gross estimates of the philanthropic output. But even when his figures are adjusted downward, we are left to explain a significant shift in Tudor behavior. Recent estimates are that in London between 1573 and 1597 the increase in philanthropic output 'per capita in real [noninflated] terms' was 13 percent. Yet, because of the growth in the proportion of the poor relative to the general population in those years, any gain for individual recipients of assistance was slight at best.[62]

Jordan's undertaking was conceptualized in the late 1950s, just a few years after G. R. Eltons's 'Tudor revolution' thesis.[63] Jordan, too, sought to show a dramatic historical 'discontinuity,' in this instance from religion-centered to secular-motivated giving. He maintained that this 'great cultural revolution' was driven ironically by Puritan preaching. In the wake of the Dissolution of the monasteries, fraternities, chantries, and other traditional charitable and alms-dispensing institutions of the church, a powerful surge of philanthropy emerged. It became a crucial supplement to the urgent attempts of local municipal corporations to set up their own social services. The empirical base of Jordan's work consists of thousands of wills drawn from ten counties and the metropolis for the years 1480 to 1660. The ten

(Bristol, Buckinghamshire, Hampshire, Kent, Lancashire, Middlesex-London, Norfolk, Somerset, Worcestershire, and Yorkshire) represent approximately one-third of the realm's area and population, but their people disposed of approximately 50 percent of England's wealth and provided 60 percent of its charitable bequests in the early modern centuries. Jordan was convinced that this sustained outpouring of charity was of such moment that it must be understood to have been the major source of direct support for the needy and the funding of meliorative social service efforts. In comparison, he insisted, funds raised by the law-mandated parish poor rate during these years never amounted to more than 7 percent of the funds expended on the poor.[64]

The social crisis of the sixteenth century brought on by the decay of the medieval order 'hastened the end of the medieval system of alms.' And, with the accession of Elizabeth, 'the whole tone of social and cultural aspiration [became] secular'; philanthropic activity increased dramatically. The result, according to Jordan, was nothing less than an enormous ourpouring of benefactions for poor relief, secular in their form and intent.[65] The Protestant clergy, whose sermons were both heard and read, 'literally bludgeoned into the English conscience an awareness of new and pressing responsibilities which it was never quite to renounce again.'[66] We might say, then, that Jordan's merchant- and gentry-driven philanthropy provided a counterpoise to Heal's declining hospitality, and the 1560s seem to be the point of their inter-section. Requiring no discontinuity thesis, however, and far more transparent in motivation were the countless thousands of testimentary bequests that, during the Reformation decades, were shifting gradually from traditional pious uses (chantry prayers or distributions to the poor at funerals) to non-pious ones. The later might include funds for employing or educating the parish's poor. These gifts were supervised by the churchwardens and vestry and supplemented the government's expanding social welfare mandates.[67]

Several of these cross-currents intersect in Thomas Harman's modest volume, *A Caveat for common cursetors vulgarely called vagabones*, that went through four editions between 1566 and 1573, and which he was wont to distinguish from a 'small brief' roughly contemporary to his, surely John Awdeley's *Fraternity of Vacabondes*.[68] Harman was a gentleman from Kent, former Justice of the Peace, and self-proclaimed student of the poor. He was concerned with the decline in hospitality, but did not attribute that to Tudor statism and urban fashion. Rather, he praised the 'many good godly profitdable laws and acts' for the 'reliefe succor, comfort and sustentation of the poor needy impotent and miserable creatures' and the 'extreme punishment of all vagrants and sturdy vagabonds' across the realm. Unfortunately, however, the impact of that legislation was far more limited than need be. Since the early 1520s the deserving poor were being deprived of their just due by an expanding cohort of bold and undeserving poor people, the 'cursetors' of Harman's title (from the Latin 'curro' for one who runs or ranges about the country). He classified almost two dozen cursetor types, from 'Bawdy-Baskets' (women who pilfered clothes drying on hedges and victuals from unguarded kitchens) to 'Up-right men' (bosses and trainers), listed the names of more than 200 practitioners, and offered a glossary of their 'pedlars' French.' He situated the cursetors in what we might call his unique history of the undeserving poor, a sequence of anti-vagancy 'moments' or preoccupations each shaped by its migratory, able-bodied poor. Thus the cursetors utilized different skills and styles of deception from the 'valiant beggars' of the medieval statutes and the more recent 'Egyptians.' By propagating his notice of the cursetors, Harman hoped that their 'highest' point had been reached and that 'as speedy a redress will be for these' as had been for the 'Gypsies,' who 'all be dispersed, vanished, & the memory of them clean extinguished.' If this can be accomplished, Harman opined, parish relief of the deserving will improve and men of means will be encouraged to keep their country houses and offer hospitality there.[69] In not choosing between voluntary and mandatory giving to the poor, but endorsing them both, Harman indicated his comfort with both *societas* and *civitas*. And he praised the Countess of Shrewesbury, the dedicatee of his volume, for casting her 'vigilant and merciful eye' on her parish poor while, at the same time, providing 'ardent and bountiful charity' to all who seek relief at her gate.[70]

Harman's little book achieved a formidable half-life. Its nomenclature of the migratory poor was incorporated into 'An Act for the Punishment of vacabondes, and for the Relief of the Poor & Impotent' (1572), which as we will see was the most comprehensive early Elizabethan anti-poverty measure. The statute was particularly harsh on vagabonds, and, interestingly, added to this category for the first time minstrels, jugglers, interlude players, bearwards, and fencers; it also made the parish poor rate unequivocally mandatory.[71] Later in the decade, William Harrison appropriated Harman's cursetor designations for his *Description of England* (1577).

Norwich: The Sick Poor in a Puritan Citadel

The real number of rogues and vagabonds, perhaps 2 percent of the population, and their actual behavior do not appear to warrant the fuss that Harman and many of his contemporaries made about them. This is especially so if we compare that figure to the 7–11 percent of the population who were the sick or morbid poor, the physically and mentally unhealthy, diseased, or chronically impaired, until recently the most overlooked cohort in early modern social welfare studies.[72] Beier and Slack put our understanding of the vagrancy issue on more solid ground several decades ago. Beier used records of 1159 people arrested for vagrancy mostly in the 1560s and 1570s, while Slack combined registers of vagabonds' passports, returns from the Book of Orders (1630), and other sources to assemble a sample of 3000 persons who were on the road in the first half of the seventeenth century. From these databases a profile of early modern vagrants emerges: one-half were single males and another one-quarter single females; and, with the exception of the Irish, they traveled mostly in singles and in twos. The patterns of travel flowed generally from highland to lowland areas and from arable districts to woodlands and pastures (although the reverse of that flow was the most cause for alarm). Urban settings were the most frequent starting and ending points for vagrants. Further, Beier's findings suggest that most of those on the roads were children, adolescents, and young adults looking for work with a smattering of players and minstrels mixed in.[73] Marjorie McIntosh notes a geographical pattern in the predisposition of local courts to enforce misconduct ordinances, the kinds of complaints often brought against vagrants. Court activity on these matters was more frequent in the southwest, northwest and north than in the Midlands and southeast.[74]

The village of Terling in Essex, from the mid-sixteenth to mid-seventeenth centuries provided improving conditions for the middling sort, but the village's expanding population was filling at the bottom. In the mid-1520s poor laborers, cottagers, and craftsmen were 27.6 percent of Terlings population; by the 1670s they had ballooned to just over 50 percent. The new migrants, many of them adolescents, seem to have been drawn to Terling for opportunities for service, employment, or even marriage.[75] Thus magistrates may have been overly concerned with vagrants, especially since the well-off people in the localities often provided them with hospitality and employment. Furthermore, Slack found no evidence of a unique migrants' subculture and concluded that 'vagrants' were the tip of the iceberg of the late sixteenth- and early seventeenth-century mobile population. For every vagrant arrested, several more were accepted into towns and regions of rural industry. The relatively small numbers of vagrants notwithstanding, their presence on the roads and in the streets of sixteenth-centry villages and towns caused much consternation, partly out fear of disease and disorder.

But, even more, it was the very mobility of the migrants ('foreigners'), their disconnectedness, their apparent living outside the accepted social, political, and religious fabric of life that contributed to the 'collective paranoia' about them in the later sixteenth and early seventeenth centuries. Richard Baxter, looking back, had noted 'the great rude unjust rabble' with their 'malignant hatred of seriousness in religion' as but one of several threats to the tranquility of the age that included the pope, the Jesuits, and witches. It was this sense of good order's vulnerability more than anything that fed the onset of 'political puritanism,' alliances between ministers and magistrates in a number of Puritan towns.[76] Historians have concluded, on balance, that most Elizabethan and early Stuart believers were both Puritan and Anglican, 'Calvinist Episcopalians' in David Tyack's apt phrase. Arcbishop Whitgift's deft touch on the matter of predesination in the Admonition Crisis became the Calvinist bonding 'cement' of the turn of the seventeenth-century church. It is helpful, nevertheless, to distinguish between 'credal' and 'experimental' predestinarianism. Practitioners of the former accepted the doctrine but had no need to take it 'into the popular pulpit or to derive a view of the Christian community from it.' The experimentalists, on the other hand, wished to put predestination, election, and assurance 'at the centre of their practical divinity...and to define the godly community (and in some cases the visible church) in terms of those who understood those doctrines and acted upon them.' It was likely experimentalist ministers and deacons in the 1560s and 1570s who struck alliances with social activist magistrates in what we have come to call the 'Puritan citadels', towns like Warwick, Norwich, York, and in Suffolk Bury St Edmunds, Ipswich, and a variety of smaller parishes.[77]

Robert Prick of Denhan, one of the Suffolk villages, published post-humously *The doctrine of superioritie and subiection* (1609), which laid out the Puritan citadel idea and its intentions clearly. Ministers and magistrates were the two 'public' superiors that enjoyed 'sparkes of glory' from the Lord and shined as 'bright stars' among humankind.

The minister of the pair was charged to lead authoritatively in his 'attire and gesture,' teaching and example, and willingness to suspend and excommunicate. The 'sacred' ordinances of the magistrate required him to choose, compel, and protect the most fit minister for his jurisdiction, enforce the people to read and practice the Ten Commandments, and to make and execute laws that his subjects may 'live together sweetly and honestly, to the mutual help and benefit one of another.' The patina of sacred magistracy on occasion could be applied beyond local confines as it was to Robert Dudley, earl of Leicester, whose importance and bearing were ensconced in the usual retinue, liveries, and palaces. However, his public displays of piety (whether or not sincere) while attending sermons in the Midlands earned him another degree of devotion and political influence from religiously inclined courtiers and their allies, godly magistrates in the counties.[78]

One of the most determined of the local ministers had to have been John More, 'the apostle of Norwich.' Noted preacher at St Andrew's for two decades, author of a popular catechism and advisor to the leading Norfolk families, More sported a great beard to lend an image of *gravitas* to his life of spiritual striving. A contemporary enthusiast for More's Norwich described it as a place of 'heavenly harmony and sweet amity' with the magistrates and ministers 'embracing and seconding one another, and the common people affording due reverence and obedience to them both.'[79] In any case, historians agree that Norwich was a particularly fulsome example of a Puritan citadel and, through its example and the role in parliament of More's ally, Mayor John Aldrich, likely influenced the poverty and vagrancy legislation of the 1570s. Bucer's call to attend the poor with firmness and generosity is certainly evident in Norwich and other sites of experimental predestinarianism. Careful discrimination between the worthy and unworthy poor was implemented, deacons were appointed, and generous outdoor relief began to be dispensed to poor households. And suspected moral deficiencies in the unworthy were addressed directly: Norfolk justices visited the local Bridewell on a regular basis and dispensed prayer and punishment to the vagrant and unruly inmates.[80] It was the city's approach to the sick poor, however, that was its most inspired undertaking.

When disease's impact on poverty, charity, and social policy has been explored by historians, attention has tended to be confined to mega-epidemics of plague or the widespread malnutrition that accompanied regular visitations of bad harvests and dearth. Nevertheless, as we have seen in the previous two chapters, we are beginning to realize that at the quotidian level pre-industrial people were much preoccupied with their own and others' health. A statute in 1542 had legitimized some opportunities for medical practitioners who claimed 'God-given' rather than learned training, even though Calvin himself and later William Perkins expressed a clear preference for trained physicians. Henry Holland, a contemporary of Perkins and a Puritan minister and medical practitioner, argued in his *An Admonition Concerning the Use of Physick* (1603) that it was the learned physician that was God-given to the sick, while Thomas Dekker characterized the trained doctor as God's lieutenant in treating disease.[81]

Local officials in at least several towns and London shared a commitment to improving the health of the sick poor 'outdoors,' that is, without resorting solely to new or reconstituted hospitals. They were convinced that illness or disability led to indigency and that appropriate medical intervention could prevent young and old from falling into decay or bring them back to productivity. And they assumed that local gatherings of aimless and filthy poor people heightened the potential for disease outbreaks and intimidated ordinary citizens. Thus, to avoid a slide into more serious social disintegration, corporations and parishes must intervene: the health and employment of the settled poor must be looked after more carefully; hardy strangers must be forced to move on, and their sick or pregnant counterparts provided some care until fit to leave. Some form of intervention was evident in Chester, Ipswich, Newcastle, Barnstable, Norwich, and London. The poor were targeted as individuals and provided treatment, as required, by practitioners or trained physicians at public expense largely, but not exclusively, outside the funding of the parish poor rates. These undertakings continued in one form or another until the era of the New Poor Law.[82]

The small, affluent London parish of St Bartholomew's Exchange was providing a two-tiered health support system for its approximately one dozen pensioners by 1570. The arrangements endured well into the later seventeenth century and probably replicated those in parishes in many of the realm's towns. One level was in the hands of the pensioners themselves; the other involved physicians or practitioners. 'Keepers of the sick' and 'searchers of the sick suspected' were designated by the vestry and provided payments for their work above and beyond their pensions. Here was one rather unusual option in the 'economy of makeshifts' that pensioners typically pursued or a marginally profitable variety of neighborliness. The other track in the St Bartholomew's program offered the services of physicians, surgeons, or chemists as needed or requested. At the initiatve of the pensioner, trained professional or practitioner care could be pursued with the expectation that the parish would absorb the costs beyond one's ability to pay. Here was a versatile set of arrangements combining the poor's own care for themselves and the provision of more professional care when necessary. The parish records also reveal that pensioner status within a family was often passed from one generation to the next and settled and known poor people received much better treatment than did strangers. The latter, if able-bodied, were forced to leave the parish; if unwell, they were put in 'the cage,' a covered pen, where they received but minimal care.[83]

The most elaborate plan we know about was Norwich's. In 1570, the city launched a general anti-poverty effort that included custodial care, discipline, skill training and some education, work, and disease pervention. The undertaking began with an extraordinary census of the city's 2359 settled poor men, women, and children. The survey seems to have been conducted house to house and included summaries of each person's health. Approximately 9 percent of those over 16 years were categorized as sick or disabled. Another 1.5 percent elderly poor were 'past work.' Women outnumbered men in the census and more of them were ill in some way. The elderly in general were 14.8 percent of the census but only 7.3 percent of Norwich's population, while the 15–24 age group represented only 5.7 percent of the census but 19.8 percent of the city's numbers.[84] Beyond the roughly one-third described merely as sick, sickly, or very sick, a number of specific maladies were identified, including: the stone, gout, fistula, lameness, broken legs and ribs, and deafness and dumbness, among others. The city was ready to respond to its diseased and ailing poor, some of whom continued to work at some level.

Those requiring care beyond their own family's capability were placed in the city's five lazarhouses or the homes of poor women. As requested and needed, additional treatment by physicians and practitioners was provided at the city's expense. In the first years of the plan's operation 34 physicians and practitioners, approximately one-eighth of the city's medical providers, were offering treatment. About one-third of them were women. Payment arrangements were by contract rather than stipend, however. For each case, a medical provider entered into a conditional contract which guaranteed that 'the practitioner would "keep the patient whole" for the rest of his or her life'; and, a provisional payment was made. When the treatment had run its course, full payment was achieved. Over the years the payment system evolved away from contracts toward stipends and retainers. The funds came from the poor patient's parish (the poor rate or a special collection) or the city's 'hamper,' the repository for its normal fines income from offenses by guilds, merchants, alehouse keepers, players, gamblers, and perpetrators of general misrule.[85]

Dearth and Economic Hardship

The extraordinay efforts of Norwich and the other citadels notwith-standing, a sense of bafflement about the 'social question' persisted more largely in the realm, both within the government and in the villages and towns. Even then, more ordinary dealings with vagrants and the settled poor were originating at the grassroots. Local officials, feeling swamped by vagrants and indigent poor in their villages and towns, had been pressing parliament for a mandatory poor rate since the later 1540s. What they got were half-way measures that embarrassed or inconvenienced noncontributors more than anything. And the resort to urging private charity and controlled begging in the Edwardian and Marian poverty statutes revealed that the default position in relief was still the old and reliable *societas christiana*. Parliamentary consensus was developing that reform in the labor market was needed; the last wage legislation had been passed in 1514–15. Although the evidence is not conclusive, it appears that the government was attempting to enforce those wage rates in the north, but allowing them to be superseded in the more prosperous south at the discretion of local officials.

The pressure from the localities for a more coherent labor policy and the government's recognition that coinage reform alone was ineffective in preserving social peace, finally turned parliament toward legislating soon after Elizabeth's accession. Several bills were introduced in 1559 on wages, apprenticeship regulations, and retention of artificers in the towns. Four years later in 1563 yet another innocuous and temporizing poor relief Act was passed, followed immediately by the far more enduring Statute of Artificers (5 Eliz., c. 4). The poverty statute renewed explicitly the 1531 and 1552 statutes and, without naming it, the Marian Act of 1555. The Artificers' statute was wide-ranging and traditional; it established the legal framework of English labor policy for the next two centuries. The Act touched artificers, laborers, servants of husbandry and apprentices. Certain categories of persons were to be forced into service; wages and hours for artificers would be settled in each county annually by the Justices of the Peace; and apprenticeship qualifications were designed to keep the social order perpetuating itself as nearly as possible.[86]

The susceptibility of the poor to demagogic excitement was displayed again at the end of the decade. The simmering resentments of the country lords burst forth in the 1569 rising of the northern earls, ostensibly behind the shield of religion, but actually 'to escape financial troubles and asuage their own hurt dignity as nobles.'[87] If the typical Elizabethan likely did not understand the subtle shifts in lordly and gentlemanly status brought on by the new civility and *politesse* at court, he or she surely noted that the earls' ranks were filled with the indigent and destitute. Northumberland and his fellow earls had used religious propaganda, the offer of wages, and threats to dragoon poor men into their ranks.[88] While the actual violence of the rising was confined to the siege of Barnard Castle and a skirmish at Hexham, the fact that the rebel numbers had been swelled by poor and destitute men probably contributed to parliament's willingness to legislate again on vagrancy.

Sir Francis Walsingham, a committed Norwich Puritan and Secretary of State after 1573, had been reporting on his city's reforms to Lord Burghley. And restless members of parliament, including John Aldrich, Norwich mayor and MP in 1572 and 1576 and former city councillor, sought a mandatory poor rate and more intervention against vagrants. The statutes of 1572, (14 Eliz., c. 5) and 1576 (18 Eliz., c. 3), may be considered a general anti-poverty undertaking in the spirit of the 1530s program and its subsequent iterations. Noting that the realm was 'exceedingly pestered' with vagrancy and crime, the 1572 statute classified vagrants eleaborately by type, in much the way that Harman had in his *Caveat for Common Cursitors*. Although the statute authorized 'grievous' whipping and other corporal punishments to hardy recalcitrant vagrants, it also acknowledged several categories of acceptable unemployment for able-bodied persons, for example: migrant farm workers, travelers who had been victims of theft, and servants discharged less than six months. Former mariners and soldiers were to be licensed to beg. And finally, and perhaps most important, a mandatory poor rate was established in every parish; from the fund gathered the impotent would be relieved and work provided for the unemployed. The 1576 Act continued the provisions of 1572 and added the requirement that Bridewells, or houses of correction, be established in every county so that youth may be 'accustomed and brought up in labor' and rogues deprived of the excuse that 'they cannot get any service or work.'[89]

Yet, another reason for the concern about vagrants and social disruption in these years was the frequent visitation of dearth: in 1555–56, 1586, and 1595–97. Beyond the difficulties and suffering that went with a poor harvest year in and of itself, other ongoing trends in population, wages, or prices could intensify and prolong its impact, sometimes into the subsequent dearth episode. For instance, the extremely poor harvests of the mid-1550s were all the more frightening because of the price inflation that was raging from the recoinage earlier. At the same time, accelerating population growth that had begun around 1540 and would persist until the Civil War already was causing a decline in real wages which became precipituous in the 1580s and did not bottom out until the second decade of the seventeenth century.[90] While the actual incidence of starvation was rare, the social and political tensions surrounding dearth were never easy to resolve. And the range of meliorative responses typically involved both *societas* and *civitas* impulses. Dearth threatened, tested, and reinforced social bonds and hierarchical authority. And the explanations for why dearth appeared at all ranged from the agency of man to God. The usual suspects for the former were the poor makers of traditional social criticism, the enclosers, hoarders, and price gougers. Nevertheless, the 'dearth as God's punishment' explanation was more compelling in the Calvinist-informed *Zeitgeist* of the Elizabethan and Jacobean years. It acknowledged that human weakness had caused the calamity, but it was the weaknesses of all, not just the greed of those directly involved in the food chain that was the problem and had brought on God's censure. Society would have to respond collectively and cooperatively to pay for its sins.

Once the initial rounds of suspicion and complaining had run their course, a kind of ritualized *quid pro quo* entered into the intra-societal dialogue: unless the poor's social and political superiors acted on their responsibilities to preserve justice and protect the grain supply, the dearth's victims would be obliged to resort to petty crime, and even riot.[91] A case in point was the dearth episode of 1586. The government seized on the 'God's judgment' explanation and acted on its implications with considerable acumen. The evidence suggests that the mandatory parish poor rate of the 1572 statute was being widely ignored, but, owing to Cardinal Wolsey's commonweal efforts 70 years earlier, there was a precedent for the government's searching for grain in the localities and ensuring that grain markets continued to function. Such measures had been taken in response to dearth in the early and mid-1550s, and, in 1586 the government went further and broadcast *Orders devised for the reliefe of the present dearth of Graine*. And very much in keeping with the God's punishment explanation, the church hierarchy took up its own iniative, a campaign for general hospitality. Preachers were to 'move the people to hearty repentence, prayer, fasting, amendment of life and liberality to the poor.' And, since God had 'begun to shake His fatherly rod already at us by some scarsity and dearth of victuals,' argued London's Bishop Aylmer, his wrath must be appeased by 'the true preaching of his word of peace and plenty.' No records of compliance with the bishops' iniative survive, although they had insisted that nonconforming clergy or parishes be reported to them.[92]

The Elizabethan Poor Law

The scare of the mid-1580s meant that the government would have to stay close to matters that could have a disruptive effect on the poor. In 1593, the Commons appointed a committee to evaluate the existing poverty statutes. The return of major grain failure and accompanying threats of risings in mid-decade meant that poverty issues would be addressed again with urgency. Another 'general hospitality' was ordered in the summer of 1596, accompanied by *Three Sermons, or Homelies to Move Compassion towards the Poor and Needy*. The bishops and county and urban magistrates provided enthusiastic support; in some parishes churchwardens went door to door after Wednesday and Friday evening prayers collecting money and in-kind donations for those in need. And from the churchwardens' presentments available from the rural, southern county of Buckinghamshire the indication is that the response to the hospitality was 'overwhelming.'[93]

Parliament met in 1597–98 with grave responsibilities pending. That sense is captured in one MP's remarks during an exchange on enclosure: 'The eyes of the poor are upon this Parliament,' he insisted, 'this place is an epitome of the whole realme; the trust of the poore committed to us, whose persons we supply.' London's Recorder,

John Croke, pointed out to the Commons that they were the 'chief Carpenters of the Kingdom,' whose task was to fashion and carve bills 'from a rude to a polished form.' Francis Bacon urged the revival of legislation against enclosure, to which he attributed depopulation, idleness, decay of tillage, withering of charitable insitutions, and ultimately the impoverishment of the realm.[94] No less than 17 bills related to poverty were considered, some likely products of the 1593 deliberations, and an experienced committee was appointed to review them and make recommendations. It included Bacon, Thomas Cecil, Edward Coke, Sir Robert Wroth (a Puritan social reformer), Miles Sandys, Edward Hext (a Somerset justice), and Anthony Cope (familiar with Lincolnshire efforts to employ the able-bodied poor).[95] In addition to new Acts on enclosure (two), construction of workhouses, and vagrancy, a definitive bill on poor relief was reported from the committee, after considerable work and debate, and passed. The statute, 39 Eliz., c. 3 (1598) and its slighty expanded successor, 43 Eliz., c. 2 (1601), constitute the Elizabethan Poor Law. The policy called for parish churchwardens to designate four overseers of the poor to assist them in raising a parish fund and in-kind donations 'by taxing inhabit-ants and occupiers of land in the parish.' The overseers were to dispense the funds for relief of the 'lame impotent old blind' and to put poor children and unemployed and healthy adults to work. The infirm and sick were to be housed in 'convenient houses or dwellings.' Only if grandparents, parents, or children were unable to maintain them were family members to be turned over to the parish. And 'wandering and begging' were prohibited, unless the begging was for food and approved by the overseers. The statute also carried forward the prin-ciple that Justices of the Peace could tax more broadly for poor relief funds to assist beleaguered parishes and established that all parishes were responsible for the support of county hospitals and almshouses.[96] The next important Act (39 Eliz., c. 4) punished vagabonds and sturdy beggars.

The Poor Laws of 1598 and 1601 affirmed the parish's role in social welfare. But, as we have noted several times already, this responsibility certainly was not new. For more than 200 years by this time, a very important contact point, but certainly not the only one, between dispensers and recipients of alms had been the parish. What distinguished the codifying anti-poverty legislation of Elizabeth's reign was the coercive nature and thoroughness of the mandate that it added to the

1572 statute. Brian Tierney, in his invaluable study of the canon-law foundations of late medieval parish-centered poor relief, in a moment of historiographic exuberance, posited a direct causal connection between the 'medieval' and the Elizabethan Poor Laws.[97] Extravagant as his claim can be shown to be in any literal sense, it merits our attention nevertheless. The parish as the primary dispenser of assistance to the poor, if under different mandate and circumstances in the sixteenth century, was reaffirmed.

Conclusion

For all its significance the Poor Law was more a codification of existing successful local practices with roots in the later medieval centuries or developed since the crown's appropriation of the monasteries and religious foundations in the 1530s and 1540s. Those appropriations deprived the realm initially of perhaps half of its usual alms-dispensing institutions and intensified the shock of the government's official embrace of Protestantism in these same years. The growing influence of Calvinism and its reform inclinations and the resourceful efforts by aldermen, magistrates, and churchwardens in London and several regional towns began to shape a coherent response to what may have been a social welfare crisis in the 1540s through 1560s. In these localities, censuses of the poor began to be taken, hospitals established for the sick poor, houses of correction for the hardy unemployed, and mandatory rates raised for parish-supervised relief of those poor unable to care for themselves.

Although the passing of traditional chivalric ideals was curtailing hospitality at the gates of the wealthy, philanthropy was on the rise and in the seventeenth century would become a crucial ingredient in what historians now call the 'mixed economy of welfare.' All the while, parliament was passing a series of poverty relief and anti-vagrancy statutes that essentially mandated the more successful screening and relief processes that were being developed in the localities. The first Act making the poor rate mandatory in all parishes was passed in 1572. A dozen or so towns, like Norwich with particularly strong Puritan leanings became laboratories for and models of this innovative social welfare practice. Throughout these years 'betterment' and 'subsistence' migration seems to have been increasing to London and the growing regional towns and ports.[98] Explaining this and appraising its impact on the urban centers has been a contentious matter for historians, some arguing that town life was declining into crisis-like conditions during the sixteenth century and others, mainly historians of London, disagreeing fundamentally.

Chapter 4: Implementation
(c.1610–1690)

Over the course of the 'short' seventeenth century, conditions that had been exacerbating the impact of structural poverty from the 1580s through the 1620s began to abate. While the population continued to rise through the first half of the century, reaching a peak of just over five million persons in 1651, its growth leveled off at that point and remained virtually stable until the first half of the eighteenth century. Crucially important was that by the 1630s real wages had begun to recover, if undramatically, from their low point in the first two decades of the century. So gradual was the improvement, however, that wages would not attain their previous highs of the early Elizabethan years until the 1730s. Prices, too, leveled off in the 1630s and then held quite steady through the remainder of the century. The Phelps, Brown and Hopkins price index of consumables hovered between −0.5 and +0.5 percent annual rates of change, until the 1730s, when a precipitous rise set in comparable to that of the later sixteenth century.[1]

Puritans and Policy

As we begin to look more closely at the achievement of social welfare in the seventeenth century, it is worth noting again that the poor and non-poor alike were situated in a force field of sometimes competing, sometimes cooperative options for their participation, the *societas–civitas* choices, the 'mixed economy' of social welfare.[2] Implementation of the policy was slow and difficult at the start for a variety of reasons, some having to do with the limitations of the mechanism, some with impeding or alternative commitments for caring for the poor. Half a century ago, Marxist and Whig historians emphasized the growing economic and political power of the middle classes to explain the major transitions in early modern England (the Reformation, the Civil War, and deepening statism throughout). Difficulties in confirming the bourgeoisie empirically, however, subsequently led to an emphasis on splits and tensions within elite ranks to explain these processes. A third stance in the historiography, 'history from below,' posited a society polarized between the elite and the rest with no buffer cohort between them.[3]

None of these perspectives bore a close resemblance to the four-tiered social order of gentlemen, citizens and burgesses in the cities, yeomen in the countryside, and poor laborers, artisans, husbandmen, and servants that appeared in descriptions of England by Sir Thomas Smith and William Harrison in the sixteenth century and Sir Thomas Wilson and Gregory King in the seventeenth.[4] More than two decades ago, Keith Wrightson identified a discourse of 'sorts' of people that was emerging in the sixteenth century. Better said, this language looks to be an early modern iteration of distinctions we have seen already in medieval civic discourse.[5] And, consistent with the medieval categories, the sixteenth-century descriptions were general, binary, and unflattering to those at the bottom, thus: 'richer sort' and 'poorer sort'; 'wiser sort' and 'ignorant sort'; and 'better' sort and 'meaner' sort.[6] These usages described practical groupings that conformed to social experience, and they alluded not only to social differentiation but to polarization as well. The designations richer, wiser, and better conveyed the respectability and authority of those who hewed closely to proper religion and the rule of law, while the implication was that the poorer, ignorant, and meaner sorts required discipline, prodding, and assistance toward those standards. The better sort were, in effect, a 'composite local ruling group,' the mayors, vicars, vestrymen, merchants, and comfortable yeomen and artisans.

The term 'middle sort' or 'middling sort,' which implicitly acknowledged the presence of the gentry above and beyond the local ruling groups, first may have appeared in Henry Brinkelow's *The Complaynt of Roderyck Mors* in 1542 and had entered common usage a century later. Typically those who were described as middling sort were prominent for their long-term residence, above average wealth, and parish vestry leadership in their villages and towns. They often referred to themselves as the 'principall inhabitants,' 'most substantial inhabitants,' or 'chief men' and were inclined to adopt a paternal stance toward their social inferiors. And, as the government intruded more into the localities in the seventeeth century, the chief men were the mediators between innovative policies and local resistance or alternatives to them. In their roles as parish vestrymen, churchwardens, and overseers they had frequent contact with, and made crucial decisions about, the local poor.

Elizabethan social welfare policies were taken up at different paces and in a variety of ways that suited each parish or locality. And, as we will see, there were regional variations as well. Implementation, then, was a process of initiative and negotiation across jurisdictional levels in regional and local contexts.[7] The most subtle and crucial of all the requirements for the Poor Law's success was the degree to which the government's authority could be appropriated and applied locally. The implementors had to be able to justify the Poor Law's assumptions in acceptable moral and political ways. When this was done effectively, the appropriate county, town, village, and parish officials were involved and implicated in the governance process (*civitas*). Yet the many levels of interlocking responsibility, cohort and individual volition that had to converge to implement the Poor Law, illustrated well Cynthia Herrup's observation that governing was 'a repeated exercise in compromise, co-operation, co-option and resistance.'[8]

As we begin to look more closely at the Poor Law's implementation, we must remember that testamentary, non-recurring bequests to the poor and long-term philanthropic benefactions continued to provide the larger outlay for poor relief in urban and rural localities. Later in this chapter we will discuss the place of charity in rural social welfare. A very helpful look at the private–public mix in an urban setting is Connie S. Evans's overview of poor relief funding in Exeter in the late sixteenth and early seventeenth centuries. She finds that miscellaneous testamentary bequests to the poor ranged from distributing bread or cash at the testator's funeral, to aid for poor laborers or widows, dowries for indigent girls, burial expenses for prisoners, and small donations to the sick poor in almshouses. However, long-term or recurring benefactions brought much more wealth to bear on poor relief and were in three primary configurations: support for almshouses and hospitals (45 percent); revolving loan funds to help young artisans and craftsmen get started in business (14 percent); and sustenance for specific goals (38 percent). The combined annual total of private giving reached approximately 353L, which was 15 percent more than the 300L gathered by the parish funds. Eventually the Exeter corporation, which was managing most of these benefactions, began to borrow from or redirect a portion of their worth toward city improvement projects, thus blurring the private – public distinction in another way.[9]

James I's brief and enigmatic reflection on kingship, *True Lawe of Free Monarchies* (1598?), rested on scripture (1 Samuel 8.9–20), nature, and his understanding of Scottish history. Current assessments see its political theory as either a 'nuanced moderated absolutism' or a 'constitutional monarchy created by kings.'[10] Certainly the new king could not have been acclimated to the nuances of the long-evolving relationships among England's crown, parliament, and council, nor those between the center and the variegated periphery. Less compelled by policy initiatives than were his Tudor predecessors, Henry VIII and Elizabeth, James Stuart seems to have been wary of 'commonwealth' discourse, as much as anything for the heavy ideological freight it carried. He preferred the still inchoate 'public good.'[11] His aversion may also have had to do with the large edifice of Tudor social welfare policy that had been constructed in the Commonwealth's name since Wolsey's day. Thus Sir Francis Bacon, a volcano of policy ideas, found himself 'marooned' in a sea of Stuart bafflement and lack of compelling vision, even though his 'call for renewal' influenced scores of reformers in the Civil War era and beyond.[12]

On occasion, though, the king could speak in directional tones on social welfare. For example, sitting before the Star Chamber in 1616 he asked for reports on the condition of the realm, noted the continuing blight of alehouses and sturdy rogues, urged enforcement of statutes charged with curtailing London's growth, and encouraged continuing support of poor relief, schools, and hospitals. At other times he expressed interest in a variety of contemporary innovations from crop and drainage projects to urban waterworks. Yet there was little follow-through, particularly toward securing crucial financial support for these projects.[13] In his 1616 Star Chamber speech, James also had instructed the gentry to leave the city and spend Christmas, at least, on their estates dispensing 'old fashioned' hospitality and charity. And the following year, after enjoying a Sunday of bear-baiting, dancing and a masque while on a visit to Houghton in the Pennines, the king asked Thomas Morton, bishop of Chester, to draft a proclamation on Sabbatarianism, the strict religious observance of Sundays favored by many Puritans. James hoped it would clarify his ambiguous proclamation on the subject from 1603 and also mitigate a severe Sabbatarian order recently issued by the Lancashire Justices of the Peace. In his preface, James declared that such a practice was likely to yield an idle, disaffected, and unhealthy people. And, if the Puritans disagreed with him, they should leave the country.[14]

From the Reformation and social welfare legislation of the 1530s to the middle years of James I's reign, the government had imposed no fewer than 80 statutes on the counties and localities that required enforcement, the so-called 'increase in governance' that is so much a part of recent historiography.[15] It is now becoming clear that much of the response to the government's post-1572 poverty and vagrancy legislation had been achieved on the rising tide of local, middling-sort Puritan enthusiasts in their 'citadels.' Their successors in the first four decades of the seventeenth century may have attempted an even more emphatic enforcement of the legislation and consequently widened even further their social 'distance' from the lesser sorts in their parishes. In their zeal, it seems that some local Puritan leaders approached social welfare, especially the moral assessment and correction of the poor encouraged by the Poor Law, as a component of their overriding commitment to achieve a Christian common weal.

In Chapter 1, we saw that the impulse to control the poor had its roots in the immediate post-Black Death years and was revealed especially in the workings of leet courts, whose efforts in this regard extended forward to the turn of the seventeenth century.[16] Slack has suggested that some churchmen and magistrates were so roiled that they 'forced' the poor into 'the roles they had prescribed for them'; in a sense, they created the dependent poor.[17] In any case, a consensus seems to be emerging that in the last third of the sixteenth century and extending well into the seventeenth, an 'ideology of "godly rule"' was taking hold particularly in the towns that would require much discipline and order to achieve. The commitment grew out of lessons learned from the difficulties of these years combined with Puritan and Anglican moral theololgy. And, as it spread, local leaders found themselves more and more in agreement with the gentry and the government that the behaviour of the poor was socially deviant, disorderly, and dangerous. Thus the middling sort attempted to control the poor more thoroughly and to separate themselves from them culturally.[18]

By the early seventeenth century and through to the Civil War years, a number of villages and small and large towns were gravitating toward what might be called a Puritan 'confrontational reformist impulse' within their jurisdictions. In some instances it may have been motivated more by the desire to control the poor than to relieve or eliminate poverty.[19] Similarly inclined Puritan aldermen communicated frequently to encourage one another and keep abreast of evolving strategies to advance 'God's glory' and set the poor to work. One of the more ingenious corporate undertakings, for its reliance on vice to promote virtue, was Salisbury's plan to raise funds through a publicly owned and run brewhouse. The revenues raised were to help fund a comprehensive workhouse, make-work on materials supplied by local merchants, education for poor children, and a municipal storehouse from which the poor could withdraw supplies in exhange for tokens. The scheme never achieved full acceptance or implementation even though it was being pushed well into the 1640s. By the Restoration, the poor and the magistrates in Salisbury were facing conditions very much like those of the 1620s before the plan had been developed. This time, though, the magistrates fell back on the government policy of workhouses, settlement, and the poor rate.[20] David Underdown has suggested a topographical and geographical distribution of reform impulses. In the cloth-making and wood pasture districts the local culture more often promoted individualistic, confrontational parishes, dominated by new elites who wanted to manage the poor. However, in the mainly arable regions more paternalistic and deferential parishes were found in which traditional customs and rituals more likely predominated.[21]

In spite of the Puritans' energy and their resourceful structures for raising funds and managing the poor, it was their 'Utopian' rigidities (their supporters' compliment, their detractors' epithet) that ultimately did them in. The reformers' relentless, doctrinally formulaic pushing against their sometimes uncomprehending, sometimes unappreciative or resisting fellow denizens exhausted their pursuit of 'public edification' by the 1640s. The means to that end, too often 'servitude, loss of liberty [and] punishment,' in the words of the 1620s writer, Robert Burton, could not be sustained nor be successful.[22] But, perhaps a disillusioned reformer explained best the surrender from within: 'People hear much, learn little and practice less,' a matter nevertheless 'which cannot be imputed to the want of good preaching, but rather to the want of good hearing.'[23]

The Book of Orders (1630–31), an effort by Charles I's government to jump start implementation of the Poor Law was actually three books: the previously issued orders on plague (1578) and dearth (1586) distributed first and later a third, titled *Orders and Directions . . . tending to the relief of the Poor.* If the deepest precedent for issuing orders like these extended back to the initiatives of Cardinal Wolsey between 1517 and 1527, the more immediate stimulus was Bacon's proposal in 1619–20 for a series of 'commonwealth' commissions. One of them, at the behest of Henry Montagu, earl of Manchester, was to have considered 'relief of the poor and suppressing vagabonds.' Although it did not survive Bacon's fall, the continuing economic difficulties of the realm, exacerbated by the severe dearth of 1629–30, allowed Manchester, now Lord Privy Seal, to convince Charles to issue the orders. Compliance, though, like so many government policy initiatives in these years, seems to have been quite spotty; the mandated responses came from a narrow sample of counties. Slack attributes this to two perceptions of the orders on the hustings: they cast a 'spectre' of excessive direction from the center which provoked resistance; and they were too 'secular' for many Puritan Justices of the Peace.[24]

'Going on the Parish'

The pace and thoroughness of the Poor Law's implementation varied among and within the regions of the country. We have seen already that London and Norwich, among other localities, had introduced censuses of the poor and mandatory rates even before the 1572 statute. And perhaps a dozen Puritan towns had set up vigorous anti-vagrancy and poor relief efforts soon after that. Application of the government-mandated poor rate became widespread in Kent in the 1590s and was beginning in Lancashire in the 1620s and Sussex and Lincolnshire in the 1630s. Eighty-seven percent of the parishes in Kineton Hundred, Warwickshire, were implementing a poor rate in the later 1630s.[25] The most tardy region on the uptake was the northeast, Northumberland and Durham counties. There, with the exception of Newcastle, the town of Durham, and several other parishes, it was not until the 1650s that the bulk of the Justices of the Peace, local magistrates, and parish officials began serious attempts to implement the Poor Law.[26] Since each of the realm's thousands of parishes had its own unique setting, history, local culture, and particular social welfare challenge, generalizing about the implementation of the Poor Law is hazardous. At the same time, no one parish can represent them all. It would seem more useful, then, to identify several paradigmatic parishes and develop a composite sense of what implementing the policy involved.

We discussed briefly in Chapter 3 the small, 'closed' Essex village, Terling. The years 1550 to 1650 were a time of steadily improving living conditions for residents roughly in the middle ranks, but an extended period of impoverishment for those at or near the bottom. In the midst of these opposite fortunes, however, what had been 'sporadic interpersonal conflict' began in the 1620s to be transformed into 'a pattern of hostility' among middling-sort, Puritan innovators and the village poor. A modicum of stability emerged after 1640, as a more favorable ratio of population to prices and wages became established. However, these were years of quiet desperation for Terling's poor who 'endured rather than shaped' their lives and languished in cultural isolation, 'increased social regulation, new forms of dependency and public humiliation.'[27]

Affluent St Martin's-in-the-Fields in London's West End was a rapidly growing behemoth.[28] In 1671, the parish had over 35,000 members and was providing relief to 400 pensioners, just over one percent of the parish, from an annual fund of more than 1000L. In 1678, the parish numbers had become so large that two of its churches were elevated to parish status, St James Westminster and St Anne Soho. Thereafter, its numbers expanded more gradually to 45,000 parishioners and 350–400 pensioners, at an outlay of about 3700L annually by 1707. Nevertheless, as was Terling, St Martin's in these years was attempting to realize in its own way the Elizabethan objectives of curtailing vagrancy, disciplining the able-bodied unemployed, and providing pensions for the impotent and elderly poor.

Still other parishes, located primarily in the previously mentioned northeast counties of Northumberland and Durham, were a challenge because of their sparse populations and huge geographical areas. The parish at Prestburg, for example, ranged over 63,000 acres and required an administrative structure of 28 settlements and ten chapels. A steady flow of migrants from upland areas to the more low-lying settlements prevailed throughout these years, and large, porous or 'open' parishes like Prestburg or St Peter's Bywell faced steep odds against developing the 'community of commitment' that was necessary to be successful in implementing the Poor Law.[29] If we add to the mix the region's historical resistance to religious and policy legislation (recall the Pilgrimage of Grace) and the fact that the border region of Northumberland had a tradition of scanty law enforcement, it is small wonder that the Prestburgs and Bywells were initially unmoved by, or unable or unwilling to respond to, the Poor Law.

Social historians use the early modern parish as a fruitful site to explore the 'political dimensions of everyday life.' In its role as the government's agent in dispensing social welfare within the Elizabethan policy framework, the parish was a 'system of social relations in motion' that can deepen our understanding of the contingency and complexity of relations between the poor and non-poor. Or, put another way, to reach pensioner status in a parish was a 'political achievement, sometimes hard fought at the local level.'[30] Most decisions on who would receive a weekly pension or one-time 'casual' assistance were made by the parish overseers, with input from the churchwardens and vestry members as needed or appropriate. Particularly difficult cases might require that the local Justice of the Peace intervene. In this mix, however, the overseers' decisions carried the most weight. The office was an annually appointed one, and in a large parish like St Martin's with many details to manage and personal liability for financial errors it required considerable accounting and organizational skills. And, as we will see later in this chapter, overseers took most of the blame when the parishioners were dissatisfied with local poor relief. The vestry, though, had the overall responsibility for deciding the behavior that was to be expected from the poor and the amount and timing of pension payments. It was not unusual for vestries to challenge the overseers' decisions or to direct them more carefully.[31] And, since the vestry members answered to the parishioners for the amount of the poor rate and the number of pensioners, they typically sought to limit both. The traditional leet court objective of fining those who harbored unsettled poor persons was taken up by parishes in the northeast and in Hertfordshire. Similarly, orders were issued in northeastern parishes that restricted all hiring to known, local workers and excluded single women from service. Occasionally vestries would order that homes be searched for hidden migrants. Some parishes farmed out pensioners to kin or other willing supervisors for a fixed fee, a procedure known as 'tabling.' And often sustenance for the local poor who were teetering on the brink of pensioner status was available through privately funded charities administered by the parish, a practice with medieval roots that was becoming much more frequent since the Reformation and is now getting its due attention from historians.[32]

Most often those seeking pensions brought their pleas for assistance to the parish overseers in face-to-face encounters. And, as Keith Wrightson reminds us, these were fraught with enormous consequences. The overseers, representatives of 'the best sort of the parish,' in a sense guarded the community's 'boundaries'. They had the power to admit some as pensioners and to consign others to the unsettled and unentitled ranks beyond the pale. Petitioners, of course, made their case in ways that emphasized their uprightness. For instance, one Thomas Jarvis, petitioning the overseers at St Martin's in 1665, asked their 'Worships' to behold him with compassion, noted his 23 years of residence in the parish 'without being chargeable to any,' and pointed out that only because 'he is past his labor' now did he need assistance lest he perish.[33] There were times when a petitioner's interview with an overseer or overseers took place in front of the assembled vestry or the size of a pension was settled there. In addition to their formal appeal, petitioners had other means of influencing a positive decision, including sheer persistance, the intervention of an influential patron, or playing off against one another the various participants in the decision.

Even if successful, new pensioners 'going on the parish' faced continuing uncertainty. For example, they surrendered all rights to the disposal of their property. Goods usually were not confiscated until after death, but then were either sold or passed on to other pensioners. At the whim of the vestry, pensioners' behavior could be held to ever-stricter standards or narrow parameters placed on when and where to pick up their pensions. For example, if pensioners were observed among the poor who typically gathered in the churchyard clamoring for assistance while the churchwardens and overseers were collecting rates from the parishioners at the church door, they could be dropped from the rolls.[34] The intensely puritanical elders in Terling often went to court to prosecute the village's poor and pensioners for their perceived idleness, ungodliness, and inclination to disorder. And Henry Smith's charity established there in 1626 excluded from assistance those with less than five years' residence in Terling, pensioners, and persons 'guilty of excessive drinking, profane swearing, pilfering and other scandalous crimes,' along with the idle, vagrant, and incorrigible. Beneficiaries who received clothing from the fund were to wear a badge with the initials 'H.S.' on the right sleeve. In some parishes, all pensioners were required to display badges.[35]

Local censuses of the poor for the years 1582–1630 from seven villages in North Yorkshire, Kent, and Norfolk, and the smallish towns, Thirsk and Warwick, reveal how overseers and local officials assessed the poor and near poor.[36] In these records, 'poverty' was usually determined by whether or not a household was able to pay the poor rate. Local magistrates tended to divide households into four classifications: those able to pay the rate, whose numbers accounted for 60 percent to 80 percent of the local population; those unable to pay but who were self-supporting, from 20 percent to 30 percent; poor households not given aid, from 6 percent to 16.5 percent; and households given assistance or apprenticed by the parish, from 2 percent to 14 percent. Correlating family reconstitutions with poor relief records for the village of Aldenham in Hertfordshire indicates that 35 percent of the sedentary households were on the parish at one time or another. The second decade of a marriage, presumably when young children were expanding family size, typically was the most precarious economically for this group. Just half of Aldenham's families were assessed consistently for the rate. The contemporary vocabulary applied in making these assessments is particularly revealing. For example, those comprising the second category, not contributing to the rate but self-supporting, were referred to in one locality as 'indifferent,' in another as 'the poorer sort of people which as yet are able to work and do neither give nor take.' The third category, those identified as poor but not receiving assistance, were described in a number of ways: 'ready to decay,' 'not so poor,' 'the other poor,' and 'the poor able laboring folk.' The economic uncertainty at the grass roots that this vocabulary conveys is unmistakable. Family reconstitutions and individual biographies from two quite different villages in Suffolk in the latter seventeenth century add to this picture. In Cratfield, a relatively prosperous dairy farming settlement, 15 percent of the population consistently was considered 'marginally poor,' too pressed economically to pay the rate but not indigent enough to qualify for a parish pension. Poslingford, the smaller and harsher of the two, had a proto-industrial economy in cloth-making tied to the larger cycles of trade. There the numbers of marginally poor persons ranged from 39 percent to 79 percent.[37]

Whether one was identified as being on the parish or not in these years, remaining viable in the poor's 'economy of makeshifts' was problematic at best. In the county of Norfolk, once a petitioner achieved 'collectioner' status, he or she typically stayed on the parish for life. The size of the pension varied, though, depending on the collectioner's gender, point in the life-cycle, and household or family size. The pension usually increased when family size grew with young children, but, as the children matured and entered the economy, its size was reduced. When the collectioner entered old age and 'past labor,' however, the pension again increased. Women alone or widows had the most difficult time in the economy and were dependent on the parish in disproportionate numbers. In Norfolk, for example, they were 40 percent to 60 percent or more of the collectioners in some parishes and 25 percent of those exempt from the hearth tax. In the south by the mid-seventeenth century day-laborers' wages had risen 36.5 percent from their 1590s levels and weekly poor relief levels nearly doubled from 6d. to 1s. Toward the end of the century some parishes began supplementing pensions to address fuel, rent, medical care, and schooling expenses.[38]

The 'Commerce of Benefits'

A consensus on three matters has developed among most social and economic historians of early modern social welfare. First is the view that at least through the Civil War years, Elizabethan policy offered the opportunity for 'middling-sort' local officials to try to 'control the misbehavior' of the poor. This involved a new and significant 'distancing' between the middling sort and the poor that was particularly damaging to the poor's political acumen and sense of themselves. The second agreement is that a consolidating national culture emanating from London was seeping into the periphery. In the process it was attracting and converting local gentry and prosperous commoners and, all the while, dissolving local singularity, community, and custom. And third, it is assumed that, beginning in the middle of the seventeenth century, the realm's worst crises and sources of instability were abating. By the turn of the eighteenth century a less volatile order had become established, but it was the expedient stability of a deeply divided society. The image of the poor embedded in this historiography also is widely agreed upon and, interestingly, conforms to the jaundiced appraisal of the Poor Law and its deleterious impact on the poor first promulgated by the titans of early twentieth-century social welfare historiography, E. M. Leonard, R. H. Tawney, and Sidney and Beatrice Webb. The English poor at the turn of the eighteenth century were broken, mired in parish pensions, and disparaged by their middling-sort and oligarchic providers.[39]

Levine and Wrightson highlighted a Dickensian puritanism to explain the harsh anti-poverty (perhaps, better said 'anti-poor') regime established in Terling. The bleakness of that village notwithstanding, we need not assume that in other localities more moderate Puritans and Anglicans, humanists and even neo-Stoics exercised no presence. Nor should we conclude that across the realm the attitudes of gentry and middling-sort people toward the lesser sorts matched the vitriol of several Terling elders.[40] Levine and Wrightson appropriately emphasize the disorienting effect of the national demographic, social, and economic developments that enveloped Terling and countless other localities and that most of the benefits of these transitions redounded to the benefit of the 'upper and middling ranks.' And surely, with the arrival of Elizabethan policy, the elite were less than pleased with the 'new and heavier burden of the poor rate.' They suggest also, however, that the 'educational achievements' of the 'better sort' added a 'further sense of social distance' between the comfortable and the poor. So much was this the case, that J. Stalham, witness to these developments, distinguished between the 'professors' and the literate of the village and the 'ignorant and profane multitude.'[41]

Nevertheless, the educational achievements and resources of the realm's better sorts offered them other models of human aspiration than a narrow puritanism, as compelling as that may have seemed to some. By the turn of the seventeenth century a veritable explosion in educational aspirations and institutions had been under way for almost three-quarters of a century. At the top of the system so many students were attending Oxford, Cambridge, and London's Inns of Court that overcrowding had become routine in spite of expanding facilities. Grammar schools had been springing up, particularly in market towns, some endowed by single benefactors and others by groups of residents. In Solihull, Warwickshire, for instance, the inhabitants endowed a schoolhouse in 1615 and required the master to instruct the pupils in 'Catechism & good manners, & to read write & understand English, Latin & Greek, & to cast accounts the best he can … to fit them for the university.' Petty schools, too, abounded even more widely to cultivate reading and writing skills in the children, since the possession of those abilities was becoming an important component of gentry and middling-sort culture. By the 1640s, the cumulative effect of these undertakings was an adult male literacy rate of perhaps 30 percent, heavily tilted toward the gentry, with many fewer yeomen and tradesmen, and viturally no women, poor laborers or husbandmen represented.[42]

The Oxford and Cambridge curricula were full of Erasmus, More, and Vives. However, the Christian humanists' disdain for Aristotle's *Politics, Ethics*, and scientific works led to a steady eclipse of attention to the peripatetic Greek. So much so that by the 1640s, his works were no longer required in the Oxford curriculum.[43] Philip Melancthon's Lutheran version of Ciceronian Aristotelianism, much in the spirit of the 'Italian' Ciceronians, received only slight attention in Elizabethan England, but took hold in seventeenth-century Reformed centers like Strasbourg and Tubingen, where it was part of the Calvinist 'Second Reformation.' The sources most widely used by Oxbridge students in the late Elizabethan and early Stuart decades for guidance on how to conduct themselves as public figures and in home and market place were the Erasmian staples, Isocrates, Xenophon, Plutarch, Cicero, Seneca, and Quintilian. Students' commonplace books are filled with their advice on issues ranging from work to love and family, from poverty to charity and justice. And within the canon, Seneca was the most frequently cited writer on wealth, poverty, and charity; Cicero led the list on government.[44] University students were reading these materials in their original languages, but for the English-reading younger students and general public Cicero's De officiis first appeared in English translation in the 1530s and had achieved dozens of editions by the mid-seventeenth century.[45] Even more than Cicero, however, Seneca had been particularly attractive to Bucer, Zwingli, and Calvin, who thought him to be the master of ethics. Extant commonplace books, library catalogues, and correspondence of university-educated clergy indicate an overwhelming preference for Erasmus, More, Vives, and their recommended stable of ancient writers. It is likely that as much could be said for non-clerical university men as well.[46]

It is important to note, however, that in the 1580s a new Stoic and Sceptical treatment of Seneca had begun to vye with the Christian humanist appropriation of him. It was stimulated by a growing interest in Tacitus's disenchantment with government that was being refined and articulated by Justus Lipsius and Michel de Montaigne. Lipsius's mammoth edition of Seneca was put into English by Thomas Lodge in 1614, the year after John Florio had translated Montaigne's Essais.[47] Thus another 'new' humanism was afoot, this one a turn toward otium, or withdrawal and contemplation, and away from the feverish civic involvement of Erasmian negotium. At its center was 'ataraxia,' a life as free as possible from the passions, patriotism, and beliefs that raise the emotions; it was thought to be the equivalent of Seneca's apatheia, 'preservation of the self not only from external attack [but] also from the passions which might leave it open to attack.'[48]

Taken in overview, early modern ethical thought focused strongly on 'poor making,' that is, avarice and illiberality in the rich and idleness and forwardness of the poor. The most frequently cited evidence that society had lost its way were the harsh relations prevailing between the rich and the poor. Cicero and particularly Seneca offered the early modern reader a path to healing the breach between rich and poor that was considerably different from humanist 'policy' and Protestant 'reform.' Their alternatives were the cultivation of friendship, mutual regard, dependence, liberality, and reciprocality: the arts of sociability not statecraft. The Stoics encouraged behavior that, in Seneca's felicitous phrase, could lead to a 'commerce of benefits.'[49]

The discourse of benefits was less concerned with the destitute and vagrant poor, who were the major focus of government and local policy in these years, than it was with 'the other poor,' those 'ready to decay,' and 'the poor laboring folk' of the magistrates' designation. They would have matched best with Cicero's description of the poor as 'the honest, humble, and lowly...[who are] a great multitude in the common people.' It was the honesty of the poor, along with their 'hard, sad, sober, and continual toil,' that gave them their moral superiority over the rich, who would live 'delicately and easily.' 'Benefits' sought to connect people voluntarily and reciprocally within and across social distinctions, in ways that did not challenge *civitas* but did not require it either.[50]

Cicero placed the origins of a commonalty or town living (*Reipublicum*) in the bonds that developed from procreation, marriage, and household formation. These small, close and intimate affiliations were transformed by means of confederation, intermarriage, and alliances among localities into the original 'common wealth' (*rerum publicarum*), within which 'the knot of consanguinity and benevolence bindeth men in love and charity.'[51] Even though members of the commonwealth shared 'the same monuments of antiquity,' the true bonds of the new order were love, honesty, and like manners. Laws indeed were made and kings elected, according to Cicero, 'to seek right equally.' But he cautioned that the 'rulers not violate the trust and security' that they were set up to preserve.[52] As long as civil laws supported the fellowship of natural society and familiarity, they were to be preserved.

Even more important is that Cicero insisted that trust and security can be secured from the bottom up or from the inside out, if the members of the commonwealth resist the inclination to 'separate profit from honesty' in their dealings (his ultimate lesson in *De officiis*). To gain at another's expense was wrong on all accounts, and one should never prefer honors, riches, and pleasures before 'amity and friendship.' Vital and central to achieving the best of possibilities was liberality. And, the best target for one's benefits, after prudently distinguishing among those who deserve assistance and those who do not, was an honest poor man.[53] The subsequent exchange of benefits, and goods, enhanced life and deepened the commitments to friendship, mutual dependence, and amity that bound the members of society together, rich and poor.

The conceptual separation of *civitas* and *societas* was achieved with even more clarity by Seneca in *De beneficiis*. He encouraged the construction of a 'community of virtue' that would stand beside, or be surrounded by, the polity. At its heart was the free and voluntary activity of giving, receiving, reciprocating, and passing on benefits from the nobleman to the bondman and back again. First and foremost about a benefit, Seneca pointed out, was that it was an 'intention' even more than it was the thing done or given. Although the commitment should be taken 'willingly, speedily, and without hesitation, it should not be without "prudence"', a 'will grounded in reason.'[54] Perhaps the most deserving target for a benefit was one who is 'honest, simple, mindful, and grateful,' a person who does not prey on another's fortune, nor hoard his or her own or intend evil to anyone. Benefits should also be available to those who are not necessarily immediately visible or known to the benefactor, sick persons or strangers, for example. Seneca urged the use of wills to cover these eventualities.[55] In addition, recipients must also be prudent in their own way: they should take only from those to whom they would have given. The best outcome of proper giving and receiving is that 'friendship' can be undertaken afterward. This progression from giving and receiving to friendship was called by Seneca 'the Sacred Law of Benefits.'[56]

Central to the applicability of benefits' discourse to the plight of the poor commons, was Seneca's insistence that virtue knows no class, it is open to all. Fortune and its accompanying social positions captured only the body; the mind cannot be 'bought or sold,' 'restrained,' or 'held from...performing great matters, and passing beyond all bounds.' And the ability to free oneself from social station applied equally to master, bondman, poor commoner, or foreigner: all have but one parent, the world. Thus, whoever you are, wherever in society, urged Seneca, advance your minds and leap over whatever baseness lies in the way. If all this works properly, a virtual 'commerce of benefits' will be cultivated within the common weal, replete with 'mutual offices' and 'interchangeable friendships.'[57]

One behavior that is anathema to manners is ungratefulness; it is both 'loathsome' in itself and 'hateful' in the eyes of others. Nevertheless, and this makes even more evident Seneca's intent to keep *societas* and *civitas* separate, he demurred from making ungratefulness a matter of 'civil offense.' To make it a 'crime' transforms a benefit into a debt and invokes the structure of usury. 'Pay' is the 'foulest' word in giving, and whatever is good surely will perish 'if we make a merchandise of benefits.' Seneca opposed legal obligations in lending as well. Far better in both benefiting and lending would be to bring to these undertakings 'faith' and a 'mind observing equity.' Unfortunately, 'men have preferred profit over honesty' and would rather 'enforce others to be faithful, than behold them faithful.' In any case, how could a judge possibly decide these subtle matters? Would one punishment apply in all cases regardless of the dimensions of the benefits involved? He concluded that guaranteeing return through legal coercion would eviscerate the very meaning of benefits, which must include taking risk for worthy ends.[58]

Seneca's ethics offered a way to integrate the poor into the moral community through the ministrations of a non-coercive, voluntary 'commerce of benefits.' Considered in tandem with Cicero's determined call for concord through mutual regard and the devoted attention that both authors received in the educational establishement from grammar schools through the universities, the case is compelling that a revived traditional *societas* supplemented the traditional *societas christiana* in the early Stuart years.

During episodes of severe dearth, for example, in 1585, 1596–98, 1629–30, the government's Orders could provide only limited protection to the poor. The 'conjunctural poor,' near pensioners with little or no material or credit resources, lacked the 'exchange entitlements' to be able to participate in the controlled grain markets. That very few of them perished during these crises suggests the existence of a 'social economy' that paralleled or existed beneath the regular economy and its social welfare policy initiatives.[59] Softening the vertical, obligatory bonds somewhat were horizontal connections provided by kinship ties and, even more pervasively, neighborliness. The latter might be seen as the practical, on-the-ground parallel to the behaviors suggested by the Stoic 'discourse of benefits.' In this instance, however, its roots were customary, instinctual or Christian rather than Ciceronian or Senecan. Wrightson has described the reciprocity among neighbors as the 'exchange of comparable services between *effective*, if not actual, equals,' most often concerning 'occasions of simple economic aid,' including the extension of credit.[60] These relatonships resonate with the moral economy of ordinary early modern transactions that Craig Muldrew finds. Neighborliness and 'creditworthiness' were virtually synonymous. In an essentially pre-contractarian economy, individual profit was dependent on the 'direct co-operation on one's neighbours which trust entailed.' Thus, as Calvin had insisted and Cicero's and Seneca's moral theory had encouraged, buying and selling, far from fragmenting local communities, actually served to bind them together.[61]

Many ongoing economic relationships were alternatives to strictly market arrangements or the Poor Law's stipulations. For example, sharecropping or in-service work brought shelter and board to perhaps 60 percent of 15–24-year-olds who were employed. Workers hired to task or farm laborers brought on for a year were usually provided access to food; others worked for pay in kind. Some workers purchased grain from their employers in small amounts at less than market value. And 'local exchanges' were often set up at prices below market. In 1630, Hertfordshire farmers and corn-merchants were allowed to continue their regular marketing if they provided the poor with supplies beneath market prices. In general, there seem to have been many loan arrangements made with poor people that required either no interest or had no repayment schedule.[62]

Dearth was actually more difficult for poor people living in the towns. Live-in servants were fed by their employers on working days; guilds often provided assistance beyond their memberships; and town corporations sometimes extended credit or rent to their struggling tenants. Grain dealers set aside a portion of their supply, offering it to the poor at below market prices. In spite of the Poor Law's prohibition of begging, the Lord Mayor of London recommended that the Aldermen 'prescribe some fit time of day for the parish poor to seek relief from the houses of the richer sort.' Begging was allowed with much less supervision than usual in many towns during dearth episodes, and in a throwback to earlier hospitality, many more meals were made available to the poor at the doors of the rich. Parishes often raised special collections for the local poor.[63]

Cumulatively these undertakings suggest that it would be a mistake to suggest that caring for the poor took a sharp turn from voluntary to mandatory provision in these years. In Lancashire in 1623 several local courts sought to shore up mandatory provision by attempting to stifle informal relief efforts. Attempts to explain the motivations behind this social economy include 'church and conscience,' neighborliness, 'mental beliefs,' moral pressures, magistrates' directives, the menace of popular discontent, and the desire of the better sort to appear deserving of their position.[64] It seems likely that among those beliefs and promptings of conscience and morality across the social levels were the 'commerce of benefits,' custom, and tradition-embedded *societas*. Furthermore, it is now becoming evident that the poor themselves were not without agency in making their needs and expectations known and pursuing them.

Custom's Ideology

The ability of the gentry and middling sort to convert their obvious social power into acknowledged authority, to wield it without significant challenge required that their inferiors accepted what the anthropologist James C. Scott calls the 'public transcript.'[65] This was an inferred contract or agreement that bound the monarch and the people at the national level and the elites and the poor locally. The king and the middling sort orchestrated their right to rule by acknowledging that the protection of their inferiors was its primary objective.[66] The very fact that those in charge wanted to keep their right to rule as unsullied as possible opened the 'public space' into which the poor could air their 'hidden transcripts' of complaint. These took many forms, from grumbling and cursing, to impugning a superior's morality, or threatening violence. And, as we have discussed above, in times of dearth when suffering was great, interests strained, and emotions high, the poor's threats of violence seem to have been part of an expected ritual. The threat was more an invitation or a reminder to their superiors to act as they were charged to do to remedy the problem.[67]

The poor's hiddent transcripts were actually part of a more encompassing, 'ideology of custom.' On the surface very much a product of memory, customary culture's roots lay in the Anglo-Saxon law which Henry II had resuscitated; and its use in advocating for, and protecting the interests of, the lesser sort continued vibrantly into the last half of the eighteenth century. However, by the mid-seventeenth century the interests of the gentry and middling sort were increasingly legitimized by statutory law and policy. This alliance frequently challenged and eroded local rights of custom that the poor commons had long since incorporated into their economy of makeshifts. At this point the defense of custom became a more technically litigious exercise than it had been earlier. The poor and their advocates began to exhume the local court books, rolls, and manuscripts in which customary rights were originally granted or acknowledged and seek hearings and settlements from the Chancery or Exchequer courts in London.[68] These disputes focused on customs like boundary walking, wood gathering, corn gleaning, yearly doles, and miners' rights to gather ore.[69] Each locality's customary society was *sui generis*, tied as it was to its own spacial, social, and gendered arrangements. Since their claims rested in ancient grant and usage, customs were conveyed first and foremost 'in *perpetuam rei memoriam.*' A locality's customs bound together the 'values, beliefs, mechanisms, and forms,' the repertoire of responses of the poor and near poor to the world that conveyed their sense of station and entitlement.

Another register of custom's hold and its cause of discomfort among the gentry and middling sorts was the poor's continuing attachment to many of the rituals of 'merry' medieval England. The ideological assault on feasting and celebrations by the Calvinist reformers in the 1540s and 1550s had been severe and continued by Elizabethan and early Stuart Puritans. Although this produced a backlash of defiant practice and literary nostalgia in James's years, by the end of the Civil War era the austere goals of the Edwardian Calvinists had been realized. Ritual celebrations and feasting had been separated effectively from the religious life of the parish and its funds. With the advent of the Restoration, however, a 'merry equilibrium' began to emerge. The 'old festive culture' never regained its widespread presence of a century earlier, and it remained outside the parish. Overall, ritual was the source of much less contention, or much more resignation, than heretofore; a number of traditional celebrations, including midwinter entertainments, harvest suppers, Shrovetide misbehaviors, and wassail greetings (and the expected doles) continued.[70] In their own fashion, rituals and celebrations were part of the 'public transcripts' between the better and lesser sorts in any locality. And their stifling from above prompted 'hidden transcripts' from below.

Revolution and Political Arithmetic

The Civil War was preceded by long years of comparative calm nationally. The number of riots and participants had been diminishing steadily since the turn of the seventeenth century, and there had not been a major rebellion since the northern earls' in 1569.[71] When the ongoing friction of Charles I's authoritarian rule against parliament's prerogatives finally ignited, the ensuing rebellion was intended to be less a revolution than a series of correctives: to control the king, secure property, and institute a new religious conformity. For his part, the king expanded his council into one of war and established commissions to work fiscal and administrative matters through the local Justices of the Peace, sheriffs, and borough and parish officers. Parliament, not naturally an executive, was concerned with establishing its authority and ensuring that its decrees reached directly into the localities. It established central committees to administer a series of new taxes and other regulations through county commissioners who generally were arbitrary and abrasive in dealing with local officials. By 1649, though, Charles I had been executed, the House of Lords abolished, and within the Commons were advocates for the democratization of government, challenges to existing property arrangements, and the relinquishment of religious conformity.[72]

Estimates are that one-quarter to one-third of men between 16 and 50 years of age were pressed into service in the first war, and upwards of 80 000 of them were left dead from its 635 or so encounters of all dimensions. Besides this wide impact on the population, regions and localities in close proximity to either army experienced impressment of soldiers, house plundering, quartering of troops, trampling of crops, and commandeering of livestock. These out-of-the-ordinary abuses combined with escalating taxes from the two regimes' rapacious pursuit of revenues left the localities beleaguered in the face of new vagrants, war-related refugees, wounded or deserting soldiers, and widows and children, all of whom were mentioned frequently in the contemporary tracts.

We have seen that, beneath the relative calm of the pre-war decades in the villages and towns, pensioners and near pensioners struggled daily with the 'economy of makeshifts.' The middling sort calibrated their responses appropriately, all within the promptings of public and hidden transcripts of expectation. During the Civil War, riots did break out in six counties against parliament's ban on traditional Christmas celebrations and their accompanying, now secular, festivities. And the activities of the middling sort 'Clubmen' of the second war might by seen as evidence of local elites' determination to secure their customary privileges and authority by preventing military occupation of their villages and towns.[73] These may have been yet another iteration of the kind of center–periphery tensions that had played out especially in the Puritan towns after 1627, when William Laud became Archbishop of Canterbury. Laud's Catholic-seeming Arminianism in the context of Charles I's more authoritarian court alarmed ministers and magistrates and convinced them to be even more determined in enforcing their local reform agendas.[74]

The claims that customary rights could raise were both evident and transformed in the debates within the General Council of Oliver Cromwell's New Model Army at Putney church in October and November 1647.[75] At issue, among other matters, was the tract, *A Call to all the Soldiers of the Army by the Free People of England*, which defended the democratic claims of the more radical regiments. Presided over by Cromwell himself, the pointed exchanges among Cromwell, Henry Ireton, Cromwell's Commissary-General, Colonel Thomas Rainsborough, and Private Edward Sexby revealed the degree of constitutional unravelling that the rebellion had exposed (or created) and the resonance that the attempts to reconstitute order shared with the discourses of customary rights. The first contention was the significance of the Norman Conquest, the usual threshold into any attempt to claim 'ancient' precedents for contemporary rights. But it was Rainborough's subsequent remark, 'I think the poorest he that is in England hath a life to live, as the greatest he' that tipped the discussion into the less familiar and less grounded domain of political theory. 'I think,' he continued 'it's clear that every man that is to live under a government ought first by his own consent, to put himself under that government.' And Sexby told Cromwell directly that it was 'the poor and mean ... in their stations' who hold up the kingdom. Soon the law of nature was invoked by Rainsborough and the soldiers. Ireton responded bluntly that property itself is 'the most fundamental part of the constitution.' And it is only representatives of the freehold property owners, those with a stake in the social order, who can 'comprehend whatsoever is of real or permanent interest in the kingdom.' From this it was but a quick leap to the anarchic implications of the law of nature resting in 'every man's conception [of what] is just or unjust' and its consequence, 'What right hath any man to anything, if you lay not down that principle, that we keep a covenant.' There would be no agreement at Putney between the privates and the major general on this early airing of modern political theory's vexing questions.

A special committee was set up to consider the Army's recommendation to parliament on *A Call to all the Soldiers*, and it returned a report that leaned clearly toward Iretons's and Cromwell's position.[76] The agitators planned three rendezvous near Ware for subsequent weeks at which discontented regiments and thousands of laborers were to gather and press the franchise issue. But, between the plan and the event, the timeless claims of the soldiers were rendered untimely by the press of events. The king had escaped from Hampton Court, and Lord Fairfax, every soldier's general, had threatened to resign in the face of disloyal troops. A month later at Windsor Castle Cromwell and Fairfax entertained the senior officers and the elected representatives of the regimental officers at a grand feast of reconciliation.[77]

That the Levellers were a force to be contended with at all resulted from several developments in the mid-1640s. One was the leftward movement of the Long Parliament. In order to defeat the king, the originally staunch but politically moderate parliamentarians had to tap into those who opposed not only Charles's pretenses, but all birth privileges; and not only a potential Anglican religious conformity, but any sectarian conformity. By this time, the prominent Leveller agitator John Lilburne had been cutting his political teeth on these issues in the atmosphere of 'social disturbance and disharmony' in London for almost a decade. With the outbreak of the first civil war in 1642, he entered the parliamentary army as a captain and reached the rank of lieutenant colonel, before returning to civilian life in 1645 after quarrels with superior officers and his inability to subscribe to the Solemn League and Covenant. Arrested by the House of Lords and imprisoned in 1646 on charges related to his army insubordinations, Lilburne spent his remaining 11 years challenging the emerging Puritan order, defending himself in court, in forced exile or prison, and becoming a Quaker. Meanwhile, his ancient and natural rights ideas spread throughout the socially mobile New Model Army after 1645. There they fused with the soldiers' (and officers') grievances over arrears of pay, legal vulnerability for acts of war, and the conditions of future service to form a potent ideological force. At Putney, the Levellers challenged not only the command structure of the Army but the very legitimacy of present and future governments.[78] In spite of their defeat by Cromwell in 1647, the Levellers challenged again two years later inside (and outside) the Army in the wake of the king's execution and the deepening constitutional and religious indecision. Now, much depleted in leadership and with most of the Army's grievances settled, their effort collapsed quickly, as did the wider Leveller movement within several years. Their immediate failure notwithstanding, it is more to praise than to discount the Levellers in their confrontation with the powers-that-be at Putney to say that their probing eloquence was more a gift to the ages than to the moment.

Given the disruptions we cataloged above, it is surprising that very few, if any, of the thousands of local communities across the realm fell into disorder from internal tensions. Perhaps fear of the mayhem of war and confusion born of the awkward attempts of the royalists and the parliamentarians to reconstruct center–periphery connections inclined the villages and towns to cling to the familiar. This may have been helped, too, by the expanded corn supply that half a century of 'improvement' enclosure had helped to produce, even in the dearth years of 1649–51. Nevertheless, traditional anti-enclosure venom still was easily aroused. John Moore, a Leicestershire minister, branded enclosers 'make-beggars,' who in pursuit of their greed 'unpeople' the towns and 'uncorn' the fields. The many poor who congregate in market and 'fielden' towns were 'driven out of their hive, their honey,' literally 'their trade of plowing' was taken away. It is of no account, then, that more grain is available; it is inaccessible and unaffordable to the poor 'tenants, cottagers and their children.'[79]

More typically, the social commentators were fixated on the idleness that prevailed among the great numbers of vagabonds and war refugees inundating villages, towns, and the metropolis. They were less concerned with the poor-makers of old. This may be why Margaret James, the first historian to look systematically at social welfare in these years, noted a shift in attitude in the literature from less defensiveness about wealth and more inclination to view poverty as ' a crime and disgrace.'[80] The shift was more profound than that, however; a strictly religious register of analysis was giving way to a more secular one. The shibboleth behind which some commentators chose to hide this was traditional moral theology that emphasized God as judge of how the non-poor accepted their responsibilities to the poor. Both 'high and low must give an account to God,' and 'those who stop their ears at the cry of the poor, shall cry themselves and not be heard.' To entire nations who have failed in this responsibility 'his judgements have been long.'[81]

The bolder and more resourceful commentators, men like Peter Chamberlen and Leonard Lee, appealed to a complex set of authorities. As Chamberlen put it, 'It is the work of God, and of men that will be like God; which we are taught by nature, reason, and Christianity.' Men had to think more carefully about the idle poor, develop plans to respond to them, and act on those plans. Mere words were no longer enough. Lee reminded his readers of England's reputation in the world for 'excellent laws, but no execution ... good materials, but bad orders.'[82] Chamberlen went on to recommend an elaborate scheme to pay soldiers, employ idle vagrants, educate orphans, and provide hospitals for the sick poor, all of which began with disendowment. This time it was not the 'Caim's castles' of the lascivious monks and friars, but the the land and properties of the king, bishops, and deans taken in the war. Rather than sell them, they should be kept in public hands and converted into the '*work-houses, schools, hospitalls, &c.*' needed to rescue and redirect the poor and, in the process, '*so save so much money to the state in building others.*' Lee's plan would have every '*parish, town, hamlet, precinct, prison, and house of correction* ... 1. To raisse a stocke. 2. To provide materials. 3....to order the work.' Aware that some would say that there are too many poor and these arrrangemens would be too costly, Lee rests his confidence in the magistrates and the London City Council to 'resolve the prosecution thereof.'

The actual level of emergency in London remains to be ascertained definitively, but indications are that the social commentators were exaggerating somewhat, swept along perhaps by aphorisms such as 'since these unnatural wars begun, the poor do much more abound.' This led Lee to identify four categories of new poor persons created by the war: those who lost their trades in the shrinking economy; those stripped of their estates in the countryside; widows and children of dead soldiers; and lame soldiers.[83] The formal and informal relief activities in the Old City were much more intense and resourceful than various commentators suggest. The Lord Mayors had traditionally encouraged charity beyond the parameters of the Poor Law, and even with those restrictions the City had achieved a significant improvement by the mid-seventeenth century. The 'six-penny' dole, the maximum stipulated in the 1598 statute, had trebled to 1s. 6d. and in times of particular severity might reach 3s. The City's wealthier 87 parishes regularly participated in 'rate-in-aid' payments to supplement the pensioner funds of the 24 poorer ones, a practice first stipulated, as we have seen, in the statutes of 1555, 1563, and 1598. For instance, one-third of the total expenditure of St Andrew Wardrobe on its poor came from wealthier parishes.

In 1640, the City's population was approximately 180,000, and 1400 of them were involved in implementing Poor Law policies. Beyond that number, however, were the scores of yeomanry and company wardens, guild officers, hospital governors, magistrates, and churchwardens who participated in philanthropic charities across the City. And, if most but not all pensioners were householders, the 'straggling poor' were not ignored. The money given to them in a variety of informal ways may have approached one-quarter of all funds distributed to the poor.[84] Careful study of the parish funds distributed indicates that there was no appreciable drop off in the amounts distributed through the parishes during the war years. The bedeviling detail is whether the numbers of migrants and near poor increased significantly as a result of the wars. There certainly are indications that the relief establishment was strained. Rates-in-aid all but ceased; the hospitals seemed hard pressed; and the London Corporation of the Poor, about which we will speak shortly, was crippled by underfunding.[85]

London's social welfare practice exhibited a special commitment to its unusually high number of foundlings, orphans, and poor children. These efforts far exceeded the Poor Law's mandate that poor children be apprenticed. If the average yearly outlay for a pensioner in the mid-seventeenth century was 2L 10s., a child's maintenance ranged from 5L to 11L. Petty schools and some grammar schools took on poor children at no or reduced fees, and both female and male foundlings were cared for and educated at Christ's Hospital. It was not unusual for parishes to place foundlings for their care and education outside the City where they were less threatened by disease. One of the most confident and carefully elaborated plans in the Civil War years pamphlet output was Samuel Hartlib's *London's Charity inlarged, Stilling The Orphans Cry* (1650). It embodied the City's concern for poor children, and revealed a confident, matter-of-fact, and hopeful commitment not just to relieve the children, but to prepare them for morally sound and productive lives. In other words, one senses in the tract some shifting of priorities in social welfare discourse from 'reformation' to 'improvement' or, even, back to Christian humanist idealism.[86]

Hartlib was a pivotal, but evanescent figure in the 1640s and 1650s, whose importance is only now being appreciated. He figuratively occupied the center of a circle of optimistic, cutting-edge thinkers and doers inspired by Bacon's 'restauration' and the scientific and

Calvinist-filtered Aristotelianism that thrived on the continent at Strasbourg and Tubingen. Crucial to this mix was Jan Comenius's notion, *pansophia*, the quest for the communion of all knowledge. Along the way a united Protestantism, the interconnection of the physical sciences, and acknowledgment of the mutuality of matter and spirit would be achieved. Comenius's outlook offered a methodological and philosophical foundation, grounded in nature, reason, and revelation, for all branches of inquiry. And it promised unusual truth-finding capabilities and guidance to effective action. Hartlib, whose writings were few, was more a processor, a clearing-house, a collector and disseminator of the *pansophia* ideas of the mathematicians, historians, politicians, linguists, scieintists, agronomists, and philosopher-theologians with whom he maintained contact.[87]

In his *London's Charity inlarged*, Hartlib praised one of his dedicatees, Lord Fairfax, for being the model of a great soldier and man who is also a good man and (sounding almost like Vishnu instructing Arjuna in the *Bhagavadgita*) for his understanding that the death of the body does not destroy the soul. Hartlib's practical and carefully embellished proposal was for the City to cease investigating settlement claims for migrants from locations more than 30 miles away, to employ at least some of the hardy adult unemployed in a revived fishing trade, and to establish workhouse-like facilities to rescue and provide direction to the lives of foundlings and orphans. A cadre of 11 nurses, schoolmasters, foster mothers, cooks, butchers, among others, would care for every 100 children, who were to learn to read and write, make their own clothes, and become strong moral and spiritual beings. Hartlib insisted that these facilities be subjected to careful oversight and accounting. His own calculations of staff salaries and general food costs, combined with profits realized from goods the children would make, meant that for an overall investment of 1000L the city could 'save' 500 children from the streets.[88]

If the London Corporation of the Poor had at least some of its inspiration in the felicity and curiosity of the Hartlib circle, its immediate models were the discipline and make-work for vagrants in Bridewell, employment schemes in several localities, and the children's care in Christ's Hospital. Very important to its proponents was its call for central administration, mostly thwarted since 1598 by the parish-centered mandates of the Poor Law. Parliamentary ordinances in 1647 and 1649 authorized the London Alderman (and magistrates in other municipalities to do similarly if they wished) to establish the Corporation; the hospital charters would be replaced. The Corporation had an expansive governance structure including 42 elected freemen from the wards to facilitate cooperation with the parishes and, through the common council, raise funds equitably among the parishes. The initial cost projected for the undertaking was 12 000 L. However, neither this funding nor the full implementation of the possibilities inherent in the plan were achieved; and a full acounting for this remains elusive because of the absence of Corporation records. After the Stuart Restoration in 1660, the king's property which the Corporation had been occupying (recall Chamberlen's disendowment plan) was repossessed by the crown, and the Corporation disappeared. Even so, the statute (1662) that clarified the meaning of settlement also authorized the establishment of Corporations of the Poor in London, Middlesex, and Westminster. Subsequently, corporations were founded in Exeter, Bristol, Norwich, Dorchester, and Hull without parliament's authorization.[89]

Hartlib died in 1662 and with him the rare vibrancy of his circle's immediate influence. Nevertheless, extending all the way back to the 'Lybel of English Polycy' in the mid-fifteenth century and forward through Thomas Starkey, Thomas Smith, Francis Bacon, and into the Hartlib group and others in the Civil War and Commonwealth years, a tradition of essentially secular and hardheaded social, economic, political, and policy analysis had been firmly implanted in the English social welfare 'repertoire.' For instance, when Bacon speculated in his essay, 'Of Seditions and Troubles', on the relationships among the size, distribution, and productivity of the population and the resources of the realm, he was doing rudimentary political arithmetic. And earlier, Robert Hichcock in his *Politique Platt* had done somewhat the same in promoting a revived fishing industry.[90] This emerging discipline, devoid of sentiment or moral censure, sought to develop an empirical and calculating approach to the challenge of generating national wealth and, in the process, to make better use of the poor commons.

William Petty, disciple to Bacon (and Hobbes), gave political arithmetic its first mature expression in the seventeenth century. He probably had met with the 'invisible college' during the Commonwealth, was a charter member of the Royal Society in 1660, and brought a distinct scientific curiosity to his analyses of the paramount economic problems of the day. And, when Petty discussed the poor, he conceded the usual categories of the deserving indigent and the unworthy idle. The indigent must be relieved and hospitalized if necessary and the healthy malingerers punished. His real concern, though, was the large number of working poor people and frequently unemployed or underemployed laborers, whom he designated 'supernumeraries.' At the root of his proposals about them was the Baconian assumption that a 'fewness of people, especially of laborers and artificers,' will always make a realm poorer than it need be. However, he was equally aware that employment for these persons will not always be available; it will have to be contrived for them. Unless this is done, the unemployed will resort to begging or stealing for their subsistence, which, if successful, will 'for ever after indispose them to labor, even upon the greatest occasion which may suddenly and unexpectedly happen.' The poor commons, then, must be kept disciplined to toil, even if this meant building 'a useless Pyramid upon *Salisbury Plain*.'[91] Such is Petty's way of dealing with what must have seemed a capricious unemployment problem, but which actually was generated by fluctuations among population size, fertility, wages, and prices. Nevertheless, what most seventeenth-century commentators noticed was that the laborers often sought employment casually. They worked until they accrued some extra resources, then quit. Petty thought this to be a dangerous habit and urged that wages be kept as close to subsistence as possible so that laborers would not be able to accrue resources beyond what was required for their living. If this were done, he insisted, unemployment also could largely be eliminated.

Petty's calculations convinced him that the realm could afford to provide subsistence for the supernumeraries by requiring them to perform work of 'much labor, little art.' Mining, bridge-building, planting trees, even cloth manufacturing, which Petty hoped would be introduced, were within their capabilities; and they would add benefits and wealth to the nation. But, if such projects proved unable to absorb all the supernumeraries, they must be relieved. Their subsistence wages have left them with nothing on which to live without working.[92] Since 'the poor ye always have with you,' Petty recommended that it behooved the state to put them to the most profitable uses. The near indigence of the poor commons was no longer a bothersome irritant or a dangerous breeding-ground for vice that must be eliminated. It had become a national resource at the disposal of the policy-maker.

A 'Big Tent'?

By the Restoration decades the education boom had run its course. Schools at all levels no longer were bursting at the seams. The humanist ideal of the gentleman scholar was giving ground to the dilettantish 'man of quality,' and the classics-drenched curricula of the universities increasingly were judged to be irrelevant. In these same 40 years from the Restoration of Charles II to the turn of the eighteenth century, the proportion of parishes attempting to impose the rate expanded from roughly one-third to just over four-fifths. Across the realm by the latter date there were approximately 123,000 pensioners, who with their dependents, represented about 4.4 percent of the population. Altogether the parishes were raising 400,000L annually for anti-poverty efforts, and one-half of all households were involved with the Poor Law as rate payers or pensioners.[93] Elizabethan policy was making its way beyond the towns and larger villages into the nooks and crannies of the realm, and in so doing becoming a more widely shared national experience for good or ill. While vagrancy continued to be a concern for churchwardens and overseers, compared to the late Elizabethan and early Stuart years it had diminished; and the cash value of the typical pension had improved by 50 percent.

The expanding rolls and generous pensions may also indicate more lax screening of pensioners by the overseers. One J. Fransham complained in the 1720s that the Norwich overseers thought more about their image as 'good-natured, merciful, generous men' than 'the consequences of their over-liberality (as long as 'twas not their own).'[94] Likely there was more than the overseers' image at stake in this, however. It is possible that, as a consequence of the gradual improvement and relative stability in the economy since the dearth episodes and war calamities of mid-century, the percieved entry point from poverty into dependency was getting higher too. It is clear in any case, that the pressures surrounding the overseers were different than they had been earlier. The poor were acting more 'entitled' to their pensions and the rate payers more careful about what they perceived to be the expanding numbers of those 'on the parish.' As both the poor and the non-poor complained more openly about the overseers' shortcomings, the Justices of the Peace and local vestries became more active in their supervision and intervention.[95]

A local contextual disruption in the later Stuart years that has tended to be overlooked, but which was heightening politicization of all local undertakings, was the rechartering of upwards of 200 boroughs and corporations as a consequence of the collapse of the Commonwealth and the coming of Charles II to the throne.[96] If the towns were to recover their legal status in conducting elections and supervising charitable trusts, and if they were to establish their bonds of loyalty to the king, their charters would have to reworked or granted anew. The Corporation Act (1661) was intended to expedite the matter by encouraging the localities to settle their own parliamentary–royalist tensions under the threat of royal commissioners holding corporate personnel to several oaths and tests or purging them. Due to the statute's awkard and uneven administration, however, many local officials who had been deeply invested in the parliamentary cause continued in office.[97]

Seeking to resolve old tensions that were beginning to ebb into new Whig and Tory ones, many boroughs began to bypass the privy council for its lack of legal standing and proceed directly to the court of King's Bench. Its writs of *mandamus* and *quo warranto* could be used appropriately. Thus a reversal in the center–periphery dynamic that had been developing since at least the 1530s was under way. The council as the primary overseer of local government was being replaced by King's Bench, and, even more important, the 'divisions' and 'exclusions' involved were flowing inward from the periphery instead of the other way around.[98] Nevertheless, as the Popish and Rye House Plots and the Exclusion Crisis unfolded in the late 1670s and early 1680s, the king also utilized King's Bench *quo warranto* procedures. Charles II set off a round of 134 recharterings between 1682 and 1687, including the seizure of the London Corporation in 1683; and James II dismissed 103 corporations and then reinstated them in 1688. Whigs and Tories cooperated, perhaps for the last time, to reshape their local governments; but, unsettled and baffled by the royal intrusions, they watched almost unmoved James's expulsion, William's arrival and the Glorious Revolution.[99]

Historians now see John Locke's political theory, replete with its natural law-based rights to consent, property, and revolution, as less important in stirring the removal of the king, than had been assumed previously and not only because his *Second Treatise*, drafted in 1679–80, was published in 1690, well after the event. While radical writers had propagated ideas of the right to revolution, for example, most of them were 'republicans' and not advocates of natural law political theory as the Levellers had been. They called for elective or limited monarchy based on historical or 'ancient constitution' grounds.[100] What was of long-term significance, though, was the secular political momentum provided by the revolution. If government was a human construct, established to cope with the dilemmas of human sociability, *civitas* and its inherent policy-making functions were given even stronger justification.

Having said this, we nevertheless are becoming more aware of the vital role that *societas* in the form of institutionalized and private charity continued to play in sustaining the marginally poor and pensioners alike. And this sustenance, particularly in rural settings, appears to have been a constant and necessary practice, not an emergency intervention during particularly hard times, as it tended to be in the larger towns and London. Evidence of this has been accumulating since the mid-1980s and, as a result, a turn in social welfare historiography has become discernible. The earlier predisposition of historians to disdain the local relief responsibilities of the Poor Law for their inefficient and harsh outcomes has given ground to a more sanguine appraisal. Coming to the fore now is an appreciation for the discretionary capabilities of the churchwardens, overseers, and vestry members to marshal private and public resources to address the unique needs of communities and individuals.[101] As we have seen above, historians have acknowledged that traditional charity did not disappear with the arrival of the Poor Law-mandated parish fund and pensions. Slack has pointed out that the totals expended nationally on social welfare from parish funds began to exceed those from individual and foundational charities only toward the end of the seventeenth century. (This may be an overdue vindication of W. K. Jordan's contention that initially the Poor Law was conceived to be the back-up for the variety of private charitable uses.) A revival of 'private interest and private investment in public welfare' was taking place in these same years; and by the 1740s, the English had reestablished their 'mixed economy of welfare' which had been shattered by the Reformation.[102] John Broad and L. A. Botelho add much meat to the bones of Slack's observation. They show in their studies of several villages in near-south and southern counties that the role of traditional charities was crucial in a variety of social welfare arrangements, the 'parochial economy of welfare' in Broad's phrase, that continued until the later eighteenth century. At that point, the parish-centered social welfare system itself was on its last legs, unable to cope with population expansion, rising prices, industrial development in the north, and the loss of agricultural and proto-industrial employment in the south.[103]

Each of Broad's and Botelho's villages, Middle Claydon and Brill in Buckinghamshire, Ashwell in Hertfordshire, and Cratfield and Poslingford in Suffolk, had its own economic challenges, poor individuals, and private and public resources available for relief. And comparatively from that mix, emerged five distinct social welfare arrangements under what we might call the 'big tent' of the Poor Law. Both historians find that charitable gifts and foundations were not considered separate or outside the local social welfare strategy, even though their specific applications varied from locality to locality. And, throughout the later seventeenth and eighteenth centuries, 'going on the parish' was the last resort not the first for persons in need. Middle Claydon was a 'closed' village with a diminishing population (from 250 to 100), encouraged by the local, resident, gentry landlord family, the Verneys. They sought to keep the number of dependant persons and the poor rate in the village as low as possible and were successful. In their own paternalistic way the family pursued population control. With one eye on settlement regulations (see below) they prevented servants from achieving a full year of residency, and before being admitted apprentices were required to guarantee against their future dependence on the parish. The Verneys also sought to dissuade the indigent people from marriage. At the same time, they provided substantial charity to the village poor and maintained 'complex negotiations' with the overseers, often urging more assistance than the high-rent-paying tenant farmers were willing to provide.[104]

Much different goals and arrangements were evolving in the large (740 in 1700), open village of Ashwell in Hertfordshire, in the barley-growing region near the Cambridgeshire border. Without gentry until the nineteenth century, the local leaders were drawn from a group of perhaps a dozen farmers of 50 or more acres and their four dozen or so compatriots with smaller holdings. The parish vestry was active and innovative, creating a fund that much exceeded what the ordinary rate could have raised. For instance, parish funds were used to buy rental lands for the parish, the income from which was used to benefit the poor in several ways. The vestry bought homes for poor people, paid rents for hard-pressed laborers, bound out apprentices, and, after 1770, began purchasing 'clothing for the relief of such poor people as do not receive relief from the parish.' And, picking up on the rising national tide of ideological enthusiasm for workhouses in the 1720s (see Chapter 5), 11 villagers on their own set up a workhouse in Ashwell in 1728, which, also following the trend of the moment, failed in less than a year and a half. The Ashwell vestrymen and village leaders clearly were offering much assistance to those who were struggling but not receiving pensions.[105]

This vigilance for the marginally poor was shared by another relatively comfortable agricultural setting, the open and dairy farming village of Cratfield with a population of about 300 in the late 1600s. As we have noted, its credentials as an innovator in poor relief extend back to the 1530s and 1540s. The village leaders were very clear in distinguishing between charitable and public outlays for the poor, but the joint efforts were closely coordinated. The overseers dispensed pensions and the churchwardens (recall the appearance of that office in the fifteenth century in many parishes throughout the realm, discussed in Chapter 1) individual and foundational charity. Although the village was moderately Puritan, the philosophy of social welfare was much less penal than that found in Terling or 'godly cities' like Salisbury or Dorchester. The churchwardens, who often distributed their own charity, and the vestry hoped to keep as many of those too poor to pay the poor rate from going 'on the parish' themselves. This assistance included: coal and firewood; payment for medical services; annual rents; outlays for apprenticeships or schooling for poor children; and even once only gifts of cash. And, although pensions in Cratfield were at least modest compared to other Suffolk villages, recipients almost always received further charitable assistance through the churchwarden.[106]

Brill, a dairy village only ten miles from Oxford, formerly had been part of the Royal Forest of Bernwood. In 1632, however, the village's lumber products employment was devastated by Charles I's decision to disafforest the property. The woods all but disappeared within a decade, and the hard-up forest workers found themselves coping with rights to settle and graze animals on small portions of what was now called the 'Poor Folks Pasture,' managed by trustees. Subsequently many cottagers seeking cash sold their animals to larger farmers. In 1685, by decision of the court of Exchequer, the cottagers were encouraged to renounce their grazing rights; the bulk of the pasture was let to a single tenant, whose rent was to be redirected to assistance for eligible cottagers. Upwards of 100 cottagers were assisted from these funds, although much consternation ensued from the fact that the tenant enclosed his land and the pay-out to the cottagers was less than half of the rent income. At one point the trustees forced potential recipients of assistance to say they were satisfied with the management of the charity. By the second decade of the eighteenth century new leadership had emerged. Cooperation among comfortable local farmers, gentry, magistrates, and selected outsiders like the Verney's, led to additional charitable and philanthropic initiatives to fund apprenticeships and enlarge the local schools.[107]

The most forlorn of the five villages was Poslingford. With a population of no more than 200 it was close by the Stour Valley and tied into the cyclical proto-industrial cloth-making economy. So poor was the village that in the 1690s no more than 20 percent to 35 percent of the households could pay the rate and most of the parish fund was provided by the three wealthiest families. Attempts were made to increase the fund by reinvesting the scarce returns from pensioners' employment and adding in proceeds from the sale of deceased pensioners' goods and the Easter communion offering. Nevertheless no more than 2 percent of the population at any time, three or four persons, were pensioned, at the annual rate of 1L 7s. 8d. (compared to 2L 7s. 9d. in Cratfield). This left the remaining 70 percent or so of the marginally poor clinging to a slippery slope of survival provided by the other source of help, six wills and eight endowed charities. The benefits of these may have reached between one and two dozen indigents in any year and could include clothing, residence in Town House, the village hall and almshouse, the provision of a spinning wheel, and sickbed care or medical help. Unlike Cratfield, the Poslingford churchwardens were not charged to gather, focus, and dispense the village charities. Adding to the hard, scrabbling tone of life were the consequences of the village's somewhat enthusiastic Puritanism: occasional resort to whipping and stocks and the purchase of badges for pensioners in 1697.[108]

Botelho's prosopographic collection of 337 biographies from Cratfield and Poslingford leads her to offer reappraisals of several assumptions in the earlier historiography. In addition to reinforcing the view that more emphasis needs to be given to charitable uses if we are to understand fully seventeenth- and eighteenth-century social welfare, Botelho challenges prevailing generalizations about the play of age and gender. For instance, in Cratfield 'going on the parish' for an older person was not achieved with a persuasive plea to the overseer; it was the culmination of a gradual, 14 years on average, deterioration of one's marginal economic independence that may have begun at age 45 or so. And the possibility of a comfortable pension had diminished by the later seventeenth century as overseers here and elsewhere directed more parish funds to the younger working poor. Thus 'remaining independent' for as long as possible became the expectation and the practice. There were life and death costs, however. In both Suffolk villages the few pensioned poor outlived the non-pensioned poor, 72 years to 68 in Cratfield and 65 years to 63 in Poslingford.[109]

Even more compelling is Botelho's view that social welfare historians will have to rethink their assumption that the 'feminization of poverty' applies across the board in pre-industrial England. She concedes that it may be useful in addressing poverty in the large towns and the metropolis but finds it inaccurate for the 80 percent of the population in rural settings. Her biographies tell different stories for older women and men in the two villages, but their cumulative effect leads her to conclude that women were not disproportionately represented among the poor. She shows that in Cratfield women accomplished the transition from middle to old age more securely than men, were more likely to keep independent households, and began any pensions later than men. But, yes, the Cratfield men did outlive the women. By contrast, female pensioners in Poslingford, all single or widowed, began their dependence on the parish at average age 54.8 years, 11 years before the men; and, they outlived the men. For seventeenth-century, rural England Botelho suggests that 'gender equity' may prove to be more descriptive.[110]

A much different prospect for women and men was long under way in the Tyneside village of Whickham in the northeast coalfields of County Durham. This region has been characterized by Levine and Wrightson as perhaps the 'first thoroughly industrialized local economy in Britain...based as much on capital investment as on the use of wage labor.'[111] By the 1560s, coal digging in the Tyneside was already 200 years along, had achieved some technological innovation (chain-driven water pumps and lumber-trussed shafts for underground coal extraction), and by sea was supplying London with its vital fuel. Whickam's 93 households in 1563 had quadrupled to 367 a century later. And, as the village began to accommodate to the Poor Law in the mid-seventeenth century, two dozen vestrymen replaced the Halmote Court of leading copyholders (the leadership of older 'manorial' Whickham) in all aspects of the parish's administration. We get some indication of the extent of the marginally poor in the village, almost all wage-earners in the coal trades, from the fact that 78.8 percent of its households were exempted from the Hearth Tax in 1666. Approximately one-third of them migrated out of Whickham over the next decade, leaving a total of 185 of whom 88 (43.4 percent) eventually became pensioners. By comparison to the dairy-farming Cratfield, and even Poslingford with its cloth spinning, the employment opportunities for women in Whickham were few. Consequently, single women and widows made up the bulk of the pensioners, while men were much more prominent as recipients in the distributions of the parish's charitable outlay. Perhaps most unusual about Whickham's social welfare, however, was that by the 1670s the vestry was targeting the industrial employers with special assessments for the parish fund.[112]

The one significant Poor Law innovation in these decades was the attempt to formalize settlement, the criteria for establishing one's local residency and eligibility for relief. A local custom with roots in Anglo-Saxon England, its first acklowledgment in statutory law was in the aftermath of the Black Death. Later, in 1503–04, Henry VII's parliament defined it as three-years' residency in a locality. Edwardian and Elizabethan legislation shifted settlement's test to one's place of birth. The matter rested there until 1662 when an omnibus bill 'for the better relief of the poor of this kingdom' was passed, some parts of which addressed yet again the definition of settlement. This time, it was to be achieved only after 40 days' residence without challenge or the acquisition of a 10L annual rent. Newcomers to a parish who met neither of these criteria and were not related to a parishioner or townsman, could be removed if or when they seemed likely to require a pension.[113] Whether or not to authorize a removal was to be decided by two local justices sitting in petty sessions after taking depositions from the sojourner and parish officials. Historians have been mixed in their assessment of at least this first phase of 'settlement' in the Poor Law's development. Slack emphasizes its Draconian side, characterizing it as more an encouragement for removal of potentially burdensome migrants than a path to settlement. James Taylor, on the other hand, emphasizes that any mandatory relief system must have some gate-keeping possibility and, even so, petty session records indicate that removal was infrequently attempted.[114] In the next chapter we will take up settlement again in its 'merit' or 'earning settlement' form achieved through the statutes of 1691 and 1697. But, for the moment, whether or not to pursue removal of particular newcomers to a locality must have been yet another pressure on the overseers in their attempts to keep the peace in their parishes.

Conclusion

In the short seventeenth century the government faced the task of seeing to the implementation of the newly passed Elizabethan Poor Law. Expanding the *civitas* domain, government's authority in this formerly voluntary activity, was a slow and uneven process with the exception of a cohort of Puritan-dominated communities, in which parish-centered relief had been embraced well before the Poor Law made it mandatory. By the end of the seventeenth century perhaps 80 percent of the realm's parishes were implementing a poor rate. To appreciate the challenges in this undertaking, we explored how fundamental issues of size, geography, and local values affected when and how parishes began to comply. The new system presented challenges also to the poor who had to 'request' and 'negotiate' for pensioner status under the new arrangements. At the same time, the very expansion of the Poor Law's coercive and intrusive provisions spawned commitments to alternative *societas* responses to poverty by both the non-poor and poor alike. These undertakings sought to retain a voluntary, moral, or spiritual dimension to the exchanges of poverty relief. And we explored the Roman Stoic-inspired 'commerce of benefits,' that was widely available to educated gentry and middling sort, to illustrate a powerfully moral approach to poverty relief outside the spheres of government and the church.

The depredations of the Civil War in the 1640s produced much concern about neglected poor people, stubborn vagrants, and wounded soldiers, as well as widows and orphans. We found in the resulting remonstrances and tracts a curious juxtaposition. On the one hand were traditional *societas christiana* calls for more care for the deserving poor and harsh discipline for the healthy unemployed and, on the other, the beginnings of the application of political arithmetic to poverty issues. For all the disruptions and suffering caused by the wars, however, there was little intracommunal instability or violence stemming from social justice or poverty-related issues. This, even though the rights of the realm's 'little and poor men' were invoked in the Puritan Army debates of 1647–48 over the deep constitutional meanings of the rising against Charles I. Of more immediate importance were the careful proposals generated for elaborate workhouses that focused not only on the adult unemployed but also on the care, education, and work training of foundlings, orphans, and poor children. An impressive example of this was the London Corporation of the Poor, which, although unsuccessful, stood as a model for many imitators well into the eighteenth century. And recent historiography focused on the important role of charity in sustaining both the marginal and pensioned poor in rural settings has led to more interest in the Poor Law as a 'big tent' under which many different mixes of private and public assistance could be combined to address the unique circumstances of communities and individuals. This work is also raising new questions about the play of age and gender in the rural social welfare process.

In the half-century from the Civil War era through the Stuart Restoration and the Glorious Revolution of 1688, the focus of attention in the poverty discussion and practice shifted from the vagrant to the settled poor. The statute of 1662 was the first of several that attempted to clarify the criteria that established a person's eligibility for relief or 'settlement,' the one parish that would accept him or her as chargeable for a pension if that became necessary. Even though the Poor Law was in many ways an irritating and ill-fitting policy garment for English society, it was constantly being shaped and reshaped locally in its implementation.

Chapter 5: Settlement, Workhouses, and New Industry (c.1690–1780)

The population, wage, and prices patterns in the long eighteenth century indicate a sharp turn toward expanding structural poverty after the 1760s. The realm's population, after remaining virtually unchanged at about 5.1 million since 1650, began to expand rapidly in the 1730s, reaching 6.5 million by 1780 and 8 million at the turn of the nineteenth century. And in the 1740s the consumables price index also began to rise after a long steady-state of nearly a century. Prices rose quickly, outpacing population increases, until a sharp decline set in around 1805. Meanwhile wages, which had been rising slowly since the 1620s reached their temporary high point around 1740 and then began a steady decline until 1800.[1] Other developments tended to make incidents of extreme poverty and suffering less likely. For instance, widespread dearth was a less regular phenomenon in the eighteenth century. After the bad harvest years of 1657–61, it was almost 50 years until the next grain shortages of 1708 to 1711 and another 85 years to the severe breakdown of the mid-1790s. Furthermore, for all intents and purposes, the last visitation of the plague was in 1666. 'Sweating sickness' or influenza had been part of the earlier pandemics, however, and would continue in the post-plague years to contirubute to dangerous new fever outbreaks in 1677–82, 1727–29, and 1740–01.[2]

Nevertheless, the convergence of rising prices, falling wages, and expanding population in the 1760s was compounded by the emerging industrial sector of the economy. That shift to a new, innovative and more industrial economy was, for our purposes, the 'signal event' of the eighteenth century. It changed so significantly the traditional Malthusian restraints on economic expansion and population growth as to render the more than four centuries old, pre-industrial societal and economic 'foot print' almost unrecognizable by the middle of the next century. And its parish-centered social welfare was becoming obsolete, and by the 1830s expendable.

Settlement

We saw in Chapter 4 that the settlement provisions of the Poor Law of 1662, the so-called Settlement Act, sought more than anything to clarify what 'settlement' was intended to mean. It focused on a new definition of residency for settlement: 40 days passed in a locality without being challenged or the assumption of a yearly rental of at least 10L. The absence of either of these and needing a pension or approaching that condition left a newcomer vulnerable to removal by the parish. Since so much early modern social legislation seemed to codify local practices long under way, we probably can assume that these were fairly common criteria for settlement and removal. Norma Landau has noted that, prior to the imposition of Whig conformity under George I, parish officers in Kent brought many more appeals for removal orders to Quarter Sessions. They were trying to take advantage of frequent differences of political allegiance between the petty session and the county judges. Once top to bottom Whig conformity was in place, the number of appeals for removal dropped off significantly.[3] That contested removals could be decided to the disadvantage of the removing parish, very costly in legal fees and travel costs, and politically divisive, must have contributed to the mounting pressures on the overseers.

The other side of the 'unwelcome migrant' coin, however, was that both the seasonal agricultural sector of the economy and its gradually expanding manufacturing necessitated some degree of mobility. Perhaps in recognition of this, the government began to encourage at least the more confident and adventuresome migrants. In the statute of 1691, new criteria were established for achieving settlement: paying the parish rate, serving a year in public office or charge, completing an indentured apprenticeship of more than 40 days, or acquiring an annual hire. Six years later the settlement statute of 1697 stipulated that the annual hire criterion had to be completed for settlement eligibility, but much more importantly it authorized a migrant's parish of origin to provide a certificate acknowledging its relief obligations to the migrant and his descendents.[4] In theory, carrying such certificates should have attested to the uprightness of strangers as they sought better opportunities. But, a certificate's promise was one thing; it was quite another to be able to accomplish a removal, should that have become necessary. Prohibitive distances, jurisdictional boundaries, and lack of attention by necessary intermediaries made the removal of newcomers, certificated or not, extremely difficult.

William Hay, writing in 1735 and well informed on the law associated with settlement, described it as 'an *Utopian* scheme, unworthy of the legislature; good, perhaps, in theory, but, in the nature and circumstances of human affairs, impossible to be put in execution.'[5] Aligning himself with the opinion of 'many authors', Hay saw the tendency of settlement regulations to discourage migration as a kind of imprisonment, particularly unfortunate because 'so little care is taken to employ the poor.' Further, he was convinced that every man had the 'natural right' to provide for himself and his family wherever he thought best. It was 'unreasonable to molest him, and abridge him of his liberty (the chief comfort of a poor man) on the suggestion or apprehension of his being likely to become chargeable.' Even the certificate plan was faulty because it left in 'the breast of the parish officers' the decision whether or not they will grant someone a certificate. Much better would be that every migrant be declared a 'certificate-man,' removable only if he becomes chargeable, and, if he does not, that he become a legal resident.[6]

The conviction of Sidney and Beatrice Webb and R. H. Tawney that post-1660 policies represented the government's abandonment of its 'sordid and disheartening' treatment of the poor to the even worse prospects of local parishes and entrepreneurs, relegated settlement to its own historiographical black hole for most of the twentieth century.[7] Thus we are fortunate that interest has been on the rise in the last three decades, and the records themselves (examinations, removal orders, and certificates) are proving to be highly valuable, along with other Poor Law materials and overseas correspondence, in revealing the lives of the disinherited.[8] Yet the meaning of settlement and the goals to which it was put in the parishes has been contested deeply by K. D. M. Snell and Norma Landau. Snell has sampled settlement records from six mostly Southern and southeastern counties, Bedfordshire, Berkshire, Buckinghamshire, Essex, Hertfordshire, and Suffolk, and concluded that pauper settlement '*related above all to the rights of the poor to poor relief in certain parishes.*' He emphasizes the unique local conditions affecting each parish's response to settlement and particularly the cycles of seasonal employment (and unemployment) that prevailed in predominantly rural counties. That and the long chronological context in which settlement grew and declined, convinces Snell that it was always (and certainly in the eighteenth century) primarily an administrative aspect of poverty relief.[9] Landau's concentration on Kent leads her to conclude that settlement legislation between 1662 and 1697 'created a legal framework which allowed parish officials to supervise and regulate migration.' Rather than attempting to limit newcomers' access to pensions, she is convinced that parish officials were using removal to guarantee the exclusive use of wastes, woods, commons, gleaning, housing, and jobs for the local poor, thus making it less likely that they would have to go on the parish.[10]

This is not the place to attempt to resolve these alternatives or choose between them. And to see them as zero-sum options would be to miss a potentially larger and more useful point. The variety of internal and contextual conditions that distinguished the parishes from one another meant almost certainly that at different times and for different reasons the same parish would have acted closer to Snell's paradigm or to Landau's model. And there is no reason why terms like 'Poor Law administration' or 'migration management' cannot be thought of as options in any parish's repertoire of responses to its pensioners and near pensioners.

James Stephen Taylor, who in the 1970s was instrumental in reviving interest in settlement, reached more sanguine conclusions. First of all, he concluded that the most onerous decision making rested not in the breasts of the parish officers but with the petty session judges. He also resisted the assumption that settlement was ruinous either to the parishes or the poor. He noted that parliament had concluded in 1776 and 1783–85 that the costs of implementing settlement ranged from 2–5 percent of the parishes' total outlay for maintaining their poor. Furthermore, Taylor is convinced that the time expended on settlement and removal contributed, if anything, to the parishes becoming more efficient and 'business-like' in their operations. As for the poor, the spectre of removal encouraged them to assume more agency over their own situation: if they were to avoid it, they had to understand the law and learn to act in ways to protect themselves. Adam Smith observed that 'scarce a man in England of forty years...has not in some part of his life...[been] most cruelly oppressed by this ill-contrived law of settlements.' Taylor identified a young male laborer with one or more children as the most typical examinant but insisted that the vast majority of the poor were never involved in removal proceedings. For reasons we discussed in Chapter 4, the predilection of parish officers was to choose the least expensive option, which over time, as the vagaries of removal taught them, was to do nothing.[11]

Entitlement, Agency, and Age

Both the poor and the non-poor became more reconciled to the parish system in the eighteenth century. The poor not only accepted their status as pensioners, they began to believe strongly in their entitlement to it. And the non-poor, reluctantly and not without complaint about both the poor and the mechanism, accepted their role as funders. Thus a disgruntled rate payer complained in 1698 that 'the poor...thinks the parish is obliged in old age, extremities, and necessities to provide for him, who in plenty and cheap times will either work little or live without savings.'[12] An important expansion of social welfare historiography in recent years has been to learn more about the agency of the poor themselves in approaching and coping with the Poor Law. The settlement records mentioned above provide biographical information about the lives of the poor who became involved with the parish, while property inventories reveal the variety of material conditions among a parish's poor. And our capacity to decipher more about how poor people on the verge of becoming chargeable described their lives and what their expectations and apprehensions were as they faced 'going on the parish' or possible removal is being enhanced by the expanding scholarship of pauper letters.[13]

We also saw in Chapter 4 that it was not unusual in the mid-seventeenth century for the poor and non-poor alike to resort to alternative relief options when the implementation of the Poor Law was still spotty geographically and inconsistent within the parishes. James C. Scott's notion of 'public transcripts' was helpful in describing the customary *quid pro quos* that defined the senses of obligation in such circumstances.[14] A recent study of the West Riding town of Calverley-cum-Farsely offers valuable insight into the continuing resort to alternative and supplementary options in the less policy-infatuated northern counties.[15] Steven King describes Calverley as an 'inward-looking' town, with a fluid occupational and social structure. It was situated in the proto-industrial belt that swept across the base of the north country, and offered work in artisanal woolen cloth-making, agriculture, use of the common, and labor in the local service sector. Most families drew their incomes from at least two of those options. Roughly one-fifth of the townsmen had been exempt from the hearth tax in the 1670s, and a workhouse was established there about 100 years later in 1755, the same year that the common was enclosed. During the last half of the eighteenth century the number of Calverley residents 'on the parish' rose from 4 percent to 7 percent.[16]

Similar to national trends in those years, the value of the typical pension in Calverley increased not only in its monetary value but in its in-kind provision and supplements for such expenses as rent. And the number of males on the rolls increased all the while, again mirroring conditions throughout the realm. Beginning in about 1760, a marked shift nationally toward male pensioners appeared. While here was no diminishment in the numbers of elderly poor on the parishes, in many ways the economic transitions under way were making their lives even more difficult, the proportion of parish funds allocated to them was shrinking.[17] This may reflect a broad refocusing of parish relief to supplementing the income of underemployed wage earners.[18] Certainly family incomes were being impaired by the loss of employment opportunities in proto-industrial work, the inability to put enclosed commons to use, and increased competition for wage-paying work as the population expanded. When this dynamic intensified dramatically in the dearth crisis of 1794–95, the pensioner numbers in Calverley jumped to 98 from 30 in 1791, 62 percent of whom were males.[19]

At the same time, certain characteristics of poor relief in Calverley distinguished it and, more generally, the straitened north from the more prosperous south, where relief is often described as flexible and generous. For example, members of almost all social levels except the large landlords were susceptible to relief status at some point, but there were relatively few lifetime pensioners. For some, no doubt, distinctions were to be made between being poor and appearing poor. Others were in such difficulty that whatever types of assistance were available, on the parish or off, were simply options within the 'mixed economy.'[20] The average stay on the parish was a bit more than six years. Most interesting, though, was the persistent commitment to *societas*-like alternatives to going on the parish. This was not because the need was any less in the north; if anything the opposite was the case. Yet we have noted already that the north all along had been the most social policy-resistant region. Calverley residents' predispositions seem to help us understand why. They resisted going on the parish; they arranged for kin or other informal support that might have included borrowing what they needed or sharing households or pursuing any and all new earning possibilities. Compared with Terling's poor households in Essex, Calverley's families on the verge of becoming chargeable seemed to have had a thicker network of kin and local ties, some presumably vertical as well as horizontal, available to assist them. The very presence of the proto-industrial economy, weak as it was becoming in the latter decades of the eighteenth century, had tended to stabilize local populations, thus facilitating the possibility that enduring neighbourly and kin connections could develop. These counter-Poor Law predispositions were widespread enough throughout Westmorland, Wiltshire, Lancashire, and Cumberland to suggest that 'even more remains to be learnt about the role and character of relief in these areas.'[21]

As we have seen, pensioners typically surrendered to the parish the ownership, although not the use, of their real and household property. Upon a pensioner's death the goods were sold or distributed to other parish poor. Thus, the overseer took inventory when the pensioner became chargeable and after his or her death. There could be other occasions too. If a husband abandoned his wife and children, the overseers might survey the property in anticipation of putting the wife on the parish. Distraint proceedings for renters in arrears could also trigger an inventory. Peter King has tracked down 51 pauper inventories relating to pensioner status from Essex, 45 of which were taken in the years 1730 to 1799.[22] His data are drawn from nine mostly rural parishes in the central and northern parts of the county. The records of three of these were particularly full and one, Hatfield Broad Oak, provided nearly two-thirds of the post-1770 sample. Hatfield was one of the largest parishes in Essex, and included a great deal of 'commonable' areas, including a marsh and an 1100-acre forest. In his tabulated data King focused on Hatfield and compared it with aggregate totals from the other villages. These materials make clear the wide variation in property ownership that pensioners brought into their dependency on the parish. And, of course, gender, age, family size, and long-term economic trends were important as well. None of the inventories showed any silver items, knives and forks, tobacco items, or cane chairs. But in Hatfield 80 percent mentioned earthenware while only

50 percent in the other villages did so. In Hatfield 67 percent mentioned tea-related items, compared with 35 percent in the others. All the inventories in Hatfield mentioned chairs, while 92 percent in the others did. Yet clocks or watches were found in 38 percent of the outside villages and in only 13 percent of Hatfield's inventories. Likewise Hatfield's pensioners had fewer chests of drawers than their peers in the other villages, 13 percent compared to 42 percent. Twenty percent of Hatfield's inventories mentioned pictures and prints, but only 4 percent appeared in the other villages'.[23]

That the Hatfield pensioners seemed to come from slightly more fulsome economic circumstances should not be surprising given the access to common land there that likely was not duplicated in the other villages. Perhaps more surprising is what we learn from the most complete inventories descsribing the dwellings as well as the household goods. Those who became pensioners relatively late in their lives, whether workers 'past labor' or widows or widowers, often had lived in far from indigent circumstances during their working or married lives. A case in point is one Thomas Burgh of Theydon Garnon, dubbed 'Old Burgh' by the overseers who took inventory of his property on his becoming chargeable in 1775. He lived in a house of five rooms, including two bedrooms, a washhouse, and a separate kitchen and parlor equipped with a good array of household wares. In Hatfield the inventories of the widow Adams and of Edward Bird and his wife Dorothy, when they became pensioners in the 1790s, described relatively large, multi-room dwellings with outbuildings and equipped with a fair sample of useful items.[24]

The seemingly comfortable economic circumstances of these elderly pensioners might leave the twenty-first-century reader baffled that relief was given to Burgh, Adams, and the Birds, while the overseers likely would have attempted to remove a sojourner or sojourner family with few prospects for achieving economic self-sufficiency in Hatfield or Theydon Garnon. We must discard our post-welfare state and presentist lenses, however, if we are to see the 'test' involved in determining eligibility for pre-industrial social welfare. It was knowledge and experience of the potentially chargeable person, as much as the empirical facts of his or her economic situation, that influenced the overseers and vestrymen in their decisions. And the income transfer involved in raising and distributing the poor rate on a weekly basis was near at hand, direct, and replete with likely face-to-face encounters between payers and receivers. The security for the payers was knowledge that the receivers, when they were able, had previously contibuted to the well-being of the parish 'family.' The security for the receivers, on the other hand, was that in putting their need in front of those who knew and worked with them over the years, they could reasonably expect mercy in the form of a pension. To be outside that loop, as the newcomers were, was largely to be unable to establish one's worthiness to entitlement in the customary ways. John Hintermaier has explored reactions to the Huguenot emigrants in the 1680s and uncovers a many-layered attempt to move eligibility for relief in that instance from individual narrative to cohort identity.[25]

We might see in this a form of Scott's 'public transcripts' or an intra-parish *quid pro quo*: for upright living and hard work the promise of pensioner status when one fell into misfortune, 'passed labor,' or became widowed. Furthermore, Peter King wonders whether those sinking toward chargeable status, like Burgh, Adams, and the Birds (the *pauperes verecundi* [of the eighteenth century?]), were able to bargain for better pensions if they brought more goods with them, particularly if they had been rate-payers themselves.[26] Essentially the issue here is whether a kind of *societas* commitment was filtering the application of the *civitas* apparatus and mandates of the Poor Law. If so, could there have been enthusiasm for social wefare among the middling sort and near middling in a locality, as well as among its desperately poor?

At the same time, it would not be wise to think too formulaically about older people involved in and on the margins of the Poor Law, in the north or south. From all that can be gathered from censuses, parish records, pamphlets, and letters and diaries, the elderly in the eighteenth century guarded their independence and were encouraged to do so.[27] The very status 'old' was described by chronological, functional, and cultural markers, the application of which depended on where and for whom the designation was being made. But, even beyond that, there were several stops along the way from entry, 'green old age,' through various stages of diminished ability to function, and on to decrepitude. Thus, the independence of elderly people was an ongoing negotiation between their ability to function and the mates, families, work places or employers, and parishes from whom they could receive assistance.[28]

And, of course, old age, highly individualized as it could be, was also affected fundamentally not only by one's appearance and degree of vigor, but by gender and social and economic situation. In the pusuit of as much independence as possible older women of gentry status might continue to supervise their esates or property; middling-sort females often pursued business involvements, particularly in the needle trades, victualling, caring work, or retailing. Marginally poor, but still independent, older women most typically worked in charring, hawking, and nursing. Through most of the eighteenth century women on the parish outnumbered men in their age cohort. Susannah Ottaway, utilizing data from 32 parishes in all regions of the country during the 1790s, reported by Sir Frederic Morton Eden in *The State of the Poor* (1797), estimates that the 419 pensioners 60 years of age or above were approximately 40 percent of the chargeable population. Of those whose gender was identified, women outnumbered men by 284 to 128. And, older women on the parish, if they were able, were expected to work to supplement their pensions, the overseers often paying them to care for sick or more infirm parishioners.[29]

Workhouses

As we saw in William Hay's frustration with settlement procedures and the entire social welfare system, the very acceptance of responsibility within the Poor Law's mandates produced closer scrutiny of the apparatus and the search for its reform or replacement. One frequent complaint to which we have alluded already was that the overseers could 'upon frivolous pretenses' authorize more pensions than were necessary or fundable. Parliament addressed that concern in a statute in 1692 which held that only Justices of the Peace could authorize payments to non-pensioners and that vestries were to examine the pensioners' lists every Easter and determine eligibility. In 1697, the same year that 'merit' and certificates for migrants were entering the settlement legislation, parliament ordered that pensioners should wear a suitable badge on their shoulder. Paralleling the growing importance of settlement in the Poor Law's application in the first half of the century was an enthusiastic promotion of workhouses as a check on suspect parish administration in general and the enormous complications posed by settlement and removal. Between 1694 and 1705 a total of 14 bills were brought to parliament calling for change in the social welfare structure in one form or another.

The later seventeenth and early eighteenth centuries produced much speculation about improvement from the confident pens of

William Petty, John Cary, William Hay, and many others. It was not the provisions of the Poor Law that caused the discontentment so much as its faulty application. Parish administrations were perceived to be lenient in moving poor people to chargeability and relying too much on assessing real property in gathering the poor fund. Furthemore, the make-work goal was often ignored and consequently much under- and unemployment, that is idleness, seemed to be endemic. Two important reminders of the significance of these problems nationally appeared toward the end of the seventeenth century. In 1696, the Board of Trade estimated that pensions were costing upwards of 400,000L. And Gregory King published an elaborate profile of the numbers of gentry, tradesmen, laborers, and professionals in the realm and their contributions to the national income in 1688. The accuracy of King's estimates seems to be within tolerable limits, but, even more importantly, he has provided us with a detailed contemporary perception of the workings of the economy. King estimated that, of the roughly 5.5 million souls in England and Wales, 2.675 million were contributing 67 percent of the realm's annual income while the remaining 2.825 million were putting in 10.5 percent. Wages and salaries were 36 percent of the nation's income; profits, fees, and interest from loans and investments 30 percent; and rents 27 percent.[30] The contributors to the surplus were the high and low gentry, office holders, merchants, the clergy, freeholders, scientists and teachers, shopkeepers, artisans, and military officers. Decreasing the income were common sailors and soldiers, laborers and out servants, cottagers and paupers, and vagrants. There were probably no surprises there for those who already were concerned about employment and productivity issues. The challenge over the next four decades or so was to search for an agreeable set of reforms.

After the Glorious Revolution the 'center' was clearly reviving, witnessed by more frequent parliaments and the emerging Whig and Tory rivalry after their brief collaboration on the Revolution. But, keeping in mind Halliday's point that much energy was being directed from the periphery to the center since the 1660s, most of them sought parliamentary charters for local corporations of the poor. These corporations, which would be much like London's and the elaborate workhouses proposed by Leonard Lee and Samuel Hartlib in the Civil War years, were thought to be particularly suited to the perceived problem. Centralization of administration would circumvent the ill-prepared parish overseers. Workhouses not only would occupy the under- and unemployed, they readied the next generation for better lives in their schooling and work training for poor children. The London Corporation itself was revived and a dozen smaller cities and towns were authorized to establish corporations. Unlike a century earlier, however, the underlying religious and ideological inspirations were varied, from Anglicans, Quakers, Latitudinarians of all stripes, and Societies for the Reformation of Manners and Societies for the Propagation of Christian Knowledge (SPCK), to Whigs and Tories.

The first of the new coporations and the model was Bristol's, founded in 1696. John Cary, a Whig, forged a 'broad alliance' there of moderate Anglicans, Dissenters and Latitudinarians.[31] Cary was a persuasive advocate for welfare corporations, which he set in a distinctly mercantilist national economic context. Thus, while moral reform of habitually idle paupers was never ignored by Cary and others in the revived workhouse movement, the political economy calculus of Hartlib and Petty (and earlier figures like Starkey, Smith, and Bacon) is in full view. It is 'the balance of our trade,' he insisted, 'that supplies us bullion.' And, if favorable, 'it brings [bullion] to us, if otherwise, it must be carried away.' Good work habits among the nation's laborers is crucial here, however. And among Cary's six propositions for the better ordering of trade is 'Inspecting into the affairs of the poor, and putting an end to that pernicious trade of begging.' To the sceptics who say this cannot be done, he called attention to Bristol's success in training 'the poor . . . to an early delight in labor.' So much more possible, then, that '[t]his balance [of trade] is supplied by our manufactures, which keep our people at work, and enable them to maintain themselves by their own labor.' Failing that, they must 'stand still, and become a charge on our lands', but, if the laborers' work and the realm's trade are regulated effectively, 'we should soon become the richest, and consequently the greatest, people in Europe.'[32]

A total of 12 corporations were authorized in this wave of enthusiasm, including a Quaker-inspired effort in Colchester. Collaborations among Tories, Whigs, and Dissenters produced a corporation in Exeter and the revival of the London Corporation, while Tories developed a corporation in Norwich. Others were chartered in Tiverton, Crediton, Hereford, Hull, Shaftesbury, King's Lynn, Gloucester, Sudbury, Worcester, and Plymouth. The corporations were public and private ventures, as they always invited private subcribers and rewarded the most generous of them with guardianships.[33] The one significant attempt to reform the Poor Law amidst this spate of legislation was introduced in 1705 by Humphrey Mackworth, who came from a London SPCK background. Mackworth's extensive bill passed in the Commons but failed in the House of Lords. It would have consolidated existing statutes (a recommendation often articulated in the eighteenth century), emphasized labor requirements, and expanded parish social welfare governance by incorporating a paid assistant to the overseers, churchwardens, and private benefactors of charity schools to encourage philanthropic gifts to the parish fund.

Nevertheless, workhouses, sometimes 'factories' or 'charity schools' or 'houses of industry,' went through a cycle of popularity. In the 1720s private contracting of workhouses became popular in many localities, and the entrepreneur Matthew Marryott ran 20 or more. The statute of 1723 authorizing privatization, as well as the right of parishes to form union workhouses at their discretion, spurred a boomlet. Within a decade and a half, perhaps 700 new workhouses had been established, and there is some indication that in many of them local rates may have come down somewhat. Yet, grassroots discomfort with surrendering immediate overseer and vestry responsibility for which poor people were made chargeable, never wholly disappeared nor did disappointment over paltry results of the work provisions. This round of workhouse reform, then, lost its energy rather quickly and the houses came to be used more than anything as lodgings for the old and infirm.[34] However, several years of experience with parish-only relief led to yet another round of calls for reform, and workhouses, in the 1750s. And, as we will see below, their commitments to medical services and work training made them important underpinnings for the new social welfare challenges that industrialization was presenting. In the years between 1748 and 1783 parliament authorized another hundred localities to establish workhouses. East Anglia was a particular hot spot; swayed by Thomas Gilbert's rhetoric (and Gilbert's Act of 1782) as many as one-third of the parishes there may have established houses.[35]

Health Care and Gender

We have alluded several times in previous chapters to the underlying frustration with the very mandatoriness of the Poor Law that seems to have been ubiquitous and continuous. The coercive nature of the Elizabethan policy deprived the rate-payers of their sense of having helped the poor not because they were being forced to, but because they wanted to. One example of how this played out was the 'social economy' begging and charitable giving that had been a vital supplement to the government's dearth and plague orders in the sixteenth and seventeenth centuries. In 1752 and 1753, Thomas Alcock, MA, late of Oxford and a well-informed observer of the Poor Law and its various embellishments in the workhouses, published a remarkable set of pamphlets. They no doubt contributed to revival of the workhouse reform idea. Alcock encouraged yet anew the establishment of multi-purpose workhouses, this time each with three distinct parts, a work-house, a correction-house, and a hospital. In and of itself Alcock's proposal was not out of the ordinary. His discussion of motive, however, is important and revealing. The 1752 pamphlet was filled with complaints of how the Poor Law, acceptable enough in its goals, was being implemented so badly that it invited the poor into chargeable status. But, for Alcock, the worst thing about it was the mandatory nature of the rate. Interspersing his text with allusions to Juvenal, Seneca, and Alexander Pope, Alcock intoned, a 'law to enforce relief, tends to destroy the principle it proceeds from, the principle of charity.' All charity 'must be free,' he insisted, and if left to his own devices, 'I should be willing to do for the Poor to the utmost of my power: but it's grating to be obliged to it.' Under such circumstances, Alcock parted with his money 'as a tax, not as a benevolence; and there is no kindness or merit in what I do.'[36]

In his pamphlet the following year, Alcock boasted that Henry Fielding had supported his views and that two bills had been introduced in reponse to his plan, even if he was displeased with them. The first addressed poor children, which Alcock rejected because they were but one in four of the poor. The other would have established one large workhouse in each county. This called forth a lengthy quote from Bacon's advice to James I on hospitals, to the effect that great institutions 'are the more seen' while modest ones 'will be the more felt.' And he raised again the mandatory rates issue, but this time with more effect for the practical minded. As long as the rates are mandatory, 'the generality of people will think of nothing else, the landed interest will still bear the chief burden, and voluntary charities will come in but sparingly.' On the other hand, if the entire plan were put 'as much as possible' on a charitable base, Alcock was 'persuaded' that sufficient 'subscriptions, benefactions, collections, and legacies' would come in to establish it solidly after several years. Poor relief in the realm and in all countries, he concluded, must be 'voluntary, not forced, a matter of charity, not a tax.' This will also have the effect of reminding 'the rich and generous, the monied-men and opulent traders' that they have 'calls and opportunities of shewing their benevolence.'[37]

Whether attempting to fund the Poor Law apparatus with voluntary giving instead of mandatory rates would have been successful certainly was problematic. Nevertheless we should not lose sight of the substantial numbers of philanthropic and charitable outlays that had been proliferating since the Restoration. It has been estimated that in 1660 upwards of 10,000 of them had been established in the realm; and that number may have doubled or even tripled by 1740. About 40 percent of these were vested in parishes, municipal corporations and livery companies. The other three-fifths had been set up by self-perpetuating, private associations or groups, ranging from declining craft guilds transforming themselves into charities to the ever-more popular friendly societies (voluntary risk pools to which members regularly contributed funds).[38]

Institutionalized health care was yet another important outlet for private funds, and making it available in the middle and latter part of the eighteenth century was a daunting challenge. Public care applied almost exclusively to that provided for the poor; wealthier persons preferred to be treated at home by their personal physicians. That didn't stop many of these same people, however, from supporting hospitals and dispensaries for the poor.[39] These supplemented the basic medical attention that in theory was available in the workhouses. However, industrialization was both intensifying and redistributing the need. For example, population shifts into Lancashire and the upper Midlands, where wool and cotton manufacturing were picking up in formerly small towns like Leeds or Manchester, meant that they were ill-prepared initially for new burdens on their undeveloped Poor Law institutions. And relatively comfortable parishes in the south, where second-track employment had been available in cottage industries that was now drying up, found themselves faced with many more potential chargeable parishioners than had been typical. Even port towns, beneficiaries in the pre-industrial economic mix, were filling with potentially dependent migrants responding to employment prospects in the realm's newly expanding overseas trade. At least towns like Bristol and Liverpool had well-functioning Poor Law establishments upon whose experience and facilities they could build. The same applied to London with its network of hospitals, dispensaries, and Poor Law infirmaries.[40]

In London and other cities and towns, workhouse infirmaries, even though they had not been designed to do so, became part of local networks of charitable hospitals within which patients were regularly shifted back and forth among the participating institutions. The workhouses actually provided entry into this larger medical world for their pensioners.[41] And we are beginning to realize that some workhouses did offer quite thorough medical care, but, like all parish social welfare, it varied markedly from one to the next. Kevin Siena offers an example of this from two London workhouses in the 1730s, St Margaret's and St Sepulchre. St Margaret's evidently had the larger infirmary and was more ambitious in responding to its inmates' medical needs. The workhouse admitted two-thirds of the 276 injured or sick poor persons who sought care in 1735 and sent only 8.7 percent of them to outside medical facilities. The surgeons' report for 1734 recorded 192 'cures,' for a range of conditions including fevers, rheumatism, dropsy, measles, broken limbs, colic, asthma, itch, and the pox (syphilis). St Sepulchre, on the other hand, admitted less than one-third of its applicants needing medical attention and offered almost half of them either a cash dole or treatment at another hospital. Five percent were given medicine to treat themselves.[42]

Medical records of the workhouses also provide insight into the relative importance of morality and economics in the churchwardens' decision making about whom to admit and treat. By eighteenth-century standards both single pregnant women and syphilis sufferers were assumed to be in predicaments resulting from illicit sexual behavior. Settlement examinations for unmarried women (sometimes including an invasive physical inspection for signs of pregnancy by parish midwives or middling-sort matrons) were always more thorough than for 'foul' (syphilitic) patients. At stake for the parish was the possible large expense of a chargeable unmarried woman and her child compared with the far less expensive treatment of a person with syphilis. The often favored choice was to remove the single woman. Another consideration beyond the narrowly economic one was probably at play also: the fear of the public health consequences of failing to treat syphilis in the parish.[43] We also learn that the majority of patients overall in the infirmaries were young, single women. When weighed down with poverty and sickness or pregnancy, they had few choices but the workhouse and its infirmary. And, like all pensioners by this time, they felt entitled to assistance but generally loathed the conditions in which it was provided, especially the house discipline, uniforms, loss of freedom, and lack of anonymity.[44]

Private giving to the charitable hospitals with which the workhouse infirmaries often cooperated probably came closest in its motive to Alcock's call for a return to benevolence and charity in responding to the poor. The roots of this can be traced back through the high-church leaning 'Charitable Society' (1716) and the previously mentioned Society for Promoting Christian Knowledge (SPCK), begun in 1699. The Charitable Society was organized for the 'more easy and effectual relief of the sick and needy' and encouraged traditional charity toward indigents standing in for Christ himself. Even in its medical endeavors, though, the Society's goals were primarily religious, that is, 'to take care of the souls of those who are sick and needy, as well as their bodies'.[45] This is close to the 'Christus Medicus' healthy soul–healthy body assumption that shaped attitudes and treatment in medieval and sixteenth-century hospitals. Society members were well versed in Counter-Reformation French ideas promoting general hospitals and the *bureaux de charité*, supported by the *Filles* and *Dames de la Charité*, which circulated in the later seventeenth century. The post-Tridentine Catholic Church held that all deviance, whether unemployment, prostitution, or heresy, could be traced to spiritual corruption. Thus was the pauper 'respiritualized' from his or her more secular characterizations.[46] In England there was much imitation of the French charitable workers, and in 1726 an English translation of a Jesuit study of the hospitals and fraternities in Turin was sponsored by the SPCK. Also inspired by the French Huguenot hospital in London, *La Providence*, the Society and its supporters established Westminster Hospital in 1720. It is plausible that, when donors thought of the sick poor as representatives of Christ, the impulse was not so much to manage them as to show mercy and even to experience the 'edification' inherent in charitable giving and receiving.[47] At the same time, the hospitals' policies occasionally put a sharp edge on that edification. In 1738, the governors of Westminster declared the admission of patients suffering from venereal disease to be 'a subversion of the charity, or a misapplication of the money given in trust for the poor . . . for the very reason of [its] being venereal.'[48]

New Industry and Welfare

Putting the Industrial Revolution into some perspective, especially its individual and social costs, disruptions, and impact on social welfare, as well as the opportunities and benefits it made possible, is crucial for this study. This requires at the outset that we move beyond what might be called the 'rapid' or 'compressed' theory of industrialization. The movement was not a dramatic 50-year transformation of the realm from an agricultural social and economic order to an urban, commerce- and factory-dominated one between 1780 and 1830. We have seen in Chapter 4 that in Whickham industrialization involving capital investment, wage labor, technological innovation, commercial links between a raw material producing region and the growing metropolis, gradual displacement of a traditional manorial order, and strains on traditional social welfare arrangements was already four centuries under way by the 1780s. The demographer E. A. Wrigley, frustrated as most historians are with the 'Industrial Revolution' designation, nevertheless does not forego use of the term. His focus, however, is on what he considers to be the phenomenon's truly 'distinguishing feature', and not only in England. He characterizes that as a 'sustained rise in real incomes per head' which has 'transformed the lives of the inhabitants of industrialized societies.'[49]

This possibility accrued in England, according to Wrigley, by means of the long-term transition from its 'advanced organic economy' to a new 'mineral-based energy economy.' He identifies a number of telling contrasts between England and the continent in the years between 1550 and 1800 that indicate the changes that were under way. For instance, in the sixteenth century the overwhelming number of laborers in England and on the continent lived on and from the land. Two and a half centuries later, even though the majority of laborers throughout Europe still lived on the land, in England only 40 percent of adult male laborers worked in agriculture, compared to 60 to 80 percent on the continent. And England's population, which had been languishing at about 2.5 million in the 1540s, reached 8 million at the turn of the nineteenth century. The expansion was predominately in the large towns and cities. Thus the least urbanized of Europe's countries during Elizabeth's reign, with not even London a major city by international standards, England had the most rapidly growing urban sector of all by the eighteenth century. London had become Europe's largest city, and the realm was second only to The Netherlands in its degree of urbanization. In these comparisons rests Wrigley's central point about early industrial revolutions: increased agricultural productivity allowed commercial and industrial expansion to take place. It was the doubling of food output per head and per acre in England during the seventeenth and eighteenth centuries that allowed a shrinking agricultural workforce to provide adequate foodstuffs for a population that was doubling and urbanizing.[50] Those developments also explain the knotty structural poverty problems of these centuries as well.

In their *Population History*, Wrigley and Schofield maintain that the causal feedback links among population, wages, and prices posed by Thomas Robert Malthus are important to historical demography if applied to the 250 years *before* he published *An Essay on the Principle of Population* in 1798. And they accept Malthus's two explanations of how population size was kept in check. The first, 'positive' or 'high pressure' restraint, was simple and stark: mortality rates began to exceed births. The second, 'preventive' or 'low pressure' curtailment, involved human agency or decision making; for a variety of reasons, people decided to delay marriages and thus reduce fertility. Wrigley and Schofield are convinced that across the centuries of their study (1541 to 1871) the preventative check dominated.[51] And the distinctive characteristic of a pre-industrial economy is that its 'movements of incipient expansion' cannot develop into 'sustained exponential growth.' A feedback cycle puts a stop to economic expansion, most often by preventative checks but occasionally positive ones, in spite of the fact that rising incomes stimulate demand for services and manufactured goods in towns and cities. An important contributing factor to these slowdowns is the limited availability of food and industrial raw materials; the essential remedy, then, is the development of 'technological' devices or solutions to overcome supply bottlenecks. If these appear, the rate of food and goods production can outstrip the rate of the population's expansion and exponential growth or 'an industrial revolution' becomes possible. Wrigley and Schofield find that preventative checks disappeared only in the last quarter of the nineteenth century, but that as early as the seventeenth century the positive check had become all but irrelevant. Consequently, over the years 1750 to 1810 English agriculture 'was able to raise production in step with population.' The critical transition from pre-industrial to industrial relationships among population, wages, and prices began in the early eighteenth century and intensified in the later part of the century 'as the industrial sector was gathering momentum.'[52]

This interpretive edifice, built from 3.7 million birth, death and marriage entries from 404 parishes, gathered over the years by the Cambridge Group, is not without its critics. John Hatcher, one of the most trenchant of them, challenges the 'orthodoxy' conferred on the project and more particularly Wrigley and Schofield's reliance on Malthus's preventive, low pressure check to explain too much pre-industrial population history. Hatcher finds many more instances when endogamous, positive checks, including mortality and the Poor Law, are the most obvious explanatory choices. And, for that reason, he is very skeptical of claims that Wrigley and Schofield's model would apply to the late medieval centuries were the data available.[53] And from a historiographical standpoint, Hatcher is convinced that England's population history requires more local clarity and less national compre-hensiveness than the Cambridge Group's data have thus fare yielded. Wrigley and Schofield, for instance, approach population history 'with a mere handful of variables, and ... at almost every stage it is held to have operated in a manner which was simple, predictable and linear, rather than complex, volatile and non-linear.' Their approach defies current methodological trends 'which increasingly stress localism and particularism, assert the importance of social and cultural factors, and acknowledge complexity and unpredictability in the relationship between cause and effect.' And even though Wrigley and Schofield acknowledge the importance of the political and ideological dimensions of familial, social, and inter-personal relations, they have not applied this awareness to 'instil more intricacy, pliancy and unpredictability' into their work.[54]

This methodological dispute notwithstanding, the importance of population history and its immersion in relevant social, economic, and political data is crucial to understanding the Industrial Revolution. So, too, is attention to the innovative and resourceful undertakings that facilitated the transition to an industrial economy. Focusing as we are in this study on pre-industrial England's social welfare traditions can lead to a certain myopia. For instance, we can begin to conclude that the Ciceronian revival in the sixteenth century impacted only on social policy or that Puritan moral theology was concerned with nothing other than the behavior of the poor. Similarly, the obvious importance of 'improvement' (bred of Baconian empirical science and 'Second Reformation' Calvinism from the continent) for social welfare thinking in the late seventeenth and eighteenth centuries does not mean that its contagion was confined to those preoccupied with the poor. 'Improve-ment,' like Ciceronian humanism and puritanism, affected a wide range of matters with half-life results that may appear at some later point as serendipitous. Thus, when we seek to explain the cumulative innovations and changes that began to restructure the realm's economy and society in the last half of the eighteenth century, we have to look at 'improvement's' central place in the broader economy since the Stuart Restoration. Scientists then were interacting with landed and commercial interests in the blossoming scientific and philosophical societies and becoming part of the innovative, essentially secular-minded establishment that came to power with the pragmatic William III and the Glorious Revolution.[55]

By the early and middle eighteenth century, results from those collaborations were beginning to appear. And Schumpeterian entrepreneurs were finding ways to incorporate into production processes the output of an expanding cohort of 'brilliant technical designers,' the likes of James Watt, Richard Awkwright, and John Smeaton. Industrial modernization was in motion. As we have noted, the subsequent 'revolution' was not dramatic or precipitous. Large factories grew from smaller more informal undertakings in converted rooms, houses, or barns, but almost right away they began to shape a new work culture for men and women.[56] But a transition was under way from an economy dominated by farming, trades, and cottage industry to one of large-scale mineral processing, cloth and consumer goods production, and transportation. Actually Britain had a 'dual economy' in these years. Approximately 90 percent traditional and 10 percent modern in 1760, it was 50–50 by 1830.[57] The effects of these changes rippled throughout society. Household responsibilities, the nature of work, what people thought about themsleves and the world, the structure and functions of government, and how the poor were perceived and responded to, all would change significantly as the industrial revolution and 'modernization' gathered momentum. Another connotation of 'revolution' was the challenge that entrepreneurial and technological innovation was making to the established pre-industrial order of things which had been in place since at least the fourteenth century. From this perspective, we can appreciate Adam Smith's view that a contention was under way between feudalism and commercialism.[58] It was not as though the two epochs had no linkages, however. In Chapter 1 and subsequent chapters, we saw that market centers and market activity were an indigenous part of the pre-industrial economy. Proto-industrial employment was commonplace in these centuries, providing the opportunity (the necessity?) for families to pursue income from two sources primarily in upland and pasture regions. And, as the coal-digging operations in Whickham demonstrate, there had been some large manufacturing facilities before 1760. Some historians speak of an '*industrious* or consumer revolution' in these years as well, referring to a growing demand for consumer goods and the requisite wage employment that this required among the middling sort and lower social levels.[59]

The Poor Law itself was yet another important connection between the 'ancient' and the 'modern'. The argument has been made that parish relief was a form of subsidization to the emerging industrial sector. Peter M. Solar, taking note of recent scholarly attention to the finances and policies of the central government that enabled the realm's development toward a manufacturing and services economy, insists that it is time to acknowledge social welfare and local government's vital contribution to the process. When wage laborers broke down from sickness or age, the rural parishes supplied their care. And, compared to relief schemes on the continent, the English system was much better organized in the countryside, uniform in its organization, and relatively certain and generous. The Poor Law and settlement not only affected the 5–15 percent of the population that received relief, but also the one-third to four-fifths who teetered at or near the poverty line. And David M. Landes in his wide-ranging study, *The Wealth and Poverty of Nations*, attempts to explain why England was first among its European equals in moving to industrialization. He concludes that the English were resourceful, individualistic, and took care of their many poor people in a way that fostered an available manufacturing labor force and a productive agricultural economy.[60]

The *longue durée* periodization of this study allows us to appreciate a significant irony in the fact that industrialization took hold first in Lancashire and the northern Midlands counties. As we discussed in Chapter 1, this was the very region whose economic fortunes fell at the outset of the pre-industrial centuries; its prosperous overseas trade in raw wool gave way to wool cloth production centered in the south. Subsequently, the northern counties languished in difficult economic and political straits until the industrial revolution; and, by the 1860s, their wage base was again preeminent.[61] And, in the rapid population build-up of the eighteenth century, five new industrial centers in the upper Midlands and the North, Manchester, Liverpool, Birmingham, Sheffield, and Leeds entered the ranks of the realm's most populous cities.[62]

Steven King has argued with convincing evidence that in the eighteenth century two 'macro-regions' of social welfare developed, the north and west and the south and east. The divider between them ran approximately from Yorkshire's East Riding south to Exeter along a line slighty bowed to the right, passing through Lincolnshire and east Leicestershire. By the end of the eighteenth century the factory system was beginning to establish itself in the north and west while proto-industrial opportunities in the south and east were disappearing. As a result of this shift, the incidence of marginal poverty increased significantly in the south and east, and the traditional social welfare generosity of the southern counties seems to have been responsive. In Wiltshire in these years, for instance, perhaps one-quarter of the adults were on their parishes.[63] In the 1740s, both regions were spending roughly similar amounts on parish pensions: 59 percent in the south and east, 56 percent in the north and west. Those amounts began to decrease considerably in the 1780s to about 40 percent in both sections; however, the decline was more than augmented by an increase in cash and in-kind supplements to pensions. A very substantial amount of that, perhaps 33 percent in the north and 25 percent in the south, was distributed for medical expenses and treatments. Other supplements went for rents, coal, clothing, and food. King concludes that when all available data from the two regions is assessed, social welfare provision was more 'generous' and 'benevolent' in the south than in the north.[64]

We have seen that the northern counties in general took a harsher approach to poor relief all through the pre-industrial centuries. We must ask, however, if the fact that this was continuing in the eighteenth century had anything to do with disciplining workers in the new factories, an attempt to change further the 'culture' and 'custom' of labor. The perspective of the Webbs and particularly Tawney may be helpful here. Recall that Tawney had perceived in enclosure and the 'agrarian problem' of the sixteenth century the first sign that capitalism was making way in the 'dense, firmly organized,' and 'intractable' world of agriculture. The 'new world,' visible as in a 'tiny mirror,' was rising 'so painfully' in England's villages. What ensued, and we can add, 'on a more fundamental level of challenge and a grander scale' in the later eighteenth century, was 'the struggle between custom and competition.' The inimitable fabricated dialogue between an enclosing steward and the soon-to-be-displaced tenants with which Tawney closes his *Agrarian Problem*, is also instructive. Their exchanges focus on: custom versus innovation, waste and efficiency, subsistence and profit, the many and the few. Ultimately the tenants say, 'We do not like your improvements which ruin half the honest men affected by them. We do not choose that the ancient customs of our villages should be changed!'[65] Surely the local agricultural laborers, women, child apprentices, and migrants who were the labor force in the new factories accommodated awkwardly and slowly to the efficiency regimen of the new factories and felt the pinch that capitalist standards were putting on their customary approaches to work. The move from natural time to clock time is but one of the basic accommodations required by modernization.[66]

The labor 'problem' for the factory employers was not so much to gather the necessary number of workers but to transform them into a loyal, disciplined, and productive body. Once they entered a factory, former proto-industrial or agricultural workers lost whatever discretion they may have had to appropriate their work-time as they saw fit. And their failure to adjust could, and often did, lead to immediate dismissal. Women and children in the early factory workforce often were providing family income for such unemployed or resisting males.[67] A worker's employment for the entire mining season in the Whickham coalfields was sought in a 'pitman's bond,' a legally enforceable commitment. Some disciplining efforts ranged into paternalistic initiatives by owners and led to arrangements that had impact on Poor Law implementation. We mentioned in Chapter 4 that in Whickham by the 1670s the new vestry was charging the different colliery managers special payments for the parish fund. One implication we might draw from this is that those funds were to provide pensions for fired or injured coal workers. On the other hand, it was not unusual for mine or factory managers to act on their paternal regard for their employees by paying directly for the care of ill or injured workers or funeral expenses for those killed on the job. Initially more out of the ordinary in early eighteenth-century Whickham, was Sir Ambrose Crowley's and his successors' efforts to acknowledge obligations to their 'people.' He sought arrangements that would make them 'quiet and easy amongst themselves and a happy and flourishing people amongst their neighbours.' This involved housing them in a factory town replete with a school and schoolmaster, a chapel with chaplain, a 'Court of Arbitrators' to settle disputes, and a doctor. By 1749, the Crowleys had established their own poor relief program; it covered all their employees, none of whom would be thereafter chargeable to the parish.

Crowley expected a *quid pro quo*, however: his workers were 'to do their utmost in the lawful promoting of my interest and answer the end of their being paid.' Combining a set of high standards of behavior with resort to Big Brother-like informers, Crowley's 'Laws' censored workers for everything from brawling, betting, drinking, swearing and smoking to failing to meet their 80 hours a week of work because of time spent at alehouses or coffee houses, reading, eating, sleeping or 'anything else foreign to my business.' Thus 'Crowley's crew' were closely watched, and his pensioners wore a 'Crowley's Poor' badge on their left sleeves.[68]

From 'Feudal' to 'Commercial' Civilization

The eighteenth century has been described variously as England's 'age of benevolence' and its 'century of law.'[69] The infatuation with benevolence existed side by side with a deepening exasperation with the structure and effects of public poor relief policies. And, even if John Brewer is correct that most eighteenth-century Englishmen 'experienced government and understood politics through their dealings with the law,' the major commentators, with the possible exception of Blackstone, saw more wrong than right in the legal system. We will be taking this up as it applies to the Poor Law in Chapter 6.

Our ability to understand the political forces at play is further complicated by the historiography of eighteenth-century politics. Instead of a relatively unchallenged and enduring oligarchic Whig conformity under Prime Minister Robert Walpole, a far more contentious ideological environment emerged. Stubborn Tory resistance survived into the last half of the century, and Whiggism existed in many forms, for instance, old, new, contractarian, republican, Scots scientist, and political economist, among others.[70] And John Pocock has been persuasive in making the case that eighteenth-century political thought was actually a 'bitter, conscious and ambivalent dialogue,' less concerned with the consequences of the political revolution of the 1680s than with the financial one of the 1690s. In the process, political thought moved from 'a law-and-rights-centered' to a 'virtue and corruption' paradigm.[71] Civic humanist discourses, promoting a propertied and armed citizenry, contended with advocacy for a government that exchanged patronage for credit and utilized professional armed forces. The crucial issue for the 'humanists' was not so much to preserve the right to resist tyrannical rule as to sustain a virtuous, independent, and civic-minded citizenry in the face of a corrupting form of politics.

One witness of this was the Tory Lord Bolingbroke. Two decades past his fall from a promising parliamentary and ministerial career for his brief service to the Stuart cause in 1715–16, he published *A Dissertation upon Parties*, 19 'letters' originally serialized in the *Craftsman* in the aftermath of one of Walpoles's rare failures on a tax bill. Bolingbroke was an admirer of Cicero and assumed that politics and political service were about building and maintaining a moral order. He sought to re-educate the British about the genius of their constitution, 'this mixture of monarchical, aristocratical and democratical power, blended together in one system.'[72] That Whigs and Tories had supported the new Acts and the Revolution, a 'new Magna Carta,' should have rendered divisive discourses irrelevant and put all politics on a new footing. Unfortunately, atavistic party posturing had survived and ruined that possibility. But, even more ominous was the corruption of parliament's independence. Ongoing collusion between the Whig parliamentary majority and the king encouraged 'the increase and continuance of taxes...multiplying officers of the revenue, and...arming them with formidable powers against their fellow-subjects.' Bolingbroke insisted that there was no 'greater error in politics' than nobles assisting a prince to take liberties away from the people. Not only was the government corrupted, but the fundamental balance of voices in the constitution was shattered. Under such conditions, a 'standing parliament' becomes as dangerous as a 'standing army.'[73]

Against this background of party division, a traditional economy transforming into a modern one, and predictably hard-pressed parish social welfare institutions, a vigorous debate was played out over the continuing merits of the Poor Law. Mackworth's reform bill in 1704 had evoked a bitter and ironic speech in parliament by Daniel Defoe, published as *Giving Alms no Charity*. Defoe, who Pocock claims was more the progenitor of the 'property' discourse than John Locke himself, argued in the speech that England, as rich as any nation in the world, was becoming poor, 'burdened with a crowd of clamoring, unemployed, unprovided for poor people.' No man of 'sound limbs and senses' can be poor any longer for want of work. The problem lay in the very workhouses, charities for employing the poor, and parish make-work efforts. They were all so many 'nuisances' and 'mischiefs' to the nation, catering to the lack of responsibility among many of the laboring poor and fostering dependence.[74] Two decades later in the *Fable of the Bees* (1723), Bernard Mandeville took Defoe's critique of the Poor Law's 'morality' to new ground by recasting 'corruption' – as self-interest or self-indulgence was typically characterized by the SPCK and other religously inspired refomers – into the necessary driving force for economic growth (the public good?).[75] He presented a 'value world turned upside down.' It challenged the array of static 'Utopian' models that had been shaping English social and political aspirations since the *societas christiana* of the thirteenth and fourteenth centuries.

Defoe and Mandeville had startled the defenders of the Poor Law as an instrument of moral reform when the presence of new industry was only beginning to appear. Subsequently, two of the emerging order's moralists, David Hume and Adam Smith, formulated a 'civic morality' that was a profound alternative to the various traditional moral codes.[76] Hume's was the essential frontal assault on habitual assumptions about how we acquire morality and what its objectives seemed to be. He argued that moralists should refocus their attention from ends to means and their epistemology from abstraction and reason to experience and sentiment. This stance also brought personal and national histories to the fore; they were the accumulations of experience upon which we should reflect and extract the wisdom essential for the cultivation of virtue. Hume's articulation of the wisdom–virtue pairing accompanied a renewed interest in Cicero and Seneca. From this mix, Smith articulated the unique values of commercial society.[77]

Crucial to the transvaluation was Smith's distinction between 'empathy,' the inclination to respond to other's pain, and 'sympathy,' actual commitment taken only after initial restraint and reflection, which he explored in the *Theory of Moral Sentiments* (1759) and *Lectures on Jurisprudence* (1766). As Nicholas Phillipson points out, Smith was much concerned with explaining the 'process by which men living in a commercial society acquire moral ideas and may be taught how to improve them.'[78] Hume had dubbed 'mutual sympathy' to be the 'hinge' of a commercial system, and Smith acknowledged that 'nothing pleases us more' than to observe in our fellows 'all the emotions of our own breasts.' But mutual sympathy or propriety had to be found; it was the outcome of the arts of friendship and conversation, that is, tolerance, detachment, moderation and respect for consensus. So it was that Smith favored the coffee house to the *polis* as the school for morality and political economy instead of politics as its field of exercise. And, on the way to proper sympathy, he insisted, one must restrain the first impulses of empathy and assume at least briefly the role of 'spectator.'[79]

The other important issue for this study was the distinction that Smith drew between 'feudal' and 'commercial' civilization. The latter challenged the 'patriarchical authority' and 'dependence' of the former. And '[n]othing,' Smith assumed in *Lectures on Jurisprudence*, 'does more to corrupt and enervate and debase the mind as dependency and nothing gives such noble and generous notions of probity as freedom and independence.' It is through voluntary participation in 'societies,' 'associations,' 'companies,' and 'clubs,' by-products of the 'ordinary commerce of the world,' that humans can begin to discover 'independence' and 'liberty.' We have seen that the medieval *societas christiana* had been a stool supported by three legs, the prayers, the warriors, and the workers. In a commerical society, according to Smith in *Wealth of Nations* (1776), the three legs were the landowners, the laborers, and the capitalists. Of the three, Smith was most sanguine about the lower gentry and middling sort, who, with effort, frugality, and the proper sympathies could become the 'natural aristocrats.' Unfortunately laborers, who generally lacked the time and inclination to be educated, failed to appreciate that their interests were at one with those of the society at large. But Smith was most wary of capitalists for their cosmopolitan rather than national loyalties and their inclinations to pervert the public interest and weaken the moral condition of the laborers.[80] For Smith and his followers, the counterforce to these vices, as well as to feudal patriarchy and dependence, was the social and ethical wisdom acquired by independent-minded participants in the the face-to-face encounters of voluntary association. The emerging order would find its way, not know its ends.

None of this was consoling for those committed to ancient rights or herediaty custom. The ability of those feeling victimized by the mandates and proscriptions of *civitas*'s Poor Law were finding the resort to custom even less effective by the middle of the eighteenth century. For instance, as the government's usual ambivalence and temporizing over enclosure turned finally to advocacy in mid-century, the poor's access to commons diminished sharply. And, since the Restoration, the better off freeholders had become more active and successful in turning away the blandishments of custom's claimants.[81]

For most of the eighteenth century the guide for achieving customary relations and festivals was a parish's or locality's annual calendar. It consisted of many repeated activities related to work, leisure, worship, parish or local administration, and interaction with the gentry. Each was a unique expression of the more general yearly rhythm found across the country. Although customs'origins and most widespread practices were rural, similar structures of work and celebration followed rural migrants into the industrial towns; the functions of customary activity were much the same for 'rustic and townsman – tradesman and industrial worker.' Custom defined a kind of contractual framework within which the 'superior' (landowners, clergy, farmers) and 'inferiors' (tenants, smallholders, laborers, the poor), in particular settings, recognized their mutual dependence.[82] Conforming to the workings of Scott's 'transcripts,' the superiors in theory accepted their responsibilities for the well-being of the inferiors and, in turn, received recognition of their status and compliance with their decisions and direction.[83] However, by the late eighteenth century the concerted undermining of custom by the requirements of the emerging industrial order was well under way. A combination of new ideologies of work discipline (for example, artificial clock-time instead of natural time), organization, and sites encouraged by evangelical prodding and rational design served to put custom on the defensive and drive a wedge between superiors and inferiors. A set of tensions developed not unlike those two centuries earlier when Puritans sought to 'control the misbehavior' of the poor. Rustics and laborers sought to preserve their customary rights to gleaning, fuel gathering, access to recreational and ritual venues, and ritualized collections of largesse from Christmas boxes and harvest levies. The levies were sometimes referred to as 'civility money,' payments to ensure compliance with the local hierarchy for the year. Evidence suggests that wassail singing (and other Merry England customs), with the expected dole payment in appreciation, was still present at the turn of the nineteenth century. Nevertheless, the middling sort and landed gentry more and more were pushing for and benefiting from statutory obstruction of customary rights claims and practices. *Civitas* was again weakening *societas*; the laws of propertied men were prevailing; custom was unwelcome in the emerging order.[84]

Writing in *The Bee* in 1759, Oliver Goldsmith praised the country that could be ruled exclusively by custom rather than written laws. His model was Rome of the early empire when 'the people [still] retained their liberty...[and] were governed by custom.' Only when they had sunk into 'oppression and tyranny' were they 'restrained by new laws and the laws of custom abolished.' Goldsmith saw parallels with Rome's fate all around him as traditional uses were being abolished or ignored and replaced by 'the multiplicity of written laws.' He bemoaned that England was imprinting on itself the 'sign of a degenerate community.'[85]

Another way of putting this is that customs' legalities were less frequently recognized, but their shaping influence ideologically and behaviorally continued. Thus E. P. Thompson, elaborating on Pierre Bourdieu's notion of *habitus*, maintained that '[a]grarian custom was never fact,' it was 'ambience.'[86] Custom inhabited a lived environment, each parish or locality replete with its own practices, expectations, norms and sanctions, limits and possibilities. And custom was understood and invoked differently (and self-servingly) by the wealthy landowner, the middling-sort yeoman, and the peasants and poor. The point is that custom was becoming more evanescent than it had been in the mid-seventeenth century and earlier but was no less a force for mobilizing a cohort's sense of itself, its past, its rights in a given situation, and its differences from the 'others.' In that sense custom was one of the parents of industrial class consciousness.

Conclusion

Refinements in settlement policy taken in the 1690s were expected to encourage the hardier and more adventuresome poor people to search out better opportunities. The statute of 1691 spelled out merit criteria for earning settlement in a new parish, and in 1697 parishes were encouraged to issue certificates pledging to fund designated parishioners and their families should they become chargeable elsewhere. But, the administrative complexities of settlement and its most difficult procedure, the removal of a newcomer to his or her 'settled parish,' led to much dissatisfaction with the effectiveness of the overseers and the system more generally.

Nevertheless, by the early eighteenth century, pensioners and rate-payers were becoming more reconciled to the Poor Law. Recent work by historians on settlement records and the correspondence of poor people is yielding a deeper understanding of how the poor, the near poor, and the elderly of all social levels thought about parish-centered policies and calculated their use of them. Rate-payers revealed much interest in improving the system, particularly its inability to implement effective make-work among the hardy unemployed. The workhouse idea, first explored in some depth in the Civil War era, periodically sparked enthusiasm for reform again in the 1680s and through the middle of the eighteenth century. Hundreds of towns of all sizes founded workhouses, often the result of 'unions' of two or more parishes, even though the central administration of the unions was a constant affront to parish overseers and vestries. The workhouses never did achieve the make-work expectations set for them. What they often did better, though, was nourish and educate poor children of all kinds and provide care for sick poor persons. In that latter capacity, the workhouses formed useful collaborations with numerous private hospitals, themsleves an important outlet in these years for philanthropic and charitable uses.

From probably as early as the 1710s the realm's economy was actually on two tracks. At first, in the much vaster traditional segment, the traces of its late medieval origins were still evident: overwhelmingly agricultural, yet driven by 'market' activity centered in conveniently located regional towns and ports; proto-industrial cottage employment in the upland and pasture regions; and *sui generis* London growing constantly, but affected only in limited ways by dynamics in the countryside. The second, the emerging track, was driven by the application of technological innovation and entrepreneurial calculation to manufacturing and commerce. And its geographical and institutional impact ultimately would overwhelm the traditional economy and obscure its feudal origins. For example, by the latter eighteenth century migrants were being drawn by the promise of employment to small towns in Lancashire and other northern Midlands counties where 'factories' were being set up. At the same time in the more prosperous south and southeast traditional proto-industrial employment was disappearing. As a consequence, social welfare institutions were being severely tested in both the growing north and the declining south.

And equally important to the fate of the Poor Law was a change of attitude about it and toward customary claims in general. David Hume and Adam Smith, among others, articulated a set of assumptions that served the emerging order. It emphasized the need to move beyond encumbering traditions, for example settlement with its disincentives for migration, and to recognize the insidious effects on self and society of feudal 'paternalism' and 'dependence.' Less certain of ends and more concerned with means, the new moralists encouraged ambitious sorts to move forward through 'association,' exchange, and consensus building.

None of these developments boded well practically or intellectually for the Poor Law, rooted as it was in the passing medieval order. By the 1780s, the era of parish-centered social welfare had entered its penultimate phase.

Chapter 6: Poverty, Policy, and History (c.1780–1810)

Disruptions caused by the industrializing economy only added to the critical uncertainty about the continuing usefulness of the Poor Law. Debate flourished and attracted scores of writers.[1] Those who sought to assess the effectiveness of the Poor Law empirically were faced with dozens of statutes modifying the Elizabethan statutes, more than 1000 King's Bench decisions refining and interpreting its meaning, unique implementations across roughly 15,000 parishes or other local units of responsibility, and an escalating national expense in the cumulative local poor rates.[2] A compilation of the appropriate statutes and King's Bench decisions filled three volumes in 1807, and by the government's own reckoning the yearly poor rate outlay had risen from 1,720,316L in 1776 to 5,348,205L by 1804.[3]

One of the most important, yet overlooked, consequences of this deep questioning was the invention of the 'history of policy,' at least in England. Three writers, Dr. Richard Burn (d. 1785), Thomas Ruggles (d. 1813), and Sir Frederic Eden (d. 1809), but particularly the latter two, were the architects of the new genre.[4] In their determination to reach some wisdom on the best fate for the Poor Law, they were compelled to search for its roots, original intentions, and subsequent development. What was the nature of poverty in the realm? What historical conditions made the Poor Law necessary? What was it designed to do? How had subsequent economic or political developments affected the Poor Law's impact? And, overall, had the Elizabethan policy been beneficial or detrimental for the realm and the poor?

173

The historians were likely stimulated, too, by the new 'philosophic' historiography of the Enlightenment and ongoing critiques of the law in general. For example, William Blackstone, convinced that the common law could meet the demands of changing conditions, urged legislative restraint and emphasized the legal mischief perpetrated by parliament.[5] Jeremy Bentham, on the other hand, took the innovator's position and disdained the common law and its pointed reliance on precedent. Much needed, he argued, was a comprehensive recodification of the statute law that would rest on rational principles and replace the common law.[6] Yet a third position, that of the statute consolidationists took inspiration from Francis Bacon's proposal for the 'regeneration and reconstruction of the laws' (*De Augmentis Scientiarum*). They strove to prune and fuse the all too numerous statutes in different categories of law, including the Poor Law.[7] Finally, the Scots Enlightenment figure, Lord Kames, advocated a 'historical' approach to legal criticism: the law became rational and intelligible only in the context of its historical development.[8]

Glimpses of Policy's Past

An early use of historical allusion to evaluate the Poor Law was part of Daniel Defoe's parliamentary rebuke of Mackworth's Poor Law reform proposal in 1704, which we discussed in Chapter 5. Defoe sought to explain the beginning of England's rise to great wealth during Elizabeth's reign. The queen had noticed in her progresses through the realm 'vast throngs of the poor, flocking to see and bless her' and she determined to study 'how to recover her people from that poverty.' Defoe concluded it was not the Poor Law but her wisdom in allowing Flemish immigrants, fleeing the Duke of Alva's persecutions, to settle in the realm that was crucial. The English learned the skills of cloth manufacturing from the Flemish. Subsequently, wherever cloth works were established, people flocked to be employed, the poor were set on work, and the ensuing expansion of commerce, wealth, and population made the nation a 'prodigy of trade.' Thus Defoe urged parliament not to add any more provisions to the Poor Law; what the poor needed was to be set to work in the many jobs available, not more oversight and regulation.[9]

Twenty-five years later John Disney published an encyclopedic work, *A View of Ancient Laws* (1729).[10] He described himself as an admirer of the Society for the Reformation of Manners and curious to know how extensively nations throughout history had attempted to contain vice by legal punishment. In the course of his 20 years of research Disney gathered data on the ancient Jews, Egyptians, Athenians, Peloponnesians, Sardinians, Italians, Germans, Asian Indians, Romans, Saxons, and Scots. The resulting volume was a nosegay of snippets from ancient and early medieval poor relief laws and practices. For example, Disney's readers learned that in ancient India's schools there was such disdain for slothful behavior that every day the students were asked to recount what they had done as a 'service to mankind.' Those who could give no good account of themselves were 'turned out of doors, and made to fast.' Or, one could discover that Macbeth in eleventh-century Scotland passed a law compelling players, Morris dancers, and idle rogues to 'fall to work in some form of mechanical business.'[11] From time to time, Disney paused to establish the appropriate lesson, such as idleness is a 'great immorality, as well as a political mischief.' Even Adam before his fall had been 'obliged to work,' and after his 'removal' from the Garden his 'sentence only made his work more necessary.'[12] And, leaving no doubt as to his agreement with the Poor Law's principles, Disney pointed out that the Roman Emperor, Alexander Severus, purged his court of those unfit for labor and shipped them in equal numbers to the cities and towns 'to be maintained at public expense, that they might not be troublesome by begging.'[13]

In 1764, the year Beccaria's *Essay on Crimes and Punishments* appeared in Italy, Richard Burn published *The History of the Poor Laws*. By this time the dynamic of expanding population, rising prices, and declining wages had been under way for more than a generation. Burn thought it necessary to 'excite attention' to the Poor Law and present 'a comprehensive view of the subject.'[14] Oxford educated and Doctor of Civil Laws, he had 30 years of experience as a vicar and magistrate in Westmorland and Cumberland; and his reputation as a legal writer had already been assured with his *Justice of the Peace* (1754). Burn's objective was to present 'the facts' of Poor Law history to the public with a minimum of intrusion on his part. Those facts were available in the statute books and pamplets in his library, which he proceeded to present quite literally.[15]

A book of unusual proportions resulted; five of the eight chapters are almost exclusively verbatim presentations of statutes and reform plans; only two are discursive. One of these offered 19 'observations' on the history of the Poor Laws; the other contained Burn's own proposals for improving the operation of the Elizabethan system. Since reformers have aimed 'at too much too soon,' and thus 'put too much to the hazard,' the present laws should 'stand.' Most important in the long run, however, would be 'to *reduce all the Poor Laws into one*.'[16] If that was not possible, all begging and private charity, which break the laws 'thro' like cobwebs' must be prohibited. And, according to Burn, since the legislature has 'provided for the poor in one way... let it be tried what the laws can do.'[17] Once this is accomplished, he insisted, 'humanity, religion, compassion, virtue, honor, decency, [and] love to our brethren' will demand better administration of the poverty relief system. Yet, to provide adequate channels for this charitable impulse will require the appointment of general superintendents of the poor over several parishes, the construction of work villages instead of elaborate workhouses, and revival of the pre-Charles II provisions for settlement, place of birth or inhabitance for one or more years.[18]

Rights of the Poor versus Abolitionism

The wider discussion of the merits of the Poor Law in these years tended to form two camps. Those who revered the Elizabethan system and wanted to add to that policy stressed the suffering of the poor and their entitlement to public provision. Writers who were dissatisfied with it emphasized the rising poor rate and the reward that it seemingly offered to improvidence. In effect, the 'rights of the poor' and 'compassion' were thrust against 'exorbitant expense' and 'unworthy recipients.' And yet, on a deeper level, the best of these exchanges carried forward the questions that had absorbed English social, moral, and political thinking at least since the fourteenth and fifteenth centuries. Was poverty the consequence of vice and weak character? Or was it created by unfair social institutions that legalized greed, as Thomas More and other anti-enclosure writers claimed?[19] Did the economic stability of the state require a pool of super-numerary laborers, kept fit 'building a useless pyramid upon *Salisbury Plain*,' in William Petty's cunning phrase, if necessary during periods of high unemployment?[20] Were tractability and acceptance of place more desirable qualities in the poor than ambition and self-direction? And, when government intervention with the poor is contemplated, what purposes are to be served: regulation and control, redress for injustice, or education and liberation?

A particularly strong formulation of the 'rights of the poor' had been made in the 1760s and 1770s by Dr Richard Woodward, Bishop of Cloyne. The laboring poor, wrote Woodward, are the victims of a property system which 'consigns to each child at birth the patrimony of his parents.' The child born to no inheritance is, for all intents and purposes, born the inhabitant of a land, every spot of which is appropriated to some other person. He cannot seize his needs without 'invading *property* and incurring the penalty of law.' But, how can the rich 'justify their exclusive property in the *common heritage* of mankind, unless they consent, in return, to provide for the subsistence of the poor.'[21] Woodward specifically challenged Lord Kames's assertion (*Sketches on the History of Man*, 1774) that providence had scattered benevolence among human beings sufficiently to care for the needy poor, and thus obviate the need for government policy on the matter. Woodward maintained that a regular, predictable, and fairly administered poor relief policy is required by the 'law of nature' and the 'law of reason.' If a similar government initiative is not also the 'plan of providence,' he implored, 'I shall readily give it up.'[22] William Paley, an Anglican clergyman and lecturer on moral philosophy at Cambridge from 1768 to 1776, propounded a 'rights of the poor' doctrine on theological utilitarian principles. His widely popular textbook, *The Principles of Moral and Political Philosophy*, (first edn., 1785), exposed several generations of students and readers to his ideas. Paley held that god had devised a social world in which the pursuit of the objects of individual happiness, for example salvation, benevolence, prudence, and health, contributed directly to the greatest happiness for the greatest number. And private property had developed from an original society of common ownership only with the crucial understanding that 'every one should have left a sufficiency for his subsistence, or the means of procuring it.'[23]

At the opposite end of the spectrum were calls to reduce the Poor Laws radically or to do away with them altogether. The 'abolitionist' case was stated forcefully in 1786 by another man of the cloth, Rev. Joseph Townsend. His *Dissertation on the Poor Laws* shared much in its outlook, if not its tone, with Defoe's parliamentary speech in 1704. Townsend held that providing make-work for the indigent would not change their habits; only increasing the 'degree of pressure' for self-reliance would do that. Make-work would, however, deprive the ambitious of work and income. He concluded that the Poor Laws should probably be abolished, or, short of that, the rate should be reduced by one-tenth each year.[24]

The 1790s: Crisis and History

In 1794–95, almost exactly two centuries after the calamities of the mid-1590s that had brought on great suffering and the fevered search in parliament for a new Poor Law, the realm again faced a crippling dearth, this time intensified by a war-economy inflation caused by the conflict with Revolutionary France. The very pressures of the moment forced to the surface reform proposals and policy innovations that otherwise might have remained inchoate. In the spring of 1795, for instance, the magistrates of Berkshire met at Speenhamland to respond to the suffering of the poor. Unable to agree on an increase in wages for agricultural laborers, they instituted a sliding scale of 'outdoor' relief based on bread prices and family size.[25] And parliament passed yet another settlement statute; it confined removal to two categories of newcomers, those who have become chargeable but are well enough to travel, and unemployed and incorrigible vagrants. Samuel Whitbread brought an agricultural wages bill to parliament that was defeated, but only after Prime Minister William Pitt promised a sweeping reform bill that would restore the Elizabethan policy to its 'original approach' and establish relief as a 'right and honour'.[26]

Pitt's Bill, introduced in December of 1796, ran to 130 headings and authorized a wide array of initiatives, including aid to the working poor, family allowances, money for the purchase of capital equipment, schools of industry for poor children, reclamation of wastelands for the poor, compulsory friendly societies (sickness and old age funds), relaxation of settlement, and an annual Poor Law budget approved by parliament.[27] If we exclude proposals for fundamental social reform, such as William Godwin's 'cultivated equality,' resting on the elimination of private property, or Thomas Paine's 'social budget for the poor' which was to be financed by a progressive tax on landed estates, Pitt's bill likely represents the fullest expression of the rights of the poor discourse as intended legislation. Parliament had not received such an audacious plan for a national policy directed at poverty since 1535, when Henry VIII introduced his draft bill that called for numerous parish relief responsibilities, supplemented by a national 'councel to avoide vagabonds,' health care for the poor, and an extensive make-work program for the able-bodied unemployed.[28] Pitt's Bill, like its Henrician predecessor, was quickly withdrawn.

Jeremy Bentham seems to have been privy to an early version of Pitt's Bill, provided to him in February 1796 by their mutual friend

William Wilberforce. The draft provoked Bentham's thinking on general principles of social welfare against which this set of proposals might be evaluated, and he speculated on an alternative plan. When the bill was presented to parliament, Bentham began to work intensely on several essays, several of which circulated only in manuscript but nevertheless were influential. For example, 'Definitions and Distinctions,' brief and likely penned in March or April 1796, was seized on by Patrick Colquhoun, who followed parts of it very closely a decade later in his *A Treatise on Indigence*.[29] Bentham's impulses favored continuing public welfare, but he veered sharply from Pitt's elaborate embellishments on the Poor Law. Rather, he insisted that the objective of the Poor Law system 'is to make provision for the relief not of *poverty*, but of *indigence*.' The former is the condition of all who, lacking subsistence, are forced to labor. The latter is the state of those lacking subsistence who are either unable to labor or, having labor, unable to acquire it. In danger of being overlooked, according to Bentham, is that as 'labour is the source of wealth, so is poverty of labour.' Poverty is the universal spur to labour; thus to set out to eliminate it would be to eliminate humankind itself.[30]

In 'Fundamental Positions in Regard to the Making Provision for the Indigent Poor' (1796), Bentham laid out two 'returns' that are due to the government for administering poor relief 'at the public charge.' These are incumbent on the individual recipient for the benefit either of him- or herself or the larger community whose resources provide the relief. The first was that the recipient of assistance works to the extent of his or her ability without risk to health or life. And second, the recipient must accept the government's determination of the place where the relief and work will occur and the mode of living in that place. Bentham offered further elaboration on the 'place' issue in another of his unpublished essays later that spring, 'Collateral Uses Derivable from a System of Industry Houses.' A sweeping proposal, it was a bit redolent of the Lollard-inspired 'Twelve Conclusions' (*c*.1395), which among other things called for the disendowment of religious houses and the use of some the funds realized to establish 100 almshouses. Bentham would collapse the social welfare of the 15 000 parishes in the 50 counties of England and Wales into 200 Industry Houses, one for each 75 parishes or so. By this time, he already had been elaborating on his idea for a panopticon prison, which embodied architecturally a 'central-inspection principle,' several floors of walled inmate cells arranged in a circular layout around the manager's apartment in the center. The inmates could not see one another, but the manager could keep all of them under constant surveillance through the cell windows facing him. Bentham never saw a panopticon built, but he adapted the concept eventually to his Industry-House plan for Poor Law reform.

Thomas Ruggles, for his part, taking note during the 1780s and early 1790s of the expanding suffering of the poor and the heavy burden of the rate, especially on rural property owners, thought it necessary to look into 'antiquity.' It was time to 'explore on what principle of legislation, from what consent, virtual or implied, of our forefathers,' from what system of human or divine laws 'this ruinous . . . paradox should happen.'[31] And he lamented that historians seldom condescend to relate '*the short and simple annals of the poor* (Grey's 'Elegy'). Ruggles's *The History of the Poor*, 49 'letters' or essays, initially serialized in Arthur Young's *Annals of Agriculture* between 1789 and 1793, appeared in two volumes (1793–94) and subsequently in one (1797). Ruggles was a country gentlemen and deputy-lieutenant of Suffolk and Essex (the Thomas Harman of his day?).

Much of Ruggles's history rests on parliamentary debates, statutes, and reform tracts. He is apologetic about the 'slim results' in sources that his use of local booksellers had produced while the 'farrago of pamphlets' in the British Museum had gone unattended by him. Identifying himself as a 'philosophical' historian, Ruggles approached his subject by 'fixing a foundation in the first principles of society, and proceeding by an historical analysis,' not unlike Aquinas's meditations on property and obligation five centuries earlier. He maintained that the maldistribution of property was the reason for poverty's appearance and continuation. Thus the working poor have 'rights' to adequate compensation for their labor and to 'maintenance from the more opulent classes' when they cannot work. Furthermore, he was convinced that '[a]nterior to, and vastly above all human laws, the obligation of the rich to the poor is prominent in the variety of religious and "social compacts," was preached by Christ and his disciples, and was early embedded in English practice in the distribution of the tithes.'[32] Ruggles buttressed his claim for the rights of the poor with a custom-like 'ancient obligation' instead of an 'ancient constitution' argument (in the Leveller rather than the Whig sense).[33]

Ruggles's dividing line between 'premodern' and 'modern' was the Reformation. And, in his view, the poor fared badly both before and after the event, but for different reasons. The invasion of William of

Normandy to wrest the kingdom from its old possessors set off several centuries of contention, during which the 'voice of law' and the 'doing of equity' were seldom heard and finally forgotten. Only with the ascent of the Tudors was the quieting of civil disruptions possible. Even so, at first the claims of the poor remained 'dormant,' if not 'extinct,' largely because of Henry VIII's break with Rome and the division of the monasteries among his 'unprincipled' courtiers.[34] It was not until Elizabeth's 'long and prosperous reign, with religious matters settled and the kingdom well managed by a Cecil and a Bacon,' that parliament focused on poverty. During these years the rights of the poor were restored. 'Some of the best moral principles of the Christian religion' were 'engrafted by degrees . . . into the statute law of the land,' and parliament 'sanctioned that, which was before only a moral duty, by a law of the state.' Ruggles correctly viewed the Elizabethan Poor Law as a 'code,' the central feature of which was the compulsory poor rate. He insisted that the provisions of the policy were still relevant to the realm's social conditions and that the current problems in the system 'cannot arise from this statute being . . . carried into strict execution.'[35]

Unfortunately, in spite of this 'god like' policy, since the Reformation the poor had become more demoralized than ever and the rich were bowing under the strain of the rate. The poor were more numerous, more exposed to the hazards of city life, more subject to the health and moral debilities of manufacturiing, and less likely to find paths to social mobility. Ruggles's proposed remedies included strict enforcement of the Poor Laws, more restrictions on alehouses, union workhouses, partial repeal of settlement, and the encouragement of friendly societies.[36]

According to Frederic Morton Eden, it was the deep suffering of the laborers in the 1794–95 dearth that 'induced' him 'from motives both of benevolence and curiosity, to investigate their condition in various parts of the kingdom.' He published his prodigious *State of the Poor* in three quarto volumes in 1797.[37] It is a much more factual and source-rich study than Ruggles's, and the empirical data in its scores of parish surveys is still mined fruitfully by historians of social welfare. Furthermore, Eden generated much deeper insights into the historical nature of policy. He was the son of the last colonial governor of Maryland and through his mother a descendant of the Lords Baltimore. An Oxford MA, Eden mixed a successful businesss career with prolific writing, mainly on economic subjects. The printed catalogue of his library shows over 7800 volumes arranged under 'Arts and Sciences,' 'British History,' 'Foreign History,' 'French,' 'Greek, Latin, and Italian,' and assorted 'Miscellanies.'[38] When Eden died in 1809 at age 43, he was chairman of the Globe Insurance Company which he had founded.

Eden's initial objective was to compile an empirical profile of the conditions of the laboring poor and the 'actual poor' as free as possible from private opinion and passions. He designed a 'query' that requested from the parishes information from the 1680s onwards on matters ranging from diet and birth and death information to demographic and poor rate figures. He visited several parishes himself and made use of a full-time research assistant and numerous correspondents.[39] The data compiled was massive; yet, it did not provide Eden with certainty on either the extent to which the increasing 'numbers' and 'distress' of the poor had been brought on by 'domestic improvidence and misconduct' or the best 'expedients by which the condition of the laboring classes might be bettered.' Such clear understanding, he conceded, not only surpasses his degree of practical knowledge, it required 'more comprehensive details than can fall within the grasp of a single individual.' And the 'little which I have to advance on these topics...I am sorry to have to add [has] been derived more from historical than from personal and local enquiries.'[40]

Thus Eden had to concede that even if the initial spirit of the Poor Law – unlikely though that was – a number of further questions would remain for politicians and philanthropists. What good and what moral and political evils have been brought by the Poor Laws? Are the 'indigent classses' now proportionally less numerous or less miserable than they were formerly? Have poorhouses, houses of industry, and friendly societies helped them? To what extent has the poverty relief system affected the progress of industry and the blessings of domestic life? To appreciate the 'effects' of the Poor Laws and to distinguish them from those of other institutions requires ingenious historical investigation, Eden insisted. One must trace these complicated patterns through the progress of society, 'if not from the earliest, at least through the most important, periods of our history.'[41] The inquirer who undertakes this task is but the 'hewer of stone' and 'drawer of water.' Certainly, the 'glory' of the builder is more enviable; but the 'drudgery' of the mason is of greater use. For, only if it is done, can public opinion be deepened and the 'edifice' of 'political knowledge' be constructed.[42]

Furthermore, very little about the intention of the Poor Laws can be ascertained from 'perusal only of the records of Parliament.' To appraise the characteristics of a law with any degree of subtlety, it is 'essential to advert to the manners and customs of the people' and 'to consider how far those evils existed, for which a legislative remedy was proposed.'[43] Thus, 'copious streams of political knowledge, of the highest kind,' important subjects for reflection by legislators, flow from the reservoir of information of the domestic economy, the manners, and the opinions of the poor.[44] But to what materials did a pathfinding historian of policy turn for this? Little wonder that few, if any, had attempted previously to untie the Gordian knot of policy history. Eden relied on Henry Home, Lord Kames for inspiration and example. Almost four decades earlier in *Historical Law Tracts* (1761), facing his own sources problem, Kames had decided 'to supply the broken links, by hints from poets and historians, by collateral facts, and by cautious conjectures, drawn from the nature of government, of the people, and of the times.' And true to his mentor, Eden made resourcrful use of Clarendon and Hume, Chaucer and Latimer, Shakespeare and Rousseau, Adam Smith and Burke, among many others, as well as the rolls of parliament, parish records, local histories, government data on prices and rates, and whatever else he could find.[45]

Eden affirmed that in general poverty originated in the universal necessity to labor for food, clothing, and shelter; and, particularly in England, it derived from the fact that the realm's soil and climate were not adquate to supply the numbers of the population without some previous labor. Thus a 'portion' of the society 'must be indefatigably employed . . . to supply the necessary want of the whole.' But, when illness, chronic disorder, or old age befall them, they lose all comfort. In the face of such distress, according to Eden, it is the 'readily admitted' duty of every man, 'according to his abilities and opportunities,' to relieve his fellows.[46]

William the Conqueror was 'despotic' and the aftermath of his conquest was civil and social disruption until *Magna Carta*. But in the medieval period Eden was attracted mainly to the villeinage economy and its transformation. In his sketch of English feudalism, Eden made allusions to slavery in North America and Russian serfdom. Nevertheless, he maintained that no matter how degraded villeins were by the system, they were still 'assured of the bare necessities of life'; and, the legislature was 'not called upon to enact laws, either for the punishment of vagrants, or the relief of the impotent and aged.' That such legislation began to appear toward the end of the fourteenth century, however, meant that villeinage was declining 'by slow degrees' and a 'new race of men' was rising who were employed in manufactures.

Even though manufacturing and commerce ultimately brought 'numberless benefits' to the realm, Eden concluded that they were the causes of 'our national poor.' Although manfactures enabled men 'to make use of the most valuable of all property, their own industry,' it also allowed them to starve 'independently' when they were incapacitated in any way.[47]

Revealing a strong 'presentism' in his analysis of earlier policy initiatives, a trait he shared with Burn and Ruggles, Eden concluded that the first statutes developed in response to public poverty rested on scanty 'knowledge of political economy,' and thus have not been 'practically useful' in subsequent times. If the legislature had had the good sense to allow 'market competition' to prevail among agricultural laborers and hourly artificers, instead of wage regulation (and later settlement), progress would have been much more rapid.[48] We are not surprised to learn, then, that the renowned Elizabethan Poor Law, 'however highly praised for its originality,' was no more than a reorganization of 'legal regulations' that had beome 'impolitic or impractical.' Unfortunately, it has continued to be the 'groundwork of every regulation affecting the poor.'[49]

Eden's understanding of the recent history of the laboring poor is quite different from Ruggles's. He was convinced that the decline of villeinage and the rise of manufactures and commerce, in spite of the public (structural) poverty that accompanied them, had created opportunities for a free labor market and initiated a general improvement in the nation's prosperity. Unfortunately, the web of wage regulations and settlement requirements that entrapped artificers and agricultural laborers prevented them from marketing their labor. If Eden saw a historical force that empowered the poor toward better possibilities, it was the influence of the constitution not the Poor Law. And he was unreserved in his praise for the Glorious Revolution, which, he believed, produced clearer understandings of prerogative and liberty, the principles of government, and the legal protection of the subjects' rights. But, ultimately, Eden put more of a 'virtue' or 'commerce' spin on this than a 'rights' one. It is in the third William, 'the master workman' (Burke), and his associates that Eden found his benefactors for the poor to match Ruggles's Elizabethans. This was not because of any immediate improvement in the 'ease and comfort' of the poor, but because William's party laid the 'foundations of future greatness,' for the rewards that can develop only from 'slow and imperceptible improvement.' The Revolution 'inspired the great mass of the nation with the spirit of thinking and acting which have been conducive towards rendering them more happy and independent.'[50] Eden seemed to claim here that the major consequence of 1688 for the history of poverty was to give impetus to a spiritual or psychological revolution which had been held back by inappropriate legislation since the fourteenth century, in spite of growth in the new economy.

Edmund Burke's *Thoughts on Scarcity* was published posthumously in 1797. Written toward the end of the dearth crisis in 1795, Burke acknowledged that wheat prices had 'risen exceedingly' within the year but argued that the consequent suffering had been minimal, 'owing to a care and superintendence of the poor, far greater than any I remember.' He had not favored Pitt's Bill, which the prime minister shared with him. His long view was that the 'laboring people did, either out of their direct gains or from charity . . . in fact fare better than they did, in seasons of common plenty, 50 or 60 years ago.' Since the 'great use' of government is as a restraint ('it can do very little positive good'), Burke urged that the men of state resist the temptation to tamper with the 'trade of provisions' or with the essentially private jurisdiction of mercy, no matter how the present conditions would seem to encourage such actions.[51]

The appearance of *An Essay on the Principle of Population* in 1798 gave abolitionism its biggest boost. 'The poor-laws of England were undoubtedly instituted for the most benevolent purpose,' wrote Malthus, 'but there is great reason to think that they have not succeeded in their intention.' The Elizabethan tradition actually created dependency; the poor marry and have children 'with little or no prospect of being able to support [their families] in independence,' while as a consequence, 'the provisions of the country must . . . be distributed to every man in smaller portions.' Most pernicious of all is that the Poor Laws, 'a code of tyrannical regulations,' enticed the poor to surrender their liberty ('going on the parish') for very little in return. The harsh fact to Malthus is that the ability to 'prevent the recurrence of misery is, alas! beyond the power of man'; nevertheless, palliatives must be attempted. In this case, to restore 'liberty and freedom of action to the peasantry' all parish laws should be abolished. Furthermore, every incentive must be given to encourage agriculture over manufactures, tillage over grazing. To relieve extreme cases of distress, county poorhouses should be authorized and funded by a national rate.[52]

Where do Ruggles and Eden fit into the 'rights of the poor' and the 'abolitionist' discourses on the Poor Law? The answer is clear with regard to Ruggles. He praised the Elizabethan policy makers for restoring the ancient rights of the indigent and was convinced that the Poor Law remained 'bottomed in humanity, justice and policy.'[53] Eden's work certainly lent itself to the 'abolitionist' cause, and, by the time of the second edition of his *Essay* in 1803, Malthus had read Eden and offered praise for his 'valuable work.' 'No man had collected so many materials for forming a judgment on the effects of the Poor Laws,' and Malthus was 'happy' for agreement with 'so practical an inquirer' that the Poor Laws had indeed brought havoc. Malthus neglected to mention, however, that Eden had eschewed the abolitionist position for being too 'bold and rash.'[54] Rather, he had chosen for himself the course of the 'temperate political specialist,' found somewhere between Pitt's elaborate proposals to extend the Elizabethan tradition and the precipitate abolitionism of Burke and Malthus. Why did he do that? The answer lies in his nascent political theory and what he had learned about policy from the Poor Law's history.

Politics, Policy, and Tradition

Eden evaluated the Poor Law's effects not only empirically but against a set of assumptions about the nature of government and good policy. For instance, he was convinced that governments are instituted 'to render mankind good, in order that they may be happy...in society.' Although government ('that is, Society in its state of perfection') rests on opinion, 'opinions on principles are not innate.' Thus the state is above all else an educational entity, a school of virtue. In offering formal schooling to the young in religion and the 'useful worldly sciences,' a government with the help of the leading members of the community 'supplies the public with the best elements of political knowledge, and the firmest foundations of moral virtue.' Yet, the purpose of this is not to cultivate the dependence of the citizens; it is rather to release them from the thrall of barbarism to the self-improving possibilities of virtue and civic life. The 'excellence' of legislation is most clearly indicated 'as it leaves the individual exertion more or less unshackled.' It is unforced effort, 'not the superintendency power of the state,' which builds the 'edifice of national grandeur.'[55]

This is as close as Eden came to defining 'policy.' He used the word frequently, along with occasional substitute terms and phrases, such as 'moral system,' 'legislative fabric,' 'system of jurisprudence,' 'the operation . . . of civil polity,' and 'political science.' When he did, he was invariably discussing the government acting on its educative responsibility in the broadest sense to initiate legislation that would cultivate 'the right,' 'moral virtue,' or 'unforced exertion' in the citizenry. Conversely, when he referred to the government using its power to stultify initiative, as in the case of the wage regulations embedded in poor relief measures, Eden used the terms 'impolicy' and 'unenlightened policy.'[56] Whatever he understood 'policy' to be precisely, in his usage the term did not describe simply any and all statutes and their effects. It carried a charge or value that separated it from mere 'police' ('regulation,' according to Dr Johnson) or 'policed' ('Regulated' and 'Formed into a regular course of administration').[57]

When Eden appraised the Poor Law against his ruminations about the virtuous intentions of government and policy, he developed his most telling critique of Pitt and Ruggles. In establishing the rights of the poor to maintenance in particular times of distress, the proponents of the Elizabethan system consigned those temporarily in need to ceaseless labor for subsistence at all other times. What is this perpetual labor with no possibility for the achievement of 'repose and recreation,' declared Eden, but 'barbarism' and the 'savage state.' The 'physical, or moral, nature of man' must not be confused with that of an 'ass in a mill,' whose only application is to 'bodily exertion from week's end to week's end.'[58] The 'ancient statutes' rest on the 'mistaken principle' that policy's goal is the 'eschewing of idleness,' and 'setting the Poor on work' and that with the 'incitements of civilization before them, the people must [nevertheless] be *compelled* to follow their own interest.' The state should have no reason to complain, Eden contended, if 'he, who can earn enough in four days to maintain him for seven, chooses to spend the remaining three in idleness and relaxation.' Thus, the rights of the poor to maintenance come at a very high cost to the poor themselves: their exclusion from the central goals of civilized society, self-possession and civil liberty.[59] Eden never actually accused the defenders of the Elizabethan policy of advocating supernumerary status for the laboring poor, but that conclusion was implicit in his argument. And it is interesting to note that John Weyland, one of the most articulate defenders of the Poor Law in the early nineteenth century, made the maintenance of a 'redundant and healthy' population of laborers and the advantages this brings to the realm, the bedrock of this case against Malthus.[60]

Finally, if their failure to realize (or acknowledge) that the Elizabethan system excluded the poor from the full benefits of civilization provoked Eden's disagreement with the 'rights of the poor' advocates, what separated him from the 'abolitionists'? Here the disagreement centered on what Eden believed to be their superficial understanding of the historical characteristics of policy. Eden's study convinced him of the great difficulty one faced in attempting to understand a developing phenomenon like the Elizabethan policy tradition. Over time, contingent forces, whether environmental, institutional, or attitudinal, combine with and alter the original intentions of a statute or code. Therefore, just as the 'philosopher of matter' must attend to the 'agency of collateral causes' in nature, so must the 'historian of society' take into consideration the 'effect of co-existing establishments.' Many institutions, 'incongruous and unconnected' in their origins, come together in harmony and cooperation as time passes. Thus, every policy initiative will be modified 'according to circumstances; imperceptible additions, adapted with reference to what is retained [and] gradually swell into a complicated machine.' The ensuing tradition 'produces effects, to which the subordinate parts have all contributed; but in what proportion each has assisted, it often becomes impractible to determine.'[61]

Thus the Elizabethan tradition by the 1790s had become a complicated and inscrutable amalgam, a 'spreading ivy' that had 'insinuated itself into every crack and aperture' of the societal edifice. The original intentions of the Elizabethan code and the society in which they were applied have been fused and transformed by the capricious and incremental developments of the succeeding two centuries. Once this complicated historical nature of policy is understood, it becomes clear that the ability of the state to affect great societal good or evil through its policies can be advanced only 'unthinkingly.' Yet, as 'faulty and defective' as the Elizabethan policy was in its construction and in its ramifications, it cannot be dismantled safely. The only prudent course is to prune the spreading ivy, not to attempt to uproot it.[62] And the pruning that Eden suggested was indeed modest. The provisions of the system that encourage 'idleness, improvidence, and immorality' must be no more extended, and the laborer must be allowed 'his right to exercise his industry...in a manner most agreeable to himself.' The rise in the poor rate should be confronted with three- or seven-year averaging, and more efficient management must be applied to the funds collected.[63]

In their struggles to make sense of the Poor Law's history, Burn and Ruggles had resorted to metaphor also. For Burn, the Poor Laws were similar to a poor persons' garment, so often repaired that the 'original coat is lost amid a variety of patch-work' and enough 'labor and materials' have been expended to have bought a new one.[64] Ruggles thought of the Elizabethan Poor Law and its tradition as an elegant piece of 'gothic architecture,' 'weakened by the flux of time' and 'the alteration of circumstances' and disfigured by crude attempts to prop it up. Nevertheless, still sound and inspiring, it 'will reflect to ages yet unborn,' a 'credit' to the country that built it.[65]

Conclusion

What can we conclude about the place of these three histories in the political and legal discourse of the British Enlightenment and the ongoing attempt to assess the viability of the Poor Law? Since by our historians' own admissions they were involved in a start-up endeavor, in their work we seem to have a narrow in focus, but nevertheless vibrant example of what John Pocock has called a 'problem-situation in the traditional explanations of the relationship of the present to the past' which gives rise to the quest for historical understanding.[66] Our three historians were no longer comfortable with the capricious accretion of poor relief statutes and customs and sought a clearer understanding of the past of that body of law and behavior and how it had become the present.

But in their work do we have as many explanations of policy as we have historians? The answer would seem to be yes and no. We have seen among the three differences in goals, methods, and historical perspectives. Burn, clearly a statute consolidationist, provided essentially a chronology of statutes, which provided the reservoir of information he wanted to make available to the public. His observations were philosophically inchoate and devoid of any narrative validation. Eden and Ruggles put much more substantive historical development on Burn's statute chronology, and more developed philosophical reflections inform their narratives. Ruggles, perhaps our Lockean, is more convinced at least of the continuing 'rights of the poor' and the inspirational and practical value of the Elizabethan statutes. Burn and Eden, far less enamored with the statute or its consequences, see no viable alternative, at least until, in Eden's words, 'the heights and the levels of the country we mean to improve' are studied much more carefully.[67]

However, their significant differences not withstanding, all three call for only modest adjustments in the system. And the sense of human agency to affect a change in policy is suffused in each with an awareness of limits. The poor relief system was perceived to have become a tradition in its own right that would be both difficult and dangerous to attempt to change dramatically. Unattractive as the prospect may have seemed to Burn and Eden and essential to Ruggles, our writers accept the perpetuation of the Elizabethan tradition and the continuing sway of the 'ancient' over the 'modern.'

Conclusion: Whither Parish Social Welfare?

It is well to note that throughout I have been addressing 'social welfare,' not simply the 'Poor Law.' The former term connotes a wider range of responses to poverty than pensions distributed from the parish fund. Some were undertaken long before the Poor Law was enacted, and they and others flourished independently or in tandem with it. Having, then, traversed more than the four centuries of England's pre-industrial social welfare history, what matters of particular significance have emerged?

Central to an understanding of the Poor Law era that benefits from the parameters of this study is that the Elizabethan legislation rested on an accumulation of parish and manor-centered efforts begun as early as the thirteenth and fourteenth centuries to discourage migration, encourage employment, and provide succor and medical care to needy persons known locally. These undertakings acquired the backing of government in the aftermath of the Black Death, when parliament acknowledged and urged local responsibility for poor relief. Experience with this essentially parish-centered activity was particularly valuable in the 1530s and 1540s when the Dissolution cut in half the number of aid-dispensing institutions in the realm. By the mid-sixteenth century, several localities had begun to implement censuses of the poor and raise funds for relief, hospitals, and houses of correction. It was such innovations that became government-mandated policy in the

Elizabethan Poor Law statutes. And the ongoing pattern of local innovation preceding government mandate persisted through the pre-industrial years.

Changing ratios and feedback effects among population size, food prices, employment, and, once industrialization was under way, the locations of work did cause the numbers of the 'structural poor' to diminish or expand in any locality. And when their numbers were growing dramatically throughout the realm as in the mid-1590s or 1790s, the pressure to respond rapidly and pragmatically was evident. Nevertheless, the primary impetus for new departures in social welfare were large and deep intellectual movements, for example: medieval Christianity; Christian humanism; Lutheran and Calvinist Protestantism; neo-Stoic 'benefits'; political arithmetic; and eighteenth-century market theory. They shaped the perceptions of poverty itself and the deliberations on goals, applications, and performance standards in social welfare practice. And it was Jeremy Bentham's utilitarian rationalism that helped turn poor relief thought and practice away from the parish's importance.

Within these shaping intellectual and institutional contexts, recipients and providers of social welfare exercised much resourcefulness. The poor were important agents on their own behalf. Their constant migrations that so irritated and frightened village and town dwellers are the most compelling data for this. And in times of particular economic distress those in need were skilled in invoking the 'hidden transcripts' and customary rights of social deference and paternal obligation that usually brought forth aid beyond that which the Poor Law obligated. In addition, it is now a commonplace that pre-industrial people in severe need could not rely exclusively on a parish pension to survive, were they able to receive one at all. Rather, through their own and local providers' efforts, and depending on age and gender, they put together combinations of work, charity, and parish support, so-called 'mixed economies' of welfare.

From recent close studies of the resources available for the 'marginally poor' in several villages, we are learning more about the degree of innovation and collaborative efforts among public (overseers) and private (churchwardens and others) relief dispensers that helped this process along. Each locality made its own arrangements between public and private resources depending on its peculiar economic circumstances. And often the recipients and dispensers put together packages of relief calibrated as much as possible to individual needs. This research also is providing a better understanding of the diminishing size of pensions for the elderly after the 1630s and the resulting pressure on them to stay employed and independent as long as possible. It appears, too, that poverty in the countryside was less 'feminized' than in the towns and cities.

Overall, the implementation of pre-industrial social welfare was more protean than had been appreciated in earlier historiography; it was an ingenious mixture of public or mandatory (*civitas*) and private or voluntary (*societas*) initiatives. The parish fund seldom was the only resource available for the desperately poor. The Poor Law seems to have been a kind of 'big tent,' under whose broad mandate for local relief many different efforts, some more humane than others, were undertaken. John Broad's phrase, 'a parochial economy of welfare,' captures well these new insights.[1] Consequently, appraisals of relief during the Poor Law years have begun to move in a more sanguine direction.

Finally, we confronted the demise of the idea of parish-centered relief in the whirlwind of legislative, historiographical, and theoretical responses to the severe dearth and underemployment episode of the mid-1790s. As resourceful as parish social welfare was – mostly in the southern counties, in the late eighteenth century – the population and employment shifts to the north, resulting from industrialization, disrupted poor relief capabilities in both regions, although for different reasons. Adding to the weakening support for the Poor Law were the crucial opinion makers, Sir Frederic Eden, Thomas Robert Malthus, and Jeremy Bentham.[2] Eden was unable to defend the Poor Law as policy, but, because of his insight into the historical nature of policy, was unwilling to recommend its abolition either. Malthus at first advocated the abolition of parish relief and settlement, encouraged agriculture over manufacturing, and urged the establishment of county workhouses for the poorest people to be funded by a national tax. However, after studying Eden's history, his position simplified: abolish the Poor Law and allow charity to care for the needy. Bentham's search for alternate first principles of social welfare yielded his distinction between indigence and poverty and a careful plan for factory-like Industry-Houses that would be profitable and encourage invention and innovation. These ideas fit well into the gathering political economy of early industrialization and achieved some form of embodiment in the workhouses established by the Poor Law reform legislation of 1834.

Thus did support for the more than four-centuries-long tradition of parish-centered social welfare reach its effective intellectual and institutional demise. As L. A. Botelho has remarked recently, in the process, 'individually tailored poor relief...would become part of the world we have lost.'[3] Of course, the best experiences of parish relief were deposited in custom's vault, one in a repertoire of alternatives to the harshness and inefficiencies of the new system. And they seemed to nourish a Romantic nostalgia for the *societas* ideal, a reaction that Charles Dickens, for one, made almost unavoidable in the grimy, heartlessly utilitarian, and class-riven industrial town that he sketched in *Hard Times*. But what can be said with more precision about the Poor Law's significance for subsequent social welfare history?

Paul Slack finds in the Poor Law's implementation an 'intriguing paradox,' the development of a 'mixed economy' of welfare, nothing less than the 'most striking example of state and community interacting creatively,' already by the eighteenth century 'in attitude and practice, a welfare state.'[4] Lynn Hollen Lees and Anthony Brundage in their studies that extend from the eighteenth century to the eve of the Welfare State have offered valuable estimates of what the Poor Law tradition bequeathed to social welfare in the nineteenth and twentieth centuries. Lees maintains that English social welfare from the late sixteenth century to 1948 was a 'residualist' system; it carried forward its original Elizabethan commitments to pensions, housing, employment, job training, and medical care.[5] Brundage holds that during the old Poor Law years English welfare development acquired its ability to be 'simultaneously consensual, contested, and contingent.'[6]

Looking back through the many layers of the parish's creation and recreation as social welfare agency from the vantage point of its imminent decline in that role at the turn of the nineteenth century, I have been struck by the 'palimpsest' effect of it all. In spite of the changes that accrued to English life and thought over the subsequent four centuries, the earliest pattern of parish-centered social welfare remained recognizable. Government's mandates and custom's momentum certainly were important in this, but likely too was the moral immediacy of local relief: people who lived cheek by jowl caring for and, yes, judging one another.

Notes

Introduction

1   Miri Rubin, *Charity and Community in Medieval Cambridge* (Cambridge, 1987), Introduction, esp. p. 3.

2   E. A. Wrigley and R. S. Schofield, *The Population History of England, 1541–1871* (Cambridge, 1989 [London, 1981]), p. 457.

3   E. M. Leonard, *The Early History of English Poor Relief* (New York, 1965 [1900]); Sidney and Beatrice Webb, *English Local Government: English Poor Law History*: Part I. *The Old Poor Law* (London, 1927); and R. H. Tawney: *The Agrarian Problem in the Sixteenth Century* (New York, 1967 [1912]); and *Religion and the Rise of Capitalism: A Historical Study* (Gloucester, MA, 1954 [1926]). For a critical overview of the work of twentieth-century historians of early modern English social welfare, see: Paul A. Fideler, 'Impressions of a Century of Historiography', *Albion* 32, 3 (Fall 2000), pp. 381–407.

4   David Thomson offers a good introduction to this issue in his, 'Welfare and the Historians', in Lloyd Bonfield, Richard M. Smith, and Keith Wrightson, eds, *The World We Have Gained* (Oxford, 1986), pp. 356–8, 365–7; see also Peter Rushton, 'The Poor Law, The Parish and the Community in North-East England, 1600–1800', in G. C. F. Forster, ed., *Northern History* xxv (1989), pp. 135–6.

5   Peter Lake, 'Periodization, Politics, and "The Social"', *Journal of British Studies* 37 (July 1998), pp. 279–80.

6   Jeremy Gregory, 'The Making of a Protestant Nation: "Success" and "Failure" in England's Long Reformation', in Nicholas Tyacke, ed., *England's Long Reformation 1500–1800* (London, 1998), pp. 314–16;

Patrick Collinson, 'England', in B. Scribner, Roy Porter, and Mikulás Teich, eds, *The Reformation in National Context* (Cambridge, 1994), p. 81.

7 Gregory, 'Protestant Nation', pp. 320–2.

8 James Masschaele, *Peasants, Merchants, and Markets: Inland Trade in Medieval England, 1150–1350* (Basingstoke, 1997), p. 60; L. R. Poos, 'The Social Context of the Statute of Laborers Enforcement', *Law and History Review* I, 1 (Spring 1983), p. 52; Joel Mokyr, ed., *The British Industrial Revolution: An Economic Perspective* (Boulder, CO, 1995), pp. 5, 10–14, 16–19.

9 Keith Wrightson, *English Society, 1580–1680* (London, 1982), p. 11; Fideler, 'Impressions', pp. 386–91.

10 Keith Wrightson, 'The Politics of the Parish in Early Modern England', in Paul Griffiths, Adam Fox, and Steve Hindle, eds, *The Experience of Authority in Early Modern England* (Basingstoke, 1996), p. 10–12.

11 Martin Rein, 'Value-Critical Policy Analysis', in D. Callahan and B. Jennings, eds, *Ethics, the Social Sciences, and Policy Analysis* (New York, 1983), pp. 96–9; emphasis mine; Paul Slack, *Poverty and Policy in Tudor and Stuart England* (London, 1988).

12 Paul Slack *From Reformation to Improvement: Public Welfare in Early Modern England* (Oxford, 1999); A. L. Beier, 'Poverty and Progress in Early Modern England', in Beier, David Cannadine, and J. M. Rosenheim, eds, *The First Modern Society: Essays in English History in Honour of Lawrence Stone* (Cambridge, 1989); Margo Todd, *Christian Humanism and the Puritan Social Order* (Cambridge, 1987); Ole Peter Grell, 'The Protestant Imperative of Christian Care and Neighbourly Love', in Grell and Andrew Cunningham, eds, *Health Care and Poor Relief in Protestant Europe 1500–1700* (London and New York, 1997); and Paul A. Fideler, 'Poverty, Policy and Providence: The Tudors and the Poor', in Fideler and T. F. Mayer, eds, *Political Thought and the Tudor Commonwealth* (London and New York, 1992), ch. 7.

13 Ronald Hutton: *The Rise and Fall of Merry England; The Ritual Year 1400–1700* (Oxford, 1994); and *The Stations of the Sun* (New York 1996); Eamon Duffy, *The Stripping of the Altars: Traditional Religion in England, c.1400–c.1580* (New Haven, CT, 1992).

14 Hutton, *Stations*, pp. 415–18, 426–7; Rubin, *Charity and Community*, pp. 294–9.

15 Duffy, *Stripping of the Altars*, pp. 2–3; Rubin, *Charity and Community*, pp. 54–8. See also Gregory's caution against exaggerating the estrangement between 'literate' and 'illiterate' religious experience ('Protestant Nation', pp. 318–19).

16 Paul A. Fideler, '*Societas, Civitas* and Early Elizabethan Poverty Relief', in Charles Carlton et al., eds, *State, Sovereigns and Society in Early Modern England: Essays in Honour of A. J. Slavin* (Stroud, 1998), pp. 59–69.

17 Wrigley and Schofield, *Population History*, p. 472–80; E. A. Wrigley, 'The Growth of Population in Eighteenth–Century England: A Conundrum Resolved', *Past and Present* 98 (Feb. 1983), p. 149.

18 Keith Wrightson, *Earthly Necessities: Economic Lives in Early Modern Britain* (New Haven, CT, and London, 2000), pp. 4–8.

Chapter 1: The Medieval Societas Christiana *(c.1350–1450)*

1 In this study we are not concerned with the manorial system's outer shell, the 'feudal system', the web that bound greater and lesser estate owners to one another and ultimately to the king through obligations of military service for land ownership.

2 Quoted in G. R. Owst, *Literature and Pulpit in Medieval England*, 2nd edn (New York, 1961), pp. 558, 292.

3 Ibid., p. 561.

4 Geoffrey Chaucer, *The Canterbury Tales*, ed. Arthur Burrell (London, 1908), p. 496.

5 Alan Dyer, *Decline and Growth in English Towns 1400–1640* (London, 1991), pp. 13–14; Christopher Dyer, ' "The Retreat from Marginal Land": The Growth and Decline of Medieval Rural Settlements', in Michael Aston, David Austin, and Christopher Dyer, eds, *The Rural Settlements of Medieval England* (Oxford, 1989), pp. 45–6.

6 R. S. Schofield, 'The Geographical Distribution of Wealth in England, 1334–1649', *Economic History Review*, 2nd ser. XVIII, 3 (December 1965), pp. 483–510. Schofield's findings challenge those of E. J. Buckatzsch that the only significant periods of wealth redistribution were 1086–1150, 1150–1283, 1503–1641, and 1693–1803; see Buckatzsch, 'The Geographical Distribution of Wealth in England, 1086–1843', *Economic History Review*, 2nd ser. III (1950), pp. 180–202.

7 J. Willard, 'Taxation Boroughs and Parliamentary Boroughs, 1294–1336', in J. G. Edwards, V. H. Galbraith, and E. F. Jacobs, eds, *Historical Essays in Honour of James Tait* (Manchester, 1933), p. 424; James Masschaele, *Peasants, Merchants, and Markets: Inland Trade in Medieval England, 1150–1350* (Basingstoke, 1997), pp. 75–7.

8 Richard Britnell, 'The Economy of British Towns, 1300–1540', *The Cambridge Urban History of Britain*, Vol. I, ed. D. M. Palliser (Cambridge, 2000), pp. 327–9.

9 Maryanne Kowaleski, *Local Markets and Regional Trade in Medieval Exeter* (Cambridge, 1995), pp. 1–3, 5, 280–1, 325–6, 330–3; and Masschaele, *Peasants, Merchants, and Markets*, pp. 3–4.

10 Ibid., pp. 3–4, 52–54; Masschaele appropriates 'central place theory' from anthropologists and economic geographers.

11 Ibid., p. 64.

12 N. Mayhew, 'Modelling Medieval Monetisation', in R. H. Britnell and B. M. S. Campbell, eds, *A Commercialising Society* (Manchester, 1995), pp. 57–60.

13 E. A. Kosminsky, *Studies in the Agrarian History of England in the Thirteenth Century*, trans. R. Kisch (Oxford, 1956), pp. 228, 230–7; Christopher Dyer, *Standards of Living in the Later Middle Ages* (Cambridge, 1989), p. 30.; Masschaele, *Peasants, Merchants, and Markets*, p. 124.

14 Ibid., pp. 60, 72; L. R. Poos, 'The Social Context of Statute of Laborers Enforcement', *Law and History Review* I, 1 (Spring 1983), p. 52; Joel Mokyr, ed., *The British Industrial Revolution: An Economic Perspective* (Boulder, CO, 1995), Intro.: pp. 5, 10–14, 16–19.

15 Gratian's and the other canonical collections are identified in Brian Tierney, *The Medieval Poor Law* (Berkeley, CA, 1959), pp. 7–8; for how recondite theology and canon law maxims were put into preachable formulations see: Miri Rubin, *Charity and Community in Medieval Cambridge* (Cambridge, 1987), pp. 58, 77.

16 Matthew 19:21: 'If you would be perfect, go, sell what you possess and give to the poor, and you will have treasure in heaven; and come, follow me'. Luke 6:20–5: 'Blessed are you poor, for yours is the kingdom of God. Blessed are you that weep now, for you shall laugh ... etc.'

17 For example, James 2:14–17: 'If a brother or sister is ill-clad and in lack of daily food, and one of you says to them, "Go in peace, be warmed and filled," without giving them the things needed for the body, what does is profit? So, faith by itself, if it has no works, is dead.'

18 'When the Son of man shall come in his glory, and all the holy angels with him, then shall he sit upon the throne of his glory: And before him shall be gathered all nations: and he shall separate them one from another, as a shepherd divideth [his] sheep from the goats: And he shall set the sheep on his right hand, but the goats on the left. Then shall the King say unto them on his right hand, Come, ye blessed of my father, inherit the kingdom prepared for you from the foundation of the world: For I was an hungred, and ye gave me meat: I was thirsty, and ye gave me drink: I was a stranger, and ye took me in: Naked, and ye clothed me: I was sick, and ye visited me: I was in prison and ye came unto me. Then shall the righteous answer him, saying, Lord when saw we thee an hungred, and fed [thee]? Or thirsty, and gave [thee] drink? When saw we thee a stranger, and took [thee] in? Or naked, and clothed [thee]? Or when saw we thee sick, or in prison, and came unto thee? And the King shall answer and say unto them, Verily I say unto you, Inasmuch as ye have done [it] unto one of the least of these my brethren, ye have done [it] unto me. Then shall he say also unto them on the left hand, Depart from me, ye cursed, into everlasting fire, prepared for the devil and his angels.... And these shall go away into everlasting punishment: but the righteous into eternal life' (25:31–46).

19 These foci of aspiration and behavior, along with the seven sacraments (Baptism, Confession, the Eucharist, Confirmation, Marriage, Holy Orders, and Extreme Unction) were propounded to the laity four times a year through the instructional scheme, *De informacione simplicium*, known better from its opening words as the *Ignorantia Sacerdotum*, that dated from Archbishop Pecham's provincial Council of Lambeth in 1281. Subsequently it was translated into English for use in the Northern Province in 1357 and in the Diocese of Wells in 1425 and reissued by Cardinal Wolsey as late as 1518; see Eamon Duffy, *The Stripping of the Altars: Traditional Religion in England, c. 1400–1580* (New Haven, CT, 1992), pp. 53–4.

20 *The Book of Vices and Virtues*, ed. W. Nelson Francis, Early English Texts Society, orig. ser. No. 217 (London, 1942), pp. 213–19.

21 Thomas Aquinas, *Summa Theologica*, trans. English Dominican Fathers (New York, 1947), II, Pt II, q. 66, art. 2, p. 1477; q. 184, art. 1, p. 1950; q. 25, art. 1, p. 1286; q. 32, arts. 1–3, pp. 1321–6; *Summa Contra Gentiles*, trans. English Dominican Fathers (London, 1923–29), III, Pt II, chs 128, 125.

22 Quoted in Tierney, *Poor Law*, pp. 37–8.

23 Aquinas, *Gentiles*, chs 125, 128, 133, 135, 141; Bonaventure, 'The Defense of the Mendicants', trans. Jose de Vinck, *The Works of Bonaventure*, Vol. IV (Patterson, NJ, 1966), pp. 31, 37–8, 48.

24 See: Howard R. Patch, *The Goddess Fortuna in Mediaeval Literature* (New York, 1967 [1927]).

25 Thomas Aquinas, *Questiones quodlibetal*, VII, art. 17c; quoted in Richard M. Douglas, 'Talent and Vocation in Humanist and Protestant Thought', in Theodore K. Rabb and Jerrold E. Seigel, eds, *Action and Contemplation in Early Modern Europe* (Princeton, NJ 1969), p. 280; *Theologica*, Vol. 2, Pt. 2, q. 25, art. 1, p. 1286; q. 66, art. 2, p. 1477, q. 184, art. 1, p. 1950.

26 *Gentiles*, chs 133, 141.

27 According to Guido de Baysio, for a charitable act to be a good work formally and canonically in the eyes of God it must adhere to three principles: *justice* (the gift should be from the donor's legally acquired property); *order* (righteousness should be in the superior place in the donor's soul); and *right intention* (the donor should be motivated by true charity, not to win praise or avoid embarrassment); see Tierney, *Poor Law*, p. 53.

28 As we will see, the government's mandating of liberality expressed through the parish was the core of the Elizabethan Poor Law.

29 Aquinas, *Theologica*, II–II, q. 81, art. 1, p. 1563; q. 66, arts. 7, 8. pp. 1480–1.

30 D. L. Douie, *The Nature and the Effect of the Heresy of the Fraticelli* (Manchester, 1932), pp. 192–3.

31 Masschaele, *Peasants, Merchants, and Markets*, pp. 51–4.

32 This insightful formulation was coined by Olwen H. Hufton (*The Poor of Eighteenth-Century France, 1750–1789* [Oxford, 1974], Introduction, chs iii and iv) and applied to the study of the poor in seventeenth-century England by Tim Wales ('Poverty, Poor Relief and the Life-Cycle: Some Evidence from Seventeenth-Century Norfolk', in *Land, Kinship and Life-Cycle*, Richard M. Smith, ed. [Cambridge, 1984], pp. 360, 364–5. A recent discussion of the 'economy of makeshifts' in the historiography of early industrial social welfare in England is Steven King and Alannah Tomkins's Introduction to their edited volume, *The Poor in England, 1700–1850: An Economy of Makeshifts* (Manchester and New York, 2003).

33 Tierney, *Poor Law*, p. 85.

34 Ibid., pp. 70, 89, 96–7, 101–4.

35 Quoted in Rubin, *Charity and Community*, p. 239.

36 Tierney, *Poor Law*, pp. 79–83.

37 Ibid., pp. 108–9, 126–8.

38 Faye Getz, *Medicine in the English Middle Ages* (Princeton, NJ, 1998), pp. 4, 5, 7, 92; Carole Rawcliffe, 'Curing Bodies and Healing Souls: Pilgrimage and Sick in Medieval East Anglia', in Colin Morris and Peter Roberts, eds, *Pilgrimage: The English Experience from Becket to Bunyan* (Cambridge, 2000), pp. 108–10.

39 Ibid., pp. 108, 110; Getz, *Medicine*, pp. 4, 5, 7, 92.

40 Nicholas Orme and Margaret Webster, *The English Hospital, 1070–1570* (New Haven, CT, 1995), pp. 22, 32–41.

41 Ibid., pp. 41, 67–8.

42 Ibid., pp. 41–2.

43 Ibid., p. 118.

44 Carole Rawcliffe, *Medicine for the Soul* (Stroud, 1999), p. 170.

45 Ibid., pp. 62, 69–75, 122–3.

46 Tierney, *Poor Law*, pp. 110–19.

47 Rubin, *Charity and Community*, p. 68.

48 Quoted in Rodney Hilton, 'Status and Class in the Medieval Town', in T. R. Slater and Gervase Rosser, eds *The Church in the Medieval Town* (Aldershot, 1998), pp. 12–13.

49 Rawcliffe, *Medicine*, p. 215.

50 Rubin, *Charity and Community*, pp. 72–3, 79–80.

51 Ibid., p. 68: 'If the theologians saw the poor as living the life of Christ, ordinary people who encountered poverty and begging all around them were inclined to be less charitable.... In practice finer distinctions of degrees of poverty were needed not only for the pious faithful but for the administrators of parochial relief and for almoners of religious institutions.... The *Glossa ordinaria*, the basic commentary on the *Decretum* throughout the late Middle Ages, surveyed all current views and settled for a scale of merit based on the recipient's virtue as well as his closeness to the giver'.

52 Rawcliffe, *Medicine*, p. 193.

53 C. Dyer, 'The "Retreat from Marginal Land"' pp. 45–46.

54 A servant was unmarried and resided in the employer's household on a yearly basis, while a laborer lived elsewhere and committed to less than an annual term; see Poos, 'Social Context', pp. 34–6, 50–2; for land value and amounts in cultivation, see D. C. Coleman, *The Economy of England, 1450–1750* (London, 1977), pp. 41–2.

55   Poos, 'Social Context', pp. 28–9.

56   Ibid., pp. 28–30.

57   Cited from C. J. Ribton-Turner, *A History of Vagrants and Vagrancy and Beggars and Begging* (London, 1887), pp. 51–2.

58   *The Statutes of the Realm*, 12 vols (London, 1963 [reprint of the 1810–28 edn]), I, pp. 307, 311.

59   Marjorie K. McIntosh, *Controlling Misbehavior in England, 1370–1600* (Cambridge, 1998).

60   Ibid., Intro., pp. 81–2; see also: Martin Ingram, 'Reformation of Manners in Early Modern England', in Paul Griffiths, Adam Fox, and Steve Hindle, eds, *The Experience of Authority in Early Modern England* (Basingstoke, 1996), pp. 47–88; and Margaret Spufford, 'Puritanism and Social Control?', in A. Fletcher and J. Stevenson, eds, *Order and Disorder in Early Modern England* (Cambridge, 1985), pp. 41–57.

61   Hostiensis: 'The meaning is this, that priests ought to admonish their parishioners about two things. First, that they should be hospitable, good almsgivers and charitable toward the poor, for it is not enough that they pay tithes in full unless they give alms from the other nine parts; and second that they should not sell more dearly [to traders].... But as to hospitality both priests and bishops shall content themselves with admonition', quoted in Tierney, *Poor Law*, pp. 126–7. The important theological point here – and an important one later for neo-Stoics and others displeased with the mandates of the Poor Law – was that the spiritual or moral value and reciprocality of almsgiving is lost if it must be coerced.

62   Jean Froissart, *Chronicles of England, France and Adjoining Countries*, trans. Thomas Jones, 4 vols (Havod, 1803–15), II, pp. 459–60.

63   Rodney Hilton, *Class Conflict and the Crisis of Feudalism* (London, 1990), pp. 143–7, 149–50.

64   Paul A. Fideler, 'Varieties of Early Modern Political Culture' (review essay), *Journal of British Studies* 41, 2 (April 2002), p. 233.

65   II.26; quoted in G. C. Coulton, *Social Life in Britain From the Conquest to the Reformation* (Cambridge, 1919), p. 353.

66   John de Burgo, 'Pupilla Oculi', Pt. V, c. ix; quoted in Coulton, pp. 341–2.

67   John Hatcher, 'England in the Aftermath of the Black Death', *Past and Present* 144 (August 1994), pp. 12–13, 20–5, 29, 31–4.

68   *The Book of Vices and Virtues*, p. 32–42.

69 William Langland, *The Vision of Piers the Plowman*, Modern English by Henry Wells (New York, 1945), Passus I, p. 17, Passus III, pp. 29–30, 36, Passus VII, p. 91.

70 A useful analysis of Robin Hood and other medieval outlaw heroes in their contexts is: Maurice H. Keen, *The Outlaws of Medieval Legend* (London, 1961).

71 Ibid., p. 101.

72 Margaret Aston, ' "Caim's Castles": Poverty, Politics, and Disendowment', in Barrie Dobson, ed., *The Church, Politics and Patronage in the Fifteenth Century* (New York, 1984), pp. 51–3.

73 Aubry Gwynn, *The English Austin Friars in the Time of Wyclif* (Oxford, 1940), pp. 67, 85.

74 H. B. Workman, *John Wyclif*, 2 vols (Oxford, 1926), I, pp. 104, 119.

75 Aston, 'Caim's Castles', pp. 46–7.

76 Quoted in ibid., pp. 48–9.

77 Ibid., pp. 49–50, 55, 57–8, 63.

78 Orme and Webster, *English Hospital*, pp. 129–31; Rubin, *Charity and Community*, pp. 294–5.

79 Orme and Webster, *English Hospital*, p. 119–20.

80 Patricia H. Cullum, ' "For Pore People Harberles": What was the Function of the Maisonsdieu?', in Dorothy J. Clayton, Richard G. Davies, and Peter MacNiven, eds, *Trade, Devotion and Governance* (Stroud, 1994), pp. 36–9, 41–6, 48, 49–51.

81 Sarah Rees Jones, 'Thomas More's *Utopia* and medieval London', in Rosemary Horrox and Sarah Rees Jones, eds, *Pragmatic Utopias: Ideals and Communities, 1200–1630* (Cambridge, 2001), pp. 117–35.

82 Arthur B. Ferguson, *The Articulate Citizen and the English Renaissance* (Durham, NC, 1965), chs 1, 3.

83 David Starkey, 'Which age of reform?', in C. Coleman and D. Starkey, eds, *Revolution Reassessed* (Oxford, 1986), pp. 15, 21–2; Mavis Mate, 'The Economic and Social Roots of Medieval Popular Rebellion: Sussex in 1450–51', *Economic History Review* XLV, 4 (Nov. 1992), pp 661–76.

84 *Statutes*, II, pp. 56, 58.

85 Quoted in Chris Given-Wilson, 'Service, Serfdom and English Labor Legislation, 1350–1500', in Anne Curry and Elizabeth Matthew, eds, *Concepts and Patterns of Service in the Later Middle Ages* (Woodbridge, 2000), pp. 21–4.

86 Ibid., pp. 25–8; Poos, 'Social Context', pp. 50–2.

Chapter 2: From God's Poor to Man's (c.1450–1540)

1 D. C. Coleman, *The Economy of England, 1450–1750 (Oxford, 1977)*, pp. 41–2; Christopher Dyer, *Everyday Life in Medieval England* (London, 1994), p. 45.

2 Cited from R. H. Tawney and Eileen Power, eds, *Tudor Economic Documents*, 3 vols (London, 1924), I, pp. 4–5.

3 C. Dyer, *Everyday Life*, pp. 34–6.

4 Ibid., pp. 37–8, 42; Margaret Spufford, *Contrasting Communities: English Villagers in the Sixteenth and Seventeenth Centuries* (Cambridge, 1974), pp. 46, 48, 55, 90–1, 94, 118, 121, 200, 205, 208, 350.

5 Richard Britnell, 'The Economy of British Towns, 1300–1540', *The Cambridge Urban History of Britain*, Vol. I (600–1540), D. M. Palliser, ed., (Cambridge, 2000), pp. 316–20.

6 Edmund Dudley, *The Tree of Commonwealth [c.1510]*, ed. D. M. Brodie (Cambridge, 1948), p. 140.

7 Coleman, *Economy*, p. 72.

8 Britnell, 'The Economy of British Towns', pp. 325–7.

9 Cited from N. B. Harte, 'State Control of Dress and Social Change in Pre-Industrial England', in D. C. Coleman and A. H. John, eds, *Trade, Government and Economy in Pre-Industrial England* (London, 1976), p. 139.

10 Ruth Mohl, *The Three Estates in Medieval and Renaissance Literature* (New York, 1933), pp. 97, 383.

11 Colin Platt, *The English Medieval Town* [London, 1976], pp. 96–102.

12 See W. C. Hazlitt, ed., *Remains of the Early Popular Poetry of England* (London, 1866), III, pp. 255ff., pp. 267ff.

13 Sir John Fortescue, *Governance of England*, ed. Charles Plummer (Oxford, 1885), p. 140.

14 John Longland, *Sermonde at Grenewiche* (London, 1538), sig. Gi, r; quoted in J. W. Blench, *Preaching in England in the Late Fifteenth and Early Sixteenth Centuries* (Oxford, 1964), p. 242.

15 Sebastian Brant, *The Ship of Fools*, trans. Alexander Barclay, ed. T. H. Jamieson, 2 vols (Edinburgh, 1874), II, pp. 31, 99–107, 184ff.; Johannes Baptista Mantuan, *The Cytezen and Uplondyshman*, trans. Alexander Barclay, ed. R. W. Fairholt, Percey Society; Early English Poetry, Vol. XXII (London, 1847), pp. 1–19, 28.

16 Clement Armstrong, 'How to Reforme the Realme in Settyng Them to Werke and to Restore Tillage [c.1535–36]', in *Tudor Economic Documents*, III, p. 127.

17 E. M. Leonard, *The Early History of English Poor Relief* (New York, 1965 [1900]), pp. 25–6.

18 *The Statutes of the Realm*, 12 vols (London, 1963 [repr. of 1810–28 edn]), III, pp. 328–32.

19 Ronald Hutton, *The Stations of the Sun: A History of the Ritual Year in Britain* (New York, 1996), pp. 412–14.

20 Useful on the liminality issues surrounding the purgatory doctrine is Stephen Greenblatt, *Hamlet in Purgatory* (Princeton, NJ, 2001), ch. 1.

21 See, for example, A. R. Hands, *Charities and Social Aid in Greece and Rome* (London, 1968), ch. 3: 'Giving for a Return'.

22 Ronald Hutton, *The Rise and Fall of Merry England* (New York, 1994), pp. 21–3, 57.

23 Colin Richmond, 'Victorian Values in Fifteenth-Century England: The Ewelme Almshouse Statutes', in Rosemary Horrox and Sarah Rees Jones, eds, *Pragmatic Utopias: Ideals and Communities, 1200–1630* (Cambridge, 2001), ch. 13.

24 Marjorie K. McIntosh, *Controlliing Misbehavior in England, 1370–1600* (Cambridge, 1998), pp. 116–19.

25 Ibid., pp. 81–3, 119–22.

26 Tim Cooper, *The Last Generation of English Catholic Clergy: Parish Priests in the Diocese of Coventry and Lichfield in the Early Sixteenth Century* (Woodbridge, 1999), pp. 30–1, 34, 35.

27 Arthur G. Dickens, *The English Reformation* (London, 1964), pp. 25–36; for active Lollard reform activity in 1490s Coventry, see P. J. P. Goldberg, 'Coventry's "Lollard" Programme of 1492 and the Making of Utopia', in *Pragmatic Utopias*, pp. 97–116.

28 Henry Parker, *Dives and Pauper* (London, 1534), p. 140b.

29 Julia Carnwath, 'The Churchwardens' Accounts of Thame, Oxfordshire, *c.*1443–1524', in Dorothy L.. Clayton, Richard G. Davies, and Peter Macviven, eds, *Trade, Devotion and Governance* (Stroud, 1994), pp. 190–4.

30 Eamon Duffy, *The Stripping of the Altars: Traditional Religion in England c.1400–c.1580* (New Haven, CT, 1992), pp. 357–66; Miri Rubin, 'The Poor', in Rosemary Horrox, ed., *Fifteenth-Century Attitudes: Perceptions of Society in Late Medieval England* (Cambridge, 1994), pp. 178–80.

31 For example, only 1.66 percent in London parishes during the 1470s, compared to 19.27 percent in the first decade of the seventeenth century. According to Gary Gibbs, by the later decade

churchwardens' accounts reveal quite different parish activities: 'Gone were chantries, relics, shrines, anchorites. Prayers for the dead had been replaced by alms for the living, private masses had given way to public sermons, and devotions to saints had been replaced by service to King and country.' See Gibbs, 'New Duties for the Parish Community in Tudor London', in Katherine L. French, Gary G. Gibbs, and Beat A. Kümin, eds, *The Parish in English Life, 1400–1600* (Manchester, 1997), pp. 164, 177.

32   Marjorie K. McIntosh, 'Local responses to the Poor in Late Medieval and Tudor England', *Continuity and Change* 3, 2 (1988), pp. 219–21.

33   For a beginning on these transitions, see: Carolly Erickson, *The Medieval Vision* (New York, 1976), pp. 117–19; Lawrence Stone, *The Crisis of the Aristocracy* (Oxford, 1976), p. 21, and *The Family, Sex and Marriage in England 1500–1800* (New York, 1977), pp. 134, 139, 148; Franklin Le Van Baumer, *The Early Tudor Theory of Kingship* (New York, 1966), pp. 18–20, 28, 37; R. Schlatter, *Private Property* (New Brunswick, NJ, 1951), pp. 72–5; Arthur B. Ferguson, *Clio Unbound* (Durham, NC, 1979), pp. 242–5, 356–61, and *The Indian Summer of English Chivalry* (Durham, NC, 1960), pp. 149–50, 219–20; F. J. Levy, *Tudor Historical Thought* (San Marino, CA, 1967), p. 287; and Dickens, *English Reformation*, pp. 136–8. For the deep insecurity of the early sixteenth century, see: A. F. Pollard, *England under Protector Somerset* (London, 1900), p. 200; and G. M. Trevelyan, *English Social History* (London, 1946), p. 117.

34   Stephen Greenblatt, *Renaissance Self-Fashioning: More to Shakespeare* (Chicago, 1980), pp. 7, 157.

35   Whitney R. D. Jones, *The Tudor Commonwealth, 1529–1559* (London, 1970); J. J. Scarisbrick, 'Cardinal Wolsey and the Common Weal', in E. W. Ives, R. J. Knecht, and J. J. Scarisbrick, eds, *Wealth and Power in Tudor England* (London, 1978), pp. 45–67; and John A. Guy: 'The Tudor Commonwealth: Revising Thomas Cromwell', *Historical Journal* 23 (1980), p. 685; and *Christopher St German on Chancery and Statute*, Seldon Society, suppl ser. 1985, Vol. 6.

36   For the primacy of social conditions, see: G. R. Elton: 'An Early Tudor Poor Law', *Economic History Review*, 2nd ser., VI (1953), p. 55, and *Reform and Renewal* (Cambridge, 1973), ch. 4; and Susan Brigden, *London and the Reformation* (Oxford, 1989), pp. 481–2. Advocates for Christian humanism's crucial role included: Paul A. Fideler,

'Christian Humanism and Poor Law Reform in Early Tudor England', *Societas* IV, 4 (1974), pp. 269–85; Scarisbrick, 'Cardinal Wolsey', pp. 45–67; Guy, 'The Tudor Commonwealth', p. 685; and Margo Todd, *Christian Humanism and the Puritan Social Order* (Cambridge, 1987), ch. 2. On 'putting the thought back in' see: Paul Slack, *Poverty and Policy in Tudor and Stuart England* (London, 1988), pp. 2–7; A. L. Beier, 'Poverty and Progress in Early Modern England', in Beier, David Cannadine, and J. M. Rosenheim, eds, *The First Modern Society: Essays in English History in Honour of Lawrence Stone* (Cambridge, 1989), pp. 236–8; and Paul A. Fideler, 'Poverty, Policy, and Providence: The Tudors and the Poor', in Fideler and T. F. Mayer, eds, *Political Thought and the Tudor Commonwealth* (London and New York, 1992), ch. 7.

37 For the importance of Lutheranism to the poverty and health care initiatives in England and Northern Europe, see: Ole Peter Grell and Andrew Cunningham, 'The Reformation and Changes in Welfare Provision in Early Modern Northern Europe', and Grell, 'The Protestant Imperative of Christian Care and Neighbourly Love', in Grell and Cunningham, eds, *Health Care and Poor Relief in Protestant Europe, 1500–1700* (London and New York, 1997), chs. 1, 2.

38 Paul Slack, *From Reformation to Improvement: Public Welfare in Early Modern England* (Oxford, 1999), pp. 8–21.

39 Ibid., pp. 10–11, n. 29; see Grell, 'Protestant Imperative', p. 52, for his agreement on this.

40 For this agreement, see also: Fideler, 'Poverty, Policy', pp. 195, 198–9.

41 Richard Tuck, *Philosophy and Government, 1572–1651*(Cambridge, 1993), pp. 21–2.

42 Cicero, *The thre bookes of Tullius offyce*, trans. R. Whittinton (London, 1534), pp. C.5.b, C.8.b, D.2.b, I.6.b.

43 For a comparison of the *Institutio* and *Utopia*, see: Alistair Fox, 'English Humanism and the Body Politic', in Fox and John A. Guy, eds, *Reassessing the Henrician Age* (Oxford, 1986), pp. 37–8.

44 Erasmus, *Education of a Christian Prince* (New York, 1936 [1516]), p. 159.

45 Thomas Elyot, *The Boke Named the Governor* [1531], ed. Henry H. S. Croft, 2 vols (London, 1883), I, pp.1–2.

46 Cicero, 'thre bookes', pp. G.1–G.8.

47 *Statutes*, II, p. 569.

48 Thomas More, *Utopia*, J. H. Hexter and Eward Surtz, eds, *The Complete Works of St. Thomas More*, Vol. 4 (New Haven, CT, 1965), pp. 127, 131–3, 147, 159, 179–81, 197–8.

49 George Logan, *The Meaning of More's Utopia* (Princeton, NJ, 1983), Prolegomena, pp. 157–9; Quentin Skinner, *The Foundations of Modern Political Thought*, 2 vols (Cambridge, 1978), vol. I, ch. 9; and 'Sir Thomas More's *Utopia* and the Language of Renaissance Humanism', in Anthony Pagden, ed., *The Languages of Political Theory in Early-Modern Europe* (Cambridge, 1987), pp. 123–57.

50 Fenlon and Skinner maintain that More did intend that European states should emulate Utopian institutions, while Hexter, Brandshaw, and Logan believe that he did not. Bradshaw summarizes his own views and those of Hexter, Fenlon, and the early Skinner in 'More on Utopia', *Historical Journal* 24 (1981), pp. 5, 27. See also: Skinner, *Foundations*, pp. 124, 156–7; and Logan, *Meaning*, p. 270.

51 For some sense of the sites, ideologies, and historiographies involved, see: Natalie, Z. Davis, 'Poor Relief, Humanism and Heresy: The Case of Lyon', *Studies in Medieval and Renaissance History* 5 (1968): 217–75; H. J. Grimm, 'Luther's Contributions to Sixteenth-Century Organization of Poor Relief', *Archiv fur Reformationsgeschichte* 61 (1970), pp. 222–34; Grell, 'Protestant Imperative', pp. 43–53; Robert M. Kingdon, 'Social Welfare in Calvin's Geneva', *American Historical Review* 76 (1971), pp. 50–69; and Brian Pullan, *Rich and Poor in Renaissance Venice* (Oxford, 1971), pp. 239–91.

52 Juan Vives, 'Concerning the Relief of the Poor' [*De subventione pauperum* 1526], trans Margaret Sherwood, *Studies in Social Work* 11 (1917), pp. 9, 21–2, 27, 33, 36, 44–7.

53 Grell, 'Protestant Imperative', pp. 47, 51; Grimm, 'Luther's Contributions'; and Martin Luther, *Ordinance for a Common Chest* (1523), in Salter, *Early Tracts*, pp. 80–96.

54 Grell, 'Protestant Imperative', pp. 52–3, 63 n. 39.

55 Luther, 'Ordinance'.

56 Martin Luther, *The Freedom of a Christian* (1520), trans. B. L. Woolf, *The Reformation Writings of Luther* (London, 1952), pp. 357–8.

57 B. A. Gerrish, *Grace and Reason: A Study in the Theology of Luther* (Oxford, 1962), pp. 13, 70–1.

58 Richard M. Douglas, 'Talent and Vocation in Humanistic and Protestant Thought', in T. K. Rabb and J. E. Seigel, eds, *Action and Conviction in Early Modern Europe* (Princeton, NJ, 1969), pp. 291–5;

D. C. Ziemke, *Love for the Neighbor in Luther's Theology* (Minneapolis, 1963), p. 72; Ernst Troeltsch, *The Social Teaching of the Christian Churches*, trans. O. Wyon, 2 vols (New York, 1931), II, pp. 540–1, 557.

59 Charles Trinkaus, 'The Religious Foundations of Luther's Social Views', in J. H. Mundy, ed., *Essays in Medieval Life and Thought* (New York, 1955), p. 72.

60 William Tyndale, *Prologue upon the Gospel of St Matthew* (1523), in H. Walter, ed., *Doctrinal Treatises and Introductions to Different Portions of the Holy Scriptures* (Cambridge, 1848), pp. 469–70; see also *The Work of William Tyndale*, G. E. Duffield, ed. (Appleford, 1964), p. xxxii; and W. A. Clebsch, *England's Earliest Protestants* (New Haven, CT, 1964), pp. 187–8.

61 William Tyndale, *An Exposition upon...Matthew*, Duffield, *William Tyndale*, pp. 283–4.

62 William Tyndale, *The Prologue into the Fourth Booke of Moses called Numeri*, in T. Russell, ed., *The Works of the English Reformers: William Tyndale and John Frith*, 3 vols (London, 1831), I, p. 43.

63 Fritz Caspari, *Humanism and the Social Order in England* (Chicago, 1954), p. 49.

64 G. R. Elton, *Policy and Police* (Cambridge, 1972), ch. 2; Keith Thomas, *Religion and the Decline of Magic* (New York, 1971), chs. 5, 6, 9, 13.

65 Thomas Starkey, *A Dialogue between Pole and Lupset* (1529–32?), T. F. Mayer, ed. (London, 1989), p. 61; the insdispensable study of Starkey is Mayer, *Thomas Starkey and the Commonweal* (Cambridge, 1989).

66 Starkey, *Dialogue*, pp. 20, 96; Mayer, *Thomas Starkey*, pp. 205–6; Thomas Starkey, *An exhortation...to unitie and obedience* (London, 1536), pp. 5b–6a; for the mixing of 'languages' or 'paradigmatic structures' into ambivalent or polyvalent expression, see: J. G. A. Pocock, *Virtue, Commerce, and History* (Cambridge, 1985), Introduction, esp. pp. 9, 25.

67 Richard Morison, *A Remedy for Sedition* [1536], ed. E. M. Cox (London, 1933), pp. 35–6.

68 Ibid., pp.16–17

69 Henry Parker, *Dives and Pauper* (London, 1534), p. 323a; Fideler, 'Christian Humanism and Poor Law Reform', pp. 279–80.

70 Starkey, *Dialogue*, pp. 54, 91ff.

71 Morison, *Remedy*, pp. 12–13.

72 Carole Rawcliffe, *Medicine for the Soul* (Stroud, 1999), pp 211–12, 217, 219; see also M. Dowling: 'Anne Boleyn and Reform', *Journal of Ecclesiastical History* XXXV (1984), and *Humanism and the Age of Henry VIII* (London, 1986); and E. W. Ives, *Anne Boleyn* (Oxford, 1986).

73 Simon Fish, *A Supplication for the Beggars* (1529?), ed. Frederick J. Furnival, Early English Text Society, Ex. ser. No. 13 (London, 1871), pp. 3, 8, 13; Greenblatt, *Hamlet in Purgatory*, pp. 35, 39–40, 145–50.

74 Thomas More, *A Supplycacion of Soulys* (London, 1529), pp. iiib, va–b, and xxiia.

75 G. R. Elton, 'An Early Tudor Poor Law', *Economic History Review*, 2nd ser., 6 (1953), pp. 55–67.

76 Elton, *Reform and Renewal*, pp. 123–4.

77 *Statutes*, vol. III, pp. 558–62.

78 Elton, *Reform and Renewal*, pp. 124–5

79 Articles 2 and 3 in the Lincoln Articles (1 October 1536); Articles 9, 13, and 14 in the Pontefract Articles (4 December 1536), in R. W. Hoyle, *The Pilgrimage of Grace and the Politics of the 1530s* (Oxford, 2001), pp. 455–6, 461–2.

80 Ibid., pp. 250–5.

81 C. S. L. Davies, 'Popular Religion and the Pilgrimage of Grace', in Anthony Fletcher and John Stevenson, eds, *Order and Disorder in Early Modern England* (Cambridge, 1985), p. 78; Scott M. Harrison, *The Pilgrimage of Grace in the Lake Counties, 1536–37* (London, 1981), p. 44.

82 Henry VIII, [to the Commissioners the Subsidy] (1536), *Letters and Papers, Foreign and Domestic*, catalogued by J. S. Brewer, 2nd rev. edn, 21 vols (Vaduz, 1965 [reprint of 1888 edn]), Vol. XI, No. 569, p. 226.

83 Pontefract Articles 12 and 15, in Hoyle, *Pilgrimage*, p. 462.

84 Davies, 'Popular Religion', p. 74.

85 Hoyle, *Pilgrimage*, pp. 450–3.

86 Davies, 'Popular Religion', pp. 76–87.

87 Nicholas Orme and Margaret Webster, *The English Hospital, 1070–1570* (New Haven, CT, 1995), p. 148.

88 Ibid., pp. 148–50.

89 Andrew Wear, 'Religious Beliefs and Medicine in Early Modern England', in Wear, ed., *Health and Healing in Early Modern England* (Aldershot, 1998), ch. V, pp. 147–9.

90   Robert Copland, *Hyeway to the Spittal House* (London, 1535–36),
     pp. B.ia–B.ivb, C.iiib–D.iva.
91   Orme and Webster, *English Hospitals*, pp. 156–7.
92   Ibid., pp. 157–9.
93   Rawcliffe, *Medicine for the Soul*, ch. VIII.

Chapter 3   Parish, Town, and Poor Law (c.1540–1610)

 1   E. A. Wrigley and R. S. Schofield, *The Population History of England:
     A Reconstruction* (Cambridge, 1989), pp. 402–4.
 2   The historians whose work is distilled in these estimates include:
     W. G. Hoskins, C. Phythian-Adams, T. J. Tronrud, J. F. Pound,
     T. Arkell, C. Husbands, and A. L. Beier. Their efforts are grace-
     fully summarized in Beier, 'Poverty and Progress in Early Modern
     England', in Beier, David Cannadine, and J. M. Rosenheim,
     eds, *The First Modern Society: Essays in English History in Honour of
     Lawrence Stone* (Cambridge, 1989), pp. 203–5.
 3   Peter Clark and Paul Slack, eds, *Crisis and Order in English Towns*
     (London, 1972), p. 9; John Patten, *English Towns 1500–1700*
     (Hamden, CT, 1978), pp. 111–12.
 4   This anomaly is one of several that is explored with perspicacity by
     Keith Wrightson in his *English Society* (London, 1982).
 5   Ibid., pp. 40–1.
 6   Ibid., pp. 126–7; Margaret Spufford, *Contrasting Communities: English
     Villagers in the Sixteenth and Seventeenth Centuries* (Cambridge, 1974),
     pp. 46, 48, 55, 90–1, 94, 118, 121.
 7   D. C. Coleman, *The Economy of England, 1450–1750* (Oxford, 1977),
     p. 34, 43–4; B. A. Holderness, *Pre-Industrial England: Economy and
     Society from 1500 to 1750* (London, 1976), pp. 32–3, 47–8, 51–5, 76–7.
 8   Ibid., p. 56; Coleman, *Economy*, p. 36; Cited in Maurice Beresford
     and John G. Hurst, eds, *Deserted Medieval Villages* (Gloucester,
     1971), p. 18.
 9   Wrightson, *English Society*, pp. 127–8.
10   Clark and Slack, *Crisis and Order*, Introduction. Three essays in the
     volume achieved a considerable half-life: Charles Phythian-Adams,
     'Ceremony and the Citizen: The Communal Year at Coventry,
     1450–1550, pp. 57–85; Clark, 'The Migrant in Kentish Towns,
     1580–1640', pp. 117–63; and Slack, 'Poverty and Politics in Salisbury,
     1597–1666', pp. 164–203.

11 See my elaborations on these matters: Paul A. Fideler, 'Impressions of a Century of Historiography', *Albion* 32, 3 (Fall 200), pp. 386–91, and 'Varieties of Early Modern Political Culture', *Journal of British Studies* 41, 2 (April 2002), pp. 232–3, 243.

12 Clark and Slack, *Crisis and Order*, pp. 4–10, 17–19.

13 Ibid., p. 20.

14 Peter Clark and Paul Slack, *English Towns in Transition, 1500–1700* (New York, 1976), pp. 124–5, 158–9.

15 David Dean, *Law-Making and Society in Late Elizabethan England: The Parliament of England, 1584–1601* (Cambridge, 1996), pp. 12–13.

16 Ian W. Archer, *The Pursuit of Stability: Social Relations in Elizabethn London* (Cambridge, 1991), pp. 11, 14–16, 28–49, 50–1.

17 See, for example, Patten, *English towns*, pp. 76–9, 124–5, 145.

18 Valerie Pearl, 'Social Policy in Early Modern London', in Hugh Lloyd-Jones, Pearl, and Blair Worden, eds, *History and Imagination: Essays in Honour of H. R. Trevor-Roper* (London, 1981), p. 17.

19 Steve Rappaport, *Worlds Within Worlds: Structures of Life in Sixteenth-Century London* (Cambridge, 1989), chs 1–4.

20 Claire S. Schen, 'Constructing the Poor in Early Seventeenth Century London', *Albion* 32, 3 (Fall 2000): 450–63.

21 Thomas Lever, 'A fruitful sermon made in Poules Church', ed. E. Arber, *Sermons* (London, 1871), pp. 24, 29; Hugh Latimer, 'Sermon of the Plough', ed. G. E. Corrie, *Works*, 2 vols (Cambridge, 1844–5), I, p. 61.

22 Henry Brinkelow, *The Complaynt of Roderyck Mors, etc.* (1542), ed. J. M. Cowper, EETS, extra ser., no. 22, pp. 73–4; and *The Lamentacyon of a Christen Agaynst the Cytye of London, etc.* (1545), ibid., pp. 119.

23 Robert Crowley, *The Way to Wealth* (1550), *Selected Works*, EETS, extra ser., no. 15, pp. 132–8, 141–2,145.

24 S. T. Bindoff, *Kett's Rebellion* (London, 1949), pp. 7, 23.

25 S. K. Land, *The Norfolk Rising of 1549* (Ipswich, 1977), p. 72.

26 Sir John Cheke, *The hurt of sedicion...to a commune welth* (London, 1549) *STC* 5109, p. B.iii.a.

27 Quoted in Ronald Hutton, *The Rise and Fall of Merry England; The Ritual Year, 1400–1700* (Oxford, 1994), pp. 86–9.

28 Thomas Becon, *News out of Heaven* (*c*.1540), ed. Rev. John Ayre, *Works*, 3 vols (Cambridge, 1843), I, p. 42. A somewhat less bleak, but still Protestant view was expressed by the scholar, statesman and Marian exile, Thomas Wilson: 'Man, by nature has a spark of

knowledge, and by the secret working of God, judges after a sort, and discerns good from evil.... For though before Adam's fall, knowledge was natural, and came without labor, yet no one man now of himself, attains the truth in all things, without help and diligent learning.' See his *The rule of reason concerning the arte of logique* (London, 1552), p. B.iii.a., which attained five editions by 1580.

29   John Calvin, *The Institutes of the Christain Religion*, ed. J. T. McNeill, trans. F. L. Battles, 2 vols (Philadelphia, 1960), Bk. III, ch. vi, par. 5, pp. 688–9; ch. ii, par. 7, p. 551; par. 28, pp. 573–4; ch. x, pars 1–4, pp. 720–2; Andre Bieler, *La Pensée Economique et Sociale de Calvin* (Geneva, 1959), ch. ii.

30   John Calvin, 'On Civil Government' [*The Institutes of the Christian Religion*, bk. IV, ch. xx] in *John Calvin on God and Political Duty*, F. T. McNeill, ed. (New York, 1950), p. 46.

31   C. H. George and K. George, *The Protestant Mind of the English Reformation* (Princeton, NJ, 1961), pp. 3, 16; Charles Trinkaus first identified the social scientific quality in Calvinism; it sought to sweep away the 'idolatrous, anthropomorphic, and mystical' distortions that interfered with the proper understanding of the world; see his 'Renaissance Problems in Calvin's Theology', *Studies in the Renaissance* (1954), I, pp. 61, 78. Valuable also on the Calvinist perception of, and stance toward, the world are: Ernst Troeltsch, *The Social Teachings of the Christian Churches*, trans. O. Wyon, 2 vols (New York, 1931), II, p. 601; R. H. Tawney, *Religion and the Rise of Capitalism: A Historical Study* (Gloucester, MA, 1954 [1926]), p. 84; Christopher Hill, *Society and Puritanism in Pre-Revolutionary England* (New York, 1964), pp. 271, 275; Ole Peter Grell and Andrew Cunningham, 'The Reformation and Changes in Welfare Provision in Early Modern Northern Europe', in *idem*, eds, *Health Care and Poor Relief in Protestant Europe, 1500–1700* (London and New York, 1997), pp. 2–4, 9–16, 27–36; and Patrick Collinson: *The Birthpangs of Protestant England: Religious and Cultural Change in the Sixteenth and Seventeenth Centuries* (Basingstoke, 1988), p. 143; and *Puritan Character, Polemics and Polarities in Early Seventeenth-Century English Culture* (Los Angeles, 1989), pp. 23–35.

32   William Perkins, *Cases of Conscience* (1606), *Works*, 3 vols (London, 1612–13), III, p. 145.

33   M. Bucer, *A Treatise, How Almose Ought to be Distributed* (*1557*?), The English Experience, No. 779 (1976), pp. 10–11, 13–14, 17–18, 24–6.

34 Paul Slack, 'Social Policy and the Constraints of Government, 1547–58', in Jennifer Loach and Robert Tittler, eds, *The Mid-Tudor Polity, c.1540–1560* (London, 1980), pp. 95–6; Holderness, *Pre-Industrial England*, pp. 53–4, 117, 120–1; Coleman, *Economy*, pp. 51–6.

35 Paul Slack, 'Hospitals, Workhouses and the Relief of the Poor in Early Modern London', in Grell and Cunningham, *Heath Care and Poor Relief*, p. 235.

36 Paul Slack, *From Reformation to Improvement: Public Welfare in Early Modern England* (Oxford, 1999), p. 26. For a sequential model of common weal thought from Christain humanist origins in More's *Utopia*, through an essentially secular-minded Cromwellian phase, and on to a Protestant 'evening glow' under Somerset, see Brendan Bradshaw, 'The Tudor Commonwealth: Reform and Revision', *Historical Journal* 22, 2 (1979), pp. 463, 466–9, 470–1.

37 Robert Tittler: 'Reformation, Resources and Authority in English Towns: An Overview', in Patrick Collinson and John Craig, eds, *The Reformation in English Towns, 1500–1640* (New York, 1998), pp. 190–201, and *The Reformation and the Towns in England* (Oxford, 1998). See also Patrick Collinson, *The Birthpangs of Protestant England: Religious and Cultural Change in the Sixteenth and Seventeenth Centuries* (Basingstoke, 1988).

38 Marjorie K. McIntosh: 'Local Responses to the Poor in Late Medieval and Tudor England', *Continuity and Change* 3, 2 (1988), pp. 225–30. Since 1980, when Paul Slack attributed the early Tudor social welfare agenda to the interplay of Christian humanist ideas and challenging social conditions ('Social Policy and the Constraints of Government', pp. 108–9), his views on the play of distinct ideologies have changed. In his *Poverty and Policy in Tudor and Stuart England* (London, 1988), Christian humanism had become 'civic humanism' (p. 114), and most recently in *From Reformation to Improvement*, Slack observes that 'humanist and Protestant (and indeed older) strands seem to me so closely intertwined in their public rhetoric, and so similar in their implications for policy, as to be impossible to disentangle' (p. 10, n. 29).

39 Slack, *Poverty and Policy*, pp. 119, 123; L. A. Botelho, *Old Age and the English Poor Law, 1500–1700* (Rochester, NY, 2004), p. 26.

40 Paul Slack, 'Hospitals, Workhouses and Relief', pp. 235–6; see also Slack: 'Social Policy and Constraints of Government', pp. 110–11, and *Poverty and Policy*, pp. 119–21.

41   Slack, 'Hospitals, Workhouses and Relief', p. 237.
42   W. K. Jordan, *Edward VI: The Young King*. (Cambridge, MA, 1968), ch. XIV.
43   *The Statutes of the Realm*, 12 vols (London, 1963; reprinted from the 1810–1828 edn), IV, part I, pp. 5–8.
44   Ibid., pp. 115–17.
45   Ibid., pp. 131–2.
46   Hutton, *Rise and Fall*, pp. 95–106; Slack, 'Social Policy and Constraints', pp. 111–13.
47   St Augustine, *Twelve sermons of Saynt Augustine, now lately Translated into English by Tho. Paynel* (London, 1555), pp. A.iiii.a, f.v.b.–vi.a., h.vii.a.
48   *Statutes*, pp. 131–2, 280–1.
49   R. Tittler, 'The Emergence of Urban Policy, 1536–58', Loach and Tittler, *Mid-Tudor Policy*, pp. 74–7.
50   Starkey, *Dialogue*, p. 40.
51   Mary Dewar, *Sir Thoms Smith: A Tudor Intellectual in Office* (London, 1964), pp. 1–7.
52   Sir Thomas Smith, *A Discourse of the Commonweal of this Realm of England* (1581), ed. Mary Dewar (Charlottsville, VA, 1969), pp. 49–54, 99–113, 121–6.
53   Ibid., pp. 83, 87–92; Neil Wood, 'Foundations of Political Economy: The New Moral Philosophy of Sir Thomas Smith', in Paul A. Fideler and T. F. Mayer, eds, *Political Thought and the Tudor Commonwealth* (London, 1992), pp. 140–3, 152.
54   Smith, *Discourse*, pp. 24–30.
55   Ibid., pp. 58–60.
56   Ibid., pp. 118.
57   Felicity Heal, *Hospitality in Early Modern England* (Oxford, 1990), pp. 15–17.
58   Ibid., p. 132.
59   Ibid., pp. 110–12.
60   Wilbur K. Jordan: *Philanthropy in England, 1480–1660* (London, 1959), *The Charities of London, 1480–1660* (London, 1960), and *The Charities of Rural England, 1480–1660* (London, 1961).
61   Jordan, *Philanthropy*, pp. 18, 19, 149, 151, 156; Heal, *Hospitality*, pp. 402.
62   The most thoughtful overall assessment of Jordan's accomplishment is: Archer, *Pursuit of Stability*, pp. 163–82, esp. 178. See also:

J. A. F. Thomson, 'Piety and Charity in Late Medieval London', *Journal of Ecclesiastical History* 16 (1965); W. B. Bittle and R. T. Lane, Inflation and Philanthropy in England: A Reassessment of W. K. Jordan's Data', *Economic History Review*, 2nd ser., 29 (1976); and F. W. Hadwin, 'Deflating Philanthropy', *Economic History Review*, 2nd ser., 31 (1978).

63 G. R. Elton, *The Tudor Revolution in Government* (Cambridge, 1953).

64 *Philanthropy*, p. 140.

65 Jordan, *Philanthropy*, pp. 19, 144, 147.

66 Jordan, *Philanthropy*, pp. 148, 151, 156.

67 Claire S. Schen, *Charity and Lay Piety in Reformation London, 1500–1620* (Aldershot, 2002), chs. 4, 5.

68 Thomas Harman, *A Caveat for commen cursetors vulgarely called vagabones* (London, 1567). John Awdeley, *Fraternity of Vacabondes* (London, 1561?, 1565?, 1565?), in Edward Viles and F. J. Furnivall, eds, *The Rogues and Vagabonds of Shakspere's Youth*, New Shakespeare Society VI, No. 7 (London, 1907).

69 Harman, *Caveat*, pp. A.iia–b, A.iii.b, A.iiii.b., B.i.b., A.3.b–A.4.b.

70 Ibid., pp. A.ii.b–Aiii.b.

71 Peter Roberts, 'Elizabethan Players and Minstrels and the Legislation of 1572 Against Retainers and Vagabonds', in Anthony Fletcher and Peter Roberts, eds, *Religion, Culture and Society in Early Modern Britain* (Cambridge, 1994), p. 33.

72 Margaret Pelling, *The Common Lot: Sickness, Medical Occupations and the Urban Poor in Early Modern England* (London, 1998), p. 13, 63–4.

73 A. L. Beier, 'Vagrants and the Social Order in Elizabethan England', *Past and Present* 64 (August 1974), pp. 3–29; and Paul Slack, 'Vagrants and Vagrancy in England, 1598–1664', *Economic History Review*, 2nd ser., 27 (August 1974), pp. 360–78. See also: Beier, *Masterless Men: The Vagrancy Problem in England, 1560–1640* (London, 1985); Peter Clark, 'The Migrant in Kentish Towns, 1580–1640', in Clark and Slack, eds, *Crisis and Order in English Towns, 1500–1700* (London, 1972).

74 Marjorie K. McIntosh, *Controlling Misbehavior in England, 1370–1600* (Cambridge, 1998), pp. 44–5.

75 David Levine and Keith Wrightson, *Poverty and Piety in an English Village: Terling, 1525–1700* (Oxford, 1995 [1979]), pp. 2, 7–8, 16–17, 34–9, 69, 80–2, 91.

76 Patrick Collinson, *The Religion of Protestants: The Church in English Society, 1559–1625* (Oxford, 1982), pp. 142, 183; Richard Baxter, *A Holy Commonwealth* (London, 1659), pp. 456–7.

77 Peter Lake, 'Calvinism and the English Church, 1570–1636', in Margo Todd, ed., *Reformation and Revolution: Politics and Religion in Early Modern England* (London and New York, 1995), pp. 184–5, Tyack's phrase cited from p. 185; Patrick Collinson, *Godly People* (London, 1983), p. 449; and Slack, *Poverty and Policy*, pp. 149–50.

78 Collinson, *Religion of Protestants*, pp. 62, 115, 124, 154–5 (includes citations from Prick), 178–88; Collinson challenges Michael Walzer's characterization of Puritans as radical and alienated from the realm's values (*The Revolution of the Saints* [Cambridge, MA, 1965]).

79 Collinson, *Religion of Protestants*, pp. 141–3.

80 Slack, 'Poverty and Social Regulation', pp. 237–8.

81 Andrew Wear, *Health and Healing in Early Modern England* (Aldershot, 1998), ch. V: 'Religious Beliefs and Medicine in Early Modern England', pp. 157–60.

82 Pelling, *Common Lot*, Introduction and pp. 63–5.

83 Wear, 'Caring for the Sick Poor in St Bartholomew's Exchange, 1580–1676', in *Health and Healing*, ch. VIII.

84 Pelling, 'Healing the Sick Poor: Social Policy and Disability in Norwich, 1550–1640', in *Common Lot*, p. 84.

85 Ibid., pp. 86–9.

86 D. Woodward, 'The Background to the Statute of Artificers: The Genesis of Labor Policy', *Economic History Review*, 2nd ser., 33 (1980), pp. 38, 41–4; *Statutes*, pp. 415–20.

87 Norman Jones, *The Birth of the Elizabethan Age* (Oxford, 1993), p. 82.

88 Anthony Fletcher, *Tudor Rebellions*, 2nd edn (London, 1973), pp. 91, 95–101.

89 *Statutes*, pp. 590–4, 611–12.

90 Wrigley and Schofield, *Population History*, p. 408.

91 John Walter and Keith Wrightson, 'Dearth and the Social Order in Early Modern England', *Past and Present* 71 (May 1976), pp. 23–4, 28–31, 33, 41–2.

92 Quoted in Slack, *Poverty and Policy*, pp. 139–40; Steve Hindle, 'Dearth, Fasting and Alms: The Campaign for General Hospitality in Late Elizabethan England', *Past and Present* 172 (August 2001), pp. 50–1.

93 Ibid., pp. 52–4, 56, 61–9.

94 Quoted in Dean, *Law-Making and Society*, p. 15; Sir Simonds D'ewes, *The Journals of All the Parliments during the Reign of Queen Elizabeth* (London, 1973 [1682]), p. 551.

95 Slack, *Poverty and Policy*, p. 126; E. M. Leonard, *The Early History of English Poor Relief* (London, 1965 [1900]), p. 74.

96 *Statutes*, pp. 896–8.

97 Brian Tierney, *Medieval Poor Law* (Berkeley, CA, 1959), pp. 131–3

98 For the 'betterment-subsistence' distinctions, which surely apply to migrants throughout the span of this study, see: Clark, 'The Migrant in Kentish Towns', pp. 117–61.

Chapter 4: Implementation (c.1610–1690)

1 E. A. Wrigley and R. S. Schofield, *The Population History of England, 1541–1871: A Reconstruction* (Cambridge, 1989 [London, 1981]), pp. 402–11, figs. 10.1–10.4.

2 For the emerging scholarship on this, see: Michael B. Katz and Christoph Sachze, eds, *The Mixed Economy of Social Welfare* (Baden-Baden, 1996), which includes essays by Jose Harris, Lynn H. Lees, Pat Thane, and David Thomson, among others.

3 Jonathan Barry, 'Introduction', in Barry and Christopher Brooks, eds, *The Middling Sort of People* (Basingstoke, 1994), pp. 9–10; for a new social historian's perspective on the limitations of Marxist and Whig treatments of the emergence of social class, see: Andy Wood, *The Politics of Social Conflict: The Peak Country, 1520–1770* (Cambridge, 1999), pp. 10–26.

4 See Keith Wrightson, *English Society, 1500–1680* (London, 1982), ch. 1, for a deft exposition of this early modern estates literature.

5 See Chapter 1 above, pp. 23–4.

6 Wrightson: *English Society*, p. 37, and ' "Sorts of People" in Tudor and Stuart England', in Barry and Brooks, *Middling Sort*, pp. 36–42. H. R. French has offered a trenchant post-Marxist and post-modern critique of those who tend to make the 'middling sort' into a catch-all, normative class; and he has sought out the uniquely local and transient meanings of the label. See his: 'The Search for the "Middle Sort of People" in England', *The Historical Journal* 43, 1 (March 2000), pp. 277, 279–81, 293, and 'Social Status, Localism and the "Middle Sort of People" in England, 1620–1750', *Past and Present* 166 (February 2000), pp. 74–5, 85–6, 93–4, 96–7.

7 Paul Slack, *Poverty and Policy in Tudor and Stuart England* (London, 1988), p. 114; Steve Hindle, *The State and Social Change in Early Modern England, c.1550–1640* (Basingstoke, 2000), pp. 21–3.

8 Cynthia B. Herrup, 'The Counties and the Country: Some Thoughts on Seventeenth-Century Historiography', in G. Eley and William Hunt, eds, *Reviving the English Revolution: Reflections and Elaborations on the Work of Christopher Hill* (London, 1988), p. 290.

9 Connie S. Evans, '"An Echo of the Multitude": The Intersection of Governmental and Private Poverty Initiatives in Early Modern Exeter', *Albion* 32, 3 (Autumn 2000), pp. 416–25, 427–8.

10 Editor's introduction to James VI and I, *Political Writings*, Johann P. Sommerville, ed. (Cambridge, 1994), p. xv; and Paul Christianson, 'Royal and Parliamentary Voices on the Ancient Constitution, *c.*1604–21', in Linda Levy Peck, ed., *The Mental World of the Jacobean Court* (Cambridge, 1991), p. 76.

11 Paul Slack, *From Reformation to Improvement: Public Welfare in Early Modern England* (Oxford, 1999), pp. 75–6.

12 Charles Webster, *The Great Instauration: Science, Medicine and Reform, 1626–1660* (London, 1975), especially pp. 360–3, 368.

13 Slack, *Reformation to Improvement*, pp. 60–74.

14 Ronald Hutton, *The Rise and Fall of Merry England, the Ritual Year 1400–1700* (Oxford, 1994), pp. 167–9.

15 David Levine and Keith Wrightson, *Poverty and Piety in an English Village: Terling, 1525–1700*), (Oxford, 1995 [1979]), pp. 7–10.

16 For additional confirmation of the commitment to control behavior before the turn of the seventeenth century, see: Margaret Spufford, 'Puritanism and Social Control?', in Anthony Fletcher and John Stevenson, eds, *Order and Disorder in Early Modern England* (Cambridge, 1985), pp. 41–57; Martin Ingram, 'Reformation of Manners in Early Modern England', in Paul Griffiths, Adam Fox, and Steve Hindle, eds, *The Experience of Authority in Early Modern England* (Basingstoke, 1996), pp. 47–88; Marjorie K. McIntosh, *Controlling Misbehaviour in England, 1370–1600* (Cambridge, 1998).

17 Slack, *Poverty and Policy*, pp. 7–8.

18 Patrick Collinson: *The Birthpangs of Protestantism: Religious and Cultural Change in the Sixteenth and Seventeenth Centuries* (London, 1988), p. 143, and *Puritan Character, Polemics and Polarities in Early Seventeenth-Century English Culture* (Los Angeles, 1989), pp. 23–35; Peter Lake, 'Periodization, Politics and "The Social"', *Journal of British Studies* 37, 3 (July 1998), pp. 279–90; McIntosh, *Controlling*

Misbehavior in England, p. 128; and Robert Tittler: *The Reformation and the Towns in England* (Oxford, 1998), pp. 5–22, 341; and 'Reformation, Resources and Authority in English Towns: An Overview', in Patrick Collinson and John Craig, eds, *The Reformation in English Towns, 1540–1640* (Oxford, 1998), pp. 190–201.

19   Levine and Wrightson, *Poverty and Piety*, pp. 164–203; Wallace MacCaffrey, *Exeter, 1540–1640* (Cambridge, MA, 1975), pp. 21–5, 199–202; David Underdown, *Fire from Heaven* (London, 1992), chs 3, 4; and Paul Slack, 'Poverty and Politics in Salisbury', in Peter Clark and Slack, eds, *Crisis and Order in English Towns 1500–1700* (London, 1972), pp. 164–203.

20   Ibid., pp. 181–4.

21   David Underdown, *Revel, Riot, and Rebellion: Popular Politics and Culture in England, 1603–1660* (Oxford, 1985), pp. 40–1.

22   Robert Burton, *The Anatomy of Melancholy*, cited from Slack, *Reformation to Improvement*, p. 52.

23   Cited from Wrightson, *English Society*, pp. 215–16, 218–20.

24   B. W. Quintrell, 'The Making of Charles I's Book of Orders', *English Historical Review* 95 (1980), pp. 553–72; Paul Slack, 'Books of Orders: The Making of English Social Policy, 1577–1631', *Transactions of the Royal Historical Society* 30 (1980), pp. 1–22.

25   Steve Hindle: *The State and Social Change* (Basingstoke, 2000), pp. 153–5, and 'The Birthpangs of Welfare: Poor Relief and Parish Governance in Seventeenth-Century Warwickshire', *Dugdale Society Occasional Papers*, No. 40 (2000), pp. 1–32.

26   Peter Rushton, 'The Poor Law, The Parish and the Community in North-East England, 1600–1800', *Northern History* XXV (1989), pp. 135–52.

27   Levine and Wrightson, *Poverty and Piety*, pp. 110–17, 140–1.

28   See: Jeremy Boulton, 'Going on the Parish: The Parish Pension and its Meaning in the London Suburbs, 1640–1724', in Tim Hitchcock, Peter King, and Pamela Sharpe, eds, *Chronicling Poverty: The Voices and Strategies of the English Poor, 1640–1840* (Basingstoke, 1997), pp. 19–46.

29   Hindle, *State and Social Change*, pp. 153–6; Rushton, 'Poor Law', pp. 149–50.

30   Keith Wrightson, 'The Politics of the Parish in Early Modern England', in Griffiths et al., *Experience of Authority*, pp. 10–12, 13, 18–22, 35–7.

31 Boulton, 'Going on the Parish', pp. 28–32, 34, 36.
32 Rushton, 'Poor Law', pp. 140–1, 143, 145; Steve Hindle, 'Exclusion Crises: Poverty, Migration and Parochial Responsibility in English Rural Communities', *Rural History* (1996), pp. 2, 7, 125–49; John Broad, 'Parish Economies of Welfare, 1650–1834', *Historical Journal* 42, 4 (1999), pp. 985–1006; Claire S. Schen, *Charity and Lay Piety in Reformation London, 1500–1620* (Aldershot, 2002), chs 3, 4; and L. A. Botelho, *Old Age and the English Poor Law, 1500–1700* (Rochester, NY, 2004), pp. 19, 117, 152.
33 Cited from Boulton, 'Going on the Parish', pp. 27, 32.
34 Ibid., p. 32.
35 Ibid., pp. 32, 35; Rushton, 'Poor Law', pp. 139–40; Levine and Wrightson, *Poverty and Piety*, pp. 179–80.
36 See: A. L. Beier, 'Poverty and Progress in Early Modern England', in Beier, David Cannadines and James M. Rosenheim, eds, *The First Modern Society: Essays in English History in Honour of Lawrence Stone* (Cambridge, 1989), pp. 203–5; Fiona Newell, 'Social Mobility in the Population of Aldenham, Hertfordshire, 1600–1800', in Doris Jones-Baker, ed., *Hertfordshire in History: Papers Presented to Lionel Munby* (Hertford, 1991), pp. 115, 122.
37 L. A. Botelho, *Old Age and the English Poor Law, 1500–1700* (Rochester, NY, 2004), pp. 77–8. For a thorough treatment of the opportunities and differing fortunes for women in dairy farming and the spinning industry, see: Deborah Valenze, *The First Industrial Woman* (New York, 1995), chs 3, 4, and 6.
38 Tim Wales, 'Poverty, Poor Relief and the Life-Cycle: Some Evidence from Seventeenth-Century Norfolk', in Richard M. Smith, ed., *Land, Kinship and Life-Cycle* (Cambridge, 1984), pp. 360, 364–5, 374, 380, 387–8.
39 See: Paul A. Fideler, 'Impressions of a Century of Historiography', *Albion* 32, 3 (Fall 2000), pp. 381–4, 391.
40 For the suggestion that historians should acknowledge links between religion and social morality when appropriate but, at the same time, avoid an overly denominational approach to religious development after the Reformation, see: Jeremy Gregory, 'The Making of a Portestant Nation: 'Success' and 'Failure' in England's Long Reformation', in Nicholas Tyacke, ed., *England's Long Reformation* (London, 1998), pp. 320–4.
41 Levine and Wrightson, *Poverty and Piety*, pp. 174–6, J. Stalham, *Vindiciae Redemptionis*, To My Beloved Brethren and Neighbors in Terling, cited from p. 176.

42 Wrightson, *English Society*, pp. 184–5, 190, 193–9.
43 Richard Tuck, *Philosophy and Government, 1572–1651* (Cambridge, 1993), pp. 20–2; Margo Todd, *Christian Humanism and the Puritan Social Order* (Cambridge, 1987), p. 81.
44 Ibid., pp. 81–84.
45 Cicero, *The three books of Tullies offices*, trans. Robert Whytinton (London, 1534).
46 Jonathan Woolfson, ed., *Reassessing Tudor Humanism* (Basingstoke, 2000), Introduction, pp. 14–15; Markku Peltonen, *Classical Humanism and Republicanism in English Political Thought, 1570–1640* (Cambridge, 1995), p. 7.
47 Seneca, *The Works of Lucius Annaeus Seneca, Both Moral and Natural*, trans. Thomas Lodge (London, 1614); *Essays written in French by Michael Lord of Montaigne*, trans. John Florio (London, 1613).
48 Cited in Tuck, *Philosophy and Government*, pp. 45–54.
49 Seneca, 'Of Benefits', *Works*, p. 75; for the *societas* orientation of the Stoics, see: Neal Wood, *Cicero's Social and Political Thought* (Berkeley, CA, 1988), and 'Cicero and the Political Thought of the Early English Renaissance', *Modern Language Quarterly* 51, 2 (June 1990), pp. 185–207; T. F. Mayer, 'Thomas Starkey's Aristocratic Reform Programme', *History of Political Thought* 7 (1986), pp. 439–61; and Margo Todd: 'Seneca and the Protestant Mind: The Influence of Stoicism on Puritan Ethics', *Archiv für Reformationsgeschichte* 74 (1983), pp. 182–99, and *Christian Humanism*.
50 Cicero, *The three bookes*, p. F.8.b.
51 Ibid., p. D.2.b..
52 Ibid., p. O.4.b.
53 Ibid., pp. T.1.b, C.6.b, V.7.b, N.3.b, N.6.b, O.2.b.
54 Seneca, 'Of Benefits', *Works*, pp. 7, 17–18.
55 Ibid., pp. 71–2.
56 Ibid., p. 29.
57 Ibid., pp. 56, 75.
58 Ibid., pp. 44–5, 48–9.
59 John Walter, 'The Social Economy of Dearth in Early Modern England', in Walter and Roger Schofield, eds, *Famine, Disease and the Social Order in Early Modern Society* (Cambridge, 1989), pp. 75–127. See also: Walter and Keith Wrightson, 'Dearth and the Social Order in Early Modern England', *Past and Present* 71 (May 1976), pp. 22–42, and Walter, 'Public Transcripts, Popular Agency and the Politics of Subsistence in Early Modern England', in M. J. Braddick and Walter, eds, *Negotiating Power in Early Modern Society* (Cambridge,

2001), pp. 123–48. I have relied heavily on John Walter for this discussion.

60   Keith Wrightson, *English Society, 1580–1680* (London, 1982), pp. 45–51.

61   Craig Muldrew, 'Interpreting the Market: The Ethics of Credit and Community Relations in Early Modern England', *Social History* 18, 2 (May 1993), pp. 164–9.

62   Walter, 'Social Economy', pp. 96–105, 112.

63   Ibid., pp. 113–16.

64   Ibid., pp. 105–10.

65   James C. Scott: *Weapons of the Weak: Everyday Forms of Peasant Resistance* (New Haven, CT, 1985), and *Domination and the Arts of Resistance: Hidden Transcripts* (New Haven, CT, 1990).

66   Walter, 'Public Transcripts', pp. 124–5.

67   Walter and Wrightson, 'Dearth and the Social Order', pp. 23–4, 33.

68   R. W. Bushaway, 'Rite, Legitimation and Community in Southern England, 1700–1850: The Ideology of Custom', in Barry Stapleton, ed., *Conflict and Community in Southern England* (Stroud, 1992), pp. 111–14; Andy Wood, 'The Place of Custom in Plebeian Political Culture: England, 1550–1800', *Social History* 22, 1 (January 1997), pp. 47, 49–51. Also important are: Bushaway, *By Rite: Custom, Ceremony and Community in England 1700–1880* (London, 1982); and E. P. Thompson, *Customs in Common* (London, 1991), especially chs i and iii.

69   Bushaway, 'Rite', pp. 117; Wood, 'Place of Custom', pp. 50–1, 53, 54, 57. See Wood's discussion of the the struggle of the Peak District miners to preserve their customary rights in his *The Politics of Social Conflict*, especially Parts II and III.

70   Ronald Hutton, *The Rise and Fall of Merry England; The Ritual Year, 1400–1700* (Oxford, 1994), chs 6, 7.

71   In what follows, I rely heavily on John Morrill, *The Revolt in the Provinces*, 2nd edn (London, 1998).

72   Ibid., pp. 5–6, 16–17, 78–80, 84, 93.

73   Ibid., pp. 200–5.

74   David Underdown, *Fire from Heaven* (London, 1992), pp. 56–60. Underdown provides a very useful description of Arminianism, which 'rejected the doctrine of predestination, emphasised the sacraments above preaching, minimised the importance of strict sabbath observance, and wished to dilute the austere simplicity of

protestant worship by the reintroduction of more elaborate rituals, in pursuit of what Laud called "the beauty of holiness" ' (p. 57).

75 H. N. Brailsford, *The Levellers and the English Revolution*, ed. Christopher Hill (Stanford, CA, 1961).

76 Ibid., ch. xiii, especially, pp. 267–8, 274–5, 280–3.

77 Ibid., ch. xiv, pp. 288–302.

78 G. E. Aylmer, ed., *The Levellers in the English Revolution* (Ithaca, NY, 1975), Introduction, pp. 9–15.

79 John Moore, *The crying sin of England, of not Caring for the Poor...* (London, 1653), pp. 7–9, 16–28.

80 Margaret James, *Social Problems and Policy during the Puritan Revolution* (London, 1966 [1930]), pp. 17–18.

81 Thomas Lawrence, *Some pity on the poor: or, a way how poor people may be supplied with labor and relief without begging...* (London, *c*.1650), p. 6.

82 Peter Chamberlen, *The poore mans advocate, or, Englands Samaritan...* (London, 1649), pp. 1–2; Leonard Lee, *A remonstrance humbly presented to the high and honourable court of Parliament...* (London, 1644), Dedication to the Lord Mayor of London, the Aldermen and the Commen Council, n.p.

83 Lee, *resmonstrance*, pp. 1–3.

84 Valerie Pearl, 'Social Policy in Early Modern London', in Hugh Lloyd-Jones, Valerie Pearl, and Blair Worden, eds, *History and Imagination: Essays in Honour of H. R. Trevor-Roper* (London, 1981), pp. 117, 123–5.

85 For the steady performance of the rate, see: Ronald Herlan, 'Poor Relief in London During the English Revolution', *Journal of British Studies* XVIII (1979); Ben Coates finds that the new demands of war-related poverty essentially overwhelmed the City's social welfare capabilities; see his: 'Poor Relief in London During the English Revolution Revisited', *The London Journal* 25, 2 (2000), pp. 48–58.

86 Slack, *Reformation to Improvement*, ch. 4.

87 Mark Greengrass, Michael Leslie, and Timothy Raylor, eds, *Samuel Hartlib and Universal Reformation* (Cambridge, 1994), Introduction, pp. 2–3, 14–15, and Howard Hotson, 'Philosophical Pedagogy in Reformed Central Europe between Ramus and Comenius', p. 39, and Dagmar Capkova, 'Comenius and His Ideals: Escape from the Labyrinth', pp. 81–3; Tuck, *Philosophy and Government*, pp. 17–20, 24–6. Hartlib's circle included: Rice Bush, John Pym, the mathematician John Pell, the linguist Theodore Haak, the historian Joachim Hubner, and the ecumenist John Drury, among others.

88 Samuel Hartlib, *London's Charity inlarged, Stilling the Orphans Cry* (1650), pp. 1–5, 12–14, 15–21.

89 Slack: *Poverty and Policy*, pp. 154–5, and *Reformation to Improvement*, pp. 77–90.

90 Robert Hitchcock, *A Pollitique Platt for the honour of the Prince, the greate profite of the publique state, etc.* (London, 1580).

91 William Petty, *A Treatise of Taxes & Contributions* (1662), in Charles Henry Hull, ed., *The Economic Writings of Sir William Petty*, 2 vols (New York, 1963), I, pp. 21, 29–31.

92 Ibid., p. 20.

93 Slack: *Poverty and Policy*, pp. 170, 171, and *The English Poor Law, 1531–1782* (Stroud, 1990), p. 26.

94 Cited from Slack, *Poverty and Policy*, p. 190.

95 Ibid., pp. 190–1.

96 See Paul D. Halliday, *Dismembering the Body Politic: Partisan Politics in England's Towns, 1650–1730* (Cambridge, 1998).

97 Ibid., p. 104.

98 Ibid., pp. 108, 131.

99 Ibid., pp. 143–4, 235–6, 348.

100 Melinda S. Zook, *Radical Whigs and Conspiratorial Politics in Late Stuart England* (University Park, PA, 1999), pp. xvi–xx, 80, 85.

101 See Rushton, 'Poor Law', pp. 135–6, for an early notice of this historiographical turn.

102 Slack: *Poverty and Policy*, pp. 169–82, and *Reformation to Improvement*, pp. 148–9.

103 John Broad, 'Parish Economies of Welfare, 1650–1834', *Historical Journal* 42, 4 (1999), pp. 985–6; and L. A. Botelho, *Old Age and the English Poor Law, 1500–1700* (Rochester, NY, 2004), pp. 19, 117, 152.

104 Broad, 'Parish Economies', pp. 992–6.

105 Ibid., pp. 996–8.

106 Botelho, *Old Age and the English Poor Law*, pp. 42–51.

107 Broad, 'Parish Economies', pp. 998–1001.

108 Botelho, *Old Age and the English Poor Law*, pp. 51–67.

109 Ibid., pp. 78–81, 112, 138–9.

110 Ibid., pp, 115–17.

111 David Levine and Keith Wrightson, *The Making of an Industrial Society: Whickham, 1560–1765* (Oxford, 1991), pp. viii–ix.

112 Ibid., pp. 80, 83, 157–64, 266–70, 341–7.

113 James Stephen Taylor, 'The Impact of Pauper Settlement, 1691–1834', *Past and Present* 73 (November 1976), pp. 47–9.

114 Slack, *Poverty and Policy*, pp. 194–5; Taylor, 'Impact', pp. 45, 50.

Chapter 5: Settlement, Workhouses, and New Industry (c.1690–1780)

1   E. A. Wrigley and R. S. Schofield, *The Population History of England, 1541–1871: A Reconstruction* (Cambridge, 1989), pp. 402–21, see tables 10.1 and 10.7.

2   B. A. Holderness, *Pre-Industrial England: Economy and Society, 1500–1750* (London, 1976), pp. 7–9, 12–13.

3   Norma Landau, 'The Laws of Settlement and the Surveillance of Immigration in Eighteenth-Century Kent', *Continuity and Change* 3, 3(1988); pp. 391–9.

4   James Stephen Taylor, 'The Impact of Pauper Settlement, 1691–1834', *Past and Present* 73 (November 1976), pp. 51–2.

5   William Hay, *Remarks on the Laws Relating to the Poor with Proposals for their better Relief and Employment* (London, 1735), p. 9.

6   Ibid., pp. 10–11.

7   Sidney and Beatrice Webb, *English Local Government: English Poor Law History: Part I. The Old Poor Law* (London, 1927), pp. 150, 350, 401; R. H. Tawney, *The Agrarian Problem in the Sixteenth Century* (New York, 1967 [1912]), pp. 2–14, 402, 408–9, and *Religion and the Rise of Capitalism: A Historical Study* (Gloucester, MA, 1954 [1926]), pp. xix, 219, 232, 239–40, 264–8.

8   So much so that K. D. M. Snell believes that, if used properly, they could help to 'ameliorate' the historiography of the poor and the family, one of several suggestions he has made to bring more innovation to the study of rural England. The others are: the study of change across long time spans; greater attention to labor's mobility; methods that combine quantitative research with materials that can yield 'attitudinal changes'; fewer polemics between optimists and pessimists; and the formulation of a 'literary sociology.' See his: *Annals of the Laboring Poor: Social Change and Agrarian England, 1660–1900* (Cambridge, 1985), Introduction, and his 'Settlement, Poor Law and the Rural Historian: New Approaches and Opportunities', *Rural History* 3, 2 (1992), pp. 145–72.

9   K. D. M. Snell, 'Pauper Settlement and the Right to Poor Relief in England and Wales', *Continuity and Change* 6, 3 (1991), pp. 377–8.

10 Norma Landau, 'The Eighteenth-Century Context of the Laws of Settlement', *Continuity and Change* 6, 3 (1991), pp. 417, 430.

11 James Stephen Taylor, 'The Impact of Pauper Settlement, 1691–1834', *Past and Present* 73 (November 1976), pp. 56–7, 58–60.

12 Quoted in Paul Slack, *Poverty and Policy in Tudor and Stuart England* (London, 1988), pp. 191–2.

13 An important contribution to this effort is: Thomas Sokoll, ed., *Essex Pauper Letters, 1731–1837* (Oxford, 2001). In addition to the texts of 758 letters, Sokoll offers three chapters of contextual perspective and methological suggestions for using them. See also: Steven King, *Poverty and Welfare in England, 1700–1850* (Manchester, 2000), pp. 117–19.

14 See above, pp. 121–2.

15 Steven King, 'Reconstructing Lives: The Poor, the Poor Law and Welfare in Calverley, 1650–1820', *Social History* 22, 3 (October 1997), pp. 318–38.

16 Ibid., pp. 319–23, 329.

17 Susannah R. Ottaway, *The Decline of Life: Old Age in Eighteenth-Century England* (Cambridge, 2004), p. 280.

18 Steven King, *Poverty and Welfare*, pp. 146–7; L. A. Botelho, *Old Age and the English Poor Law, 1500–1700* (Rochester, NY, 2004), pp. 138–9.

19 Steven King, 'Reconstructing Lives', pp. 324–6, 333–4, and *Poverty and Welfare*, pp. 123–4.

20 Ibid., pp. 136–7.

21 Steven King, 'Reconstructing Lives', p. 335–6, 338.

22 Peter King, 'Pauper Inventories and the Material Lives of the Poor in the Eighteenth and Early Nineteenth Centuries', in Tim Hitchcock, Peter King, and Pamela Sharpe, eds, *Chronicling Poverty: The Voices and Strategies of the English Poor, 1640–1840* (Basingstoke, 1997), pp. 155–91.

23 Ibid., p. 179, table 7.3.

24 Ibid., pp. 171, 180–1.

25 Ottaway, *The Decline of Life*, p. 10; John Hintermaier, 'The First Modern Refugees? Charity, Entitlement, and Persuasion in the Huguenot Immigration of the 1680s', *Albion* 32, 3 (Autumn 2000), pp. 429–49.

26 Peter King, 'Pauper Inventories', p. 182.

27 Ottaway, *Decline of Life*, pp. 2, 5, 67.

28 Ibid., pp. 17, 30.

29 Ibid., pp. 92–94, 184–85 (table 5.1).

30 Gregory King, *Natural and Political Observations on the State and Condition of England* (London, 1688); for useful summaries of King's data and their significance, see: D. C. Coleman, *The Economy of England, 1450–1750* (Oxford, 1977), pp. 5–11; Holderness, *Pre-Industrial England*, pp. 199–200.

31 For much in the next paragraphs I am dependent on Slack, *Poverty and Policy*, pp. 195–200, and *From Reformation to Improvement: Public Welfare in Early Modern England* (Oxford, 1999), ch. 5.

32 John Cary, *A Discourse on Trade, and other Matters Relative to it Wrote at the Request of several Members of Parliament* (London, 1745), pp. iv–vii.

33 Slack: *Poverty and Policy*, p. 195, and *Reformation to Improvement*, p. 113.

34 Slack, *English Poor Law*, pp. 41–2.

35 Ibid., pp. 42–4.

36 Thomas Alcock, *Observations of the Defects of the Poor laws…in a Letter to a member of Parliament* (London, 1752), p. 11.

37 Thomas Alcock, *Remarks on Two Bills for the Better Maintenance of the Poor…* (London, 1753), pp. 16–17, 29.

38 Slack, *English Poor Law*, pp. 126–30.

39 Anne Crowther, 'Health Care and Poor Relief in Provincial England', in Ole Peter Grell, Andrew Cunningham, and Robert Jütte, eds, *Health Care and Poor Relief in 18th and 19th Century Northern Europe* (Aldershot, 2001), p. 206.

40 Ibid., pp. 204–9.

41 Kevin P. Siena, *Venereal Disease, Hospitals and the Urban Poor: London's 'Foul Wards', 1600–1800* (Rochester, NY, 2004), p. 178.

42 Ibid., pp. 142–3.

43 Ibid., pp. 156–7.

44 Ibid., p. 179.

45 Quoted in Paul Slack, 'Hospitals, Workhouses and the Relief of the Poor in Early Modern London', in Ole Peter Grell and Andrew Cunningham, eds, *Health Care and Poor Relief in Protestant Europe 1500–1700* (London and New York, 1997), pp. 244–5.

46 See: Kathryn Norberg, *Rich and Poor in Grenoble, 1600–1814* (Berkeley, CA, 1985).

47 Slack, *Reformation to Improvement*, pp. 135–40.

48 Siena, *Venereal Disease*, p. 1.

49 E. A. Wrigley, *Continuity, Chance and Change* (Cambridge, 1988), pp. 8–12.

50 Ibid., pp. 12–14.

51 Wrigley and Schofield, *Population History*, pp. 414–22, 459–63, 467.

52 Ibid., pp. 463–6, 472–80.

53 John Hatcher, 'Understanding the Population History of England, 1450–1750', *Past and Present* 180 (August 2003), pp. 83–4, 88–9, 93–9, 104–16.

54 Ibid., pp. 85, 120, 124–30.

55 Joel Mokyr, 'The New Economic History and the Industrial Revolution', in Mokyr, ed., *The British Industrial Revolution: An Economic Perspective* (Boulder, CO, 1995), pp. 79–81.

56 Deborah Valenze, *The First Industrial Woman* (New York, 1995), ch. 5, provides a valuable perspective on these matters.

57 Mokyr, 'New Economic History', pp. 10–12; John Smail, *Merchants, Markets and Manufacturers* (Basingstoke, 1999), pp. 7–9, 136–8. The economist Joseph Schumpeter (d.1950) held that it was intrepreneurial activity that initiated business cycles and economic development.

58 Nicholas Phillipson, 'Adam Smith as Civic Moralist', in Istvan Hont and Michael Ignatieff, eds, *Wealth and Virtue: The Shaping of Political Economy in the Scottish Enlightenment* (Cambridge, 1983), p. 188.

59 Mokyr, 'New Economic History', pp. 66–7; J. de Vries, 'Purchasing Power and the World of Goods', in John Brewer and Roy Porter, eds, *Consumption and the World of Goods* (London, 1993), pp. 107–21.

60 Peter M. Solar, 'Poor Relief and English Economic Development before the Industrial Revolution', *Economic History Review* 48, 1 (1995), pp. 1–22; Taylor, 'The Impact of Pauper Settlement'; and David M. Landes, *The Wealth and Poverty of Nations* (New York, 1995), ch. 15.

61 Mokyr, 'New Economic History', p. 88; Steven King, *Poverty and Welfare*, p. 122.

62 Wrigley, *Continuity, Chance and Change*, pp. 15–16.

63 Steven King, *Poverty and Welfare*, pp. 141–4.

64 Ibid., pp. 154–7, 159, 170–1, 192–3, 198–204, 209–14.

65 Tawney, *Agrarian Problem*, pp. 2–14, 402, 408–9.

66 Other immanent transitions or, better said, changes of emphasis that can be at play, depending on the particular circumstances, include: from accepting one's inherited place in the social order to finding one's place; from sharing a communal or collective destiny to depending on individual self-reliance; from relying on tradition to embracing innovation; from living within a primarily religious world view to pursuing a secular one; and from embracing a primarily rural-dominated culture to accommodating to a primarily urban one.

67   Mokyr, 'New Economic History,' pp. 93–5.

68   David Levine and Ketih Wrightson, *The Making of an Industrial Society: Whickham 1560–1765* (Oxford, 1991), pp. 366–9.

69   Gertrude Himmelfarb, *The Idea of Poverty: England in the Early Industrial Age* (New York, 1984), ch. I; D. Leiberman, *The Province of Legislation Determined* (Cambridge, 1989), Intro.

70   Evelina Cruickshanks, *Political Untouchables: The Tories and the '45* (London, 1979); Linda Colley, *In Defiance of Oligarchy: The Tory Party, 1714–60* (Cambridge, 1982); J. C. D. Clark, *The Dynamics of Change: The Crises of the 1750s and English Party* (Cambridge, 1982); Isaac Kramnick, *Bolingbrode and His Circle: The Politics of Nostaligia in the Age of Walpole* (Cambridge, MA, 1968); Caroline Robbins, *The Eighteenth-Century Commonwealthmen* (Cambridge, MA, 1959); and J. G. A. Pocock, *Virtue, Commerce and History* (Cambridge, 1985).

71   Pocock, *Virtue*, pp. 48–9.

72   Lord Bolingbroke, *A Dissertation upon Parties* (1734), in David Armitage, ed., *Bolingbroke: Political Writings* (Cambridge, 1997), p. 125.

73   Ibid., pp. 5, 9, 82–3, 99, 141, 180.

74   Daniel Defoe, *Giving Alms no Charity* (London, 1704), p. 9.

75   Slack, *Reformation to Improvement*, pp. 119–25.

76   See: Phillipson, 'Adam Smith as Civic Moralist', pp. 179–202.

77   Ibid., p. 181.

78   Ibid., p. 182.

79   Ibid., pp. 183–9, 199.

80   Ibid., pp. 191–2, 198.

81   Andy Wood, 'The Place of Custom in Plebeian Politcal Culture: England, 1550–1800', *Social History* 22, 1 (January 1997), pp. 50–2.

82   R. W. Bushaway, *By Rite: Custom, Ceremony and Community in England, 1700–1880* (London, 1982), pp. 34–5, 44–5.

83   R. W. Bushaway, 'Rite, Legitimation and Community in Southern England, 1700–1850', in Barry Stapleton, ed., *Conflict and Community in Southern England* (Stroud, 1992), p. 114.

84   Ibid., pp. 115–21.

85   Cited in ibid, p. 110.

86   E. P. Thompson, *Customs in Common* (London, 1991), pp. 102–3; see: Pierre Bourdieu, *Outline of a Theory of Practice* (Cambridge, 1977), ch. 4: and also Bushaway's discussion of 'historically organic ideologies'in 'Rite, Legitimation and Community,' pp. 111–13.

Chapter 6: Poverty, Policy, and History

1 Some sense of the enormity of the debate can be acquired by perusing the 'Social Conditions' sections in Volumes 2 and 3 of the *Goldsmiths'-Kress Library of Economic Literature*, 5 vols (Woodbridge, CT, 1976–83).

2 Dorothy Marshall, *The English Poor in the Eighteenth Century* (London, 1926), pp. 6–9; J. S. Duncan, *Collections Relative to the Systematic Relief of the Poor* (Bath, 1815); Sidney and Beatrice Webb, *English Local Government: English Poor Law History; Part I. The Old Poor Law* (London, 1927), pp. 426–7.

3 Edmund Bott, *The Laws Relating to the Poor*, ed. Francis Const, 5th edn, 3 vols (London, 1807); *Report of the Select Committee of the House of Commons on the Poor Laws* (London, 1817), p. 4.

4 Richard Burn, *The History of the Poor Laws: With Observations* (London, 1764); Thomas Ruggles, *The History of the Poor, Their Rights, Duties, and the Laws Respecting Them*, 2 vols (London, 1793–94), 2nd edn in 1 vol. (London, 1797); Sir Frederic Eden, *The State of the Poor; Or, An History of the Laboring Classes in England*, 3 vols (London, 1797).

5 David Lieberman, *The Province of Legislation Determined* (Cambridge, 1989), ch. 2.

6 Ibid., Pt. IV.

7 Ibid., ch. 9.

8 Ibid., ch. 7.

9 Daniel Defoe, *Giving Alms no Charity* (London, 1704), pp. 4, 7–9.

10 John Disney, *A View of Ancient Laws against Immorality* ... (London, 1729).

11 Ibid., pp. 288, 290–1.

12 Ibid., p. 283.

13 Ibid., p. 288.

14 Burn, *History*, Preface.

15 Burn spells out his method in *Ecclesiastical Law* (London, 1763), p. xx. In this manner of using sources Burn and Eden, and to some extent Ruggles, resemble pre-Enlightenment historians like Rapin-Thoyras; see V. G. Wexler, 'David Hume's Discovery of New Scene of Historical Thought', *Eighteenth Century Studies* 10 (1976–77), p. 194.

16 Burn, *History*, p. 236; Lieberman, of course, identifies Burn as a 'consolidationist' (*Province*, pp. 190–4).

17   Ibid., pp. 202–3, 206–7.

18   Ibid., pp. 213–14, 233–5.

19   Thomas More, *Utopia* [1515], ed. J. H. Hexter and E. Surtz, S. J., *The Complete Works of St. Thomas More*, Vol. IV (New Haven, CT, 1965), p. 241.

20   William Petty, *A Treatise of Taxes and Contributions* [1662], *The Economic Writings of Sir William Petty*, ed. C. H. Hull, 2 vols (New York, 1963), I, pp. 29–31.

21   Richard Woodward, *An Argument in Support of the Right of the Poor in the Kingdom of Ireland, to a National Provision* ... (London, 1775 [1768, 1772]), pp. 30–5, bound with *An Address to the Public, on the Expediency of a Regular Plan for the Maintenance and Government of the Poor* ... (London, 1775).

22   Woodward, *Address*, pp. 75–9.

23   William Paley, *Principles of Moral and Political Philosophy*, 1st edn (London, 1785), pp. 55–9; a useful summary of Paley's position and his influence is Thomas A. Horne, ' "The poor have a claim founded in the law of nature" ...', *Journal of the History of Philosophy* XXIII, 1 (January 1985), see also Horne, *Property Rights and Poverty: Political Argument in Britain, 1605–1834* (Chapel Hill, NC, 1990).

24   Joseph Townsend, *A Dissertation on the Poor Laws* (London, 1786, 1817), p. 90–108. As Malthus would do 12 years later, Townsend maintained that hunger is the most effective check to an expanding population.

25   J. R. Poynter, *Society and Pauperism: English Ideas on Poor Relief, 1795–1834* (London, 1969), p. 79–85. Historians are divided on whether the formal granting of outdoor relief to the under-employed contributed to the ultimate breakdown of the Poor Law. The revisionists' view seems most compelling: rather than a disaster, the Speenhamland measures, applied primarily in the south and east, were an economically prudent response to declining agricultural and proto-industrial employment. The work of the revisionists, Mark Blaug, Daniel A. Baugh, Anne Digby, and George R. Boyer, is summarized in Boyer, *An Economic History of the English Poor Law, 1750–1850* (Cambridge, 1999), pp. 75–84, ch. 3, and Conclusion.

26   Poynter, *Society and Pauperism*, pp. 55–62; Eden, *State of the Poor*, Vol. III, pp. cccviii–cccxii, esp. cccx.

27   For the text of the bill see: Eden, *State of the Poor*, pp. cccxiiff.; the bill is summarized in Gertrude Himmelfarb, *The Idea of Poverty* (New York, 1984), pp. 74–6.

28   See above, pp. 89–92.

29 Editor's introduction to Jeremy Bentham, *Writings on the Poor Laws*, Vol. I, ed. Michael Quinn (Oxford, 2001), pp. xiv–v; Patrick Colquhoun, *A Treatise on Indigence...for ameliorating the Conditions of the Poor...particularly the Rising Generation* (London, 1806).

30 Bentham, *Poor Laws*, pp. 3–5.

31 Ruggles, *History of the Poor*, Vol. I, pp. xxiii–iv; unless indicated otherwise, my citations are to the two volume 1793–94 edition.

32 Ibid., pp. xii–xv.

33 For the Leveller–Whig distinction see: J. G. A. Pocock, 'The Origins of the Study of the Past: A Comparative Approach', *Comparative Studies in Society and History* 4 (1962–63), pp. 232–3.

34 Ruggles, *History of the Poor*, Vol. II, pp. 60–8; Burn, 'an able writer', nevertheless failed to explain the poor's loss of church support, according to Ruggles (Vol. I, pp. 282ff.)

35 Ibid., Vol. I, 73–5, 91–2.

36 Ibid., Vol. II, pp. 50–1, 213–15, 232–44, 313, 318–19.

37 Eden, *State of the Poor*, Vol. I, Preface, pp. i–iv. I will focus on a 400-page history, 'Of the Poor from the Conquest to the Present Period', and an 80-page essay on the underpinnings of policy, 'Of National Establishments for the Maintenance of the Poor', both found in Volume I.

38 Sir Frederic Morton Eden, *Catalogue* (1806).

39 *State of the Poor*, Vol. I, Preface, pp. ii–iv.

40 Ibid, p. 491–6.

41 Ibid., pp. 4–5.

42 Ibid., pp. xxix, 409.

43 Ibid., p. 106.

44 Ibid., p. 2.

45 Ibid., pp. xxvii. Eden seldom cites Burn and does not include his *History of the Poor Laws* in the bibliography in Volume III.

46 Ibid., p. 411.

47 Ibid., pp. 59–63.

48 Ibid., pp. 73–4. Eden cautions the reader to remember that 'in all ages, the desponding and discontented' magnify the 'excellencies of the past' and undervalue the 'blessing of their own times.'

49 Ibid., pp. 63, 128, 131.

50 Ibid., pp. 405, 407.

51 Edmund Burke, *Thoughts on Scarcity*, (London, 1800), pp. 1, 5, 18, 44.

52 Thomas Robert Malthus, *An Essay on the Principle of Population* (London, 1798), pp. 83, 91, 95–99.

53 Ruggles, *History of the Poor*, Vol. I, pp. 163–4.
54 Thomas Robert Malthus, *An Essay on Population*, new edn. (London, 1803), p. 417, ns. a, b; Eden, *State of the Poor*, Vol. I, p. 470.
55 Ibid., pp. 424, 437.
56 Ibid., pp. 5–6, 73–4.
57 Samuel Johnson, *A Dictionary of the English Language* (London, 1755).
58 Eden, *State of the Poor*, pp. 416–18, 438–44.
59 Ibid., pp. 439–40, 445, emphasis mine. A year later in the first edition of the *Essay* Malthus put the matter this way: 'We tell the common people, that if they will submit to a code of tyrannical regulations they shall never be in want; they do submit to these regulations. They perform their part of the contract: but we do not, nay cannot perform ours: and thus the poor sacrifice the valuable blessing of liberty, and receive nothing that can be called an equivalent in return' (pp. 98–9).
60 John Weyland, *A Short Inquiry into the Policy, Humanity, and Past Effects of the Poor Laws* ... (London, 1807), ch. ii.
61 Eden, *State of the Poor*, Vol. I, pp. 5–6.
62 Ibid., p. 6.
63 Ibid., p. 484–90.
64 Burn, *Poor Laws*, p. 236.
65 Ruggles, *History of the Poor*, Vol. I, pp. 163–4.
66 Pocock, 'The Origins of the Study of the Past', p. 218.
67 Eden, *State of the Poor*, Vol. I, pp. 487–8.

Conclusion: Whither Parish Social Welfare?

1 John Broad, 'Parish Economies of Welfare, 1650–1834', *Historical Journal* 42, 4 (1999), p. 985.
2 See J. R. Poynter, *Society and Pauperism* (London, 1969), ch. iv, for his agreement on this point.
3 L. A. Botelho, *Old Age and the English Poor Law, 1500–1700* (Rochester, NY, 2004), p. 73.
4 Paul Slack, *From Reformation to Improvement: Public Welfare in Early Modern England* (Oxford, 1999), pp. 148, 161–5.
5 Lynn Hollen Lees, *The Solidarities of Strangers: The English Poor Laws and the People, 1700–1948* (Cambridge, 1998), pp. 14–16, 348–9.
6 Anthony Brundage, *The English Poor Laws, 1700–1930* (Basingstoke, 2002), p. 154.

Bibliography

Abbreviations

EETS Early English Text Society

Alcock, Thomas. *Observations of the Defects of the Poor laws . . . in a Letter to a Member of Parliament* (London, 1752).
—— *Remarks on Two Bills for the Better Maintenance of the Poor . . .* (London, 1753).
Aquinas, Thomas. *Summa Contra Gentiles*, trans. English Dominican Fathers, 4 vols (London, 1923–29).
—— *Summa Theologica*, trans. English Dominican Fathers, 3 vols (New York, 1947).
Archer, Ian W. *The Pursuit of Stability: Social Relations in Elizabethan London* (Cambridge, 1991).
Armstrong, Clement. 'How to Reforme the Realme in Settyng Them to Werke and to Restore Tillage [*c*.1535–36]', in R. H. Tawney and Eileen Power, eds, *Tudor Economic Documents*, 3 vols (London, 1924), III, pp. 115–29.
Aston, Margaret. '"Caim's Castles": Poverty, Politics, and Disendowment', in Barrie Dobson, ed., *The Church, Politics and Patronage in the Fifteenth Century* (New York, 1984), pp. 45–81.
Augustine, Saint. *Twelve Sermons of Saynt Augustine, Now Lately Translated into English by Tho. Paynel* (London, 1555).
Awdeley, John. *Fraternity of Vacabondes* [1561?, 1565?, 1565?], in *The Rogues and Vagabonds of Shakspere's Youth*, Edward Viles and F. J. Furnivall, eds, New Shakespeare Society, VI, No. 7 (London, 1907).

236

Aylmer, G. E., ed. *The Levellers in the English Revolution* (Ithaca, NY, 1975).

Barry, Jonathan. 'Introduction', in Barry and Christopher Brooks, eds, *The Middling Sort of People* (Basingstoke, 1994).

Baxter, Richard. *A Holy Commonwealth* (London, 1659).

Becon, Thomas. *News out of Heaven* [*c*.1540], *Works*, ed. Rev. John Ayre, 3 vols (Cambridge, 1843), I.

Beier, A. L. 'Vagrants and the Social Order in Elizabethan England', *Past and Present*, 64 (August 1974), pp. 3–29.

——*Masterless Men: The Vagrancy Problem in England, 1560–1640* (London, 1985).

——'Poverty and Progress in Early Modern England', in Beier, David Cannadine and J. M. Rosenthal, eds, *The First Modern Society: Essays in English History in Honour of Lawrence Stone* (Cambridge, 1989), pp. 201–40.

Bentham, Jeremy. *Writings on the Poor Laws*, Vol. I, ed. Michael Quinn (Oxford, 2001).

Beresford, Maurice, and John G. Hurst, eds, *Deserted Medieval Villages* (Gloucester, 1971).

Bieler, Andre. *La Pensée Économique et Sociale de Calvin* (Geneva, 1959).

Bindoff, S. T. *Kett's Rebellion* (London, 1949).

Bittle, W. B., and R. T. Lane. 'Inflation and Philanthropy in England: A Reassessment of W. K. Jordan's Data', *Economic History Review*, 2nd ser., 29 (1976), pp. 203–10.

Blench, J. W. *Preaching in England in the Late Fifteenth and Early Sixteenth Centuries* (Oxford, 1964).

Bolingbroke, Lord. *A Dissertation upon Parties* (1734), in David Armitage, ed., *Bolingbroke: Political Writings* (Cambridge, 1997).

Bonaventure, Saint. 'The Defense of the Mendicants', trans. Jose de Vinck, *The Works of Bonaventure*, Vol. IV (Patterson, NJ, 1966).

The Book of Vices and Virtues, ed. W. Nelson Francis, EETS, Orig. ser, No. 217 (London, 1940).

Botelho, L. A. *Old Age and the English Poor Law, 1500–1700* (Rochester, NY, 2004).

Bott, Edmund. *The Laws Relating to the Poor*, Francis Const, ed., 5th edn, 3 vols (London, 1807).

Boulton, Jeremy. 'Going on the Parish: The Parish Pension and its Meaning in the London Suburbs, 1640–1724', in Tim Hitchcock, Peter King and Pamela Sharpe, eds, *Chronicling Poverty: The Voices and Strategies of the English Poor, 1640–1840* (Basingstoke, 1997), pp. 19–46.

Bourdieu, Pierre. *Outline of a Theory of Practice* (Cambridge, 1977).

Boyer, George R. *An Economic History of the English Poor Law* (Cambridge, 1990).

Bradshaw, Brendan. 'The Tudor Commonwealth: Reform and Revision' [review article], *Historical Journal*, 22, 2 (1979), pp. 455–76.

—— 'More on Utopia', *Historical Journal*, 24 (1981), pp. 1–28.

Brailsford, H. N. *The Levellers and the English Revolution*, Christopher Hill, ed. (Stanford, CA, 1961).

Brant, Sebastian. *The Ship of Fools*, trans. Alexander Barclay, ed. T. H. Jamieson, 2 vols (Edinburgh, 1874).

Brigden, Susan. *London and the Reformation* (Oxford, 1989).

Brinkelow, Henry. *The Complaynt of Roderyck Mors, etc.* (1542), ed. J. M. Cowper, EETS, extra ser., No. 22.

—— *The Lamentacyon of a Christen Agaynst the Cytye of London, etc.* (1545), ed. J. M. Cowper, EETS, extra ser., No. 22.

Britnell, Richard. 'The Economy of British Towns, 1300–1540', *The Cambridge Urban History of Britain*, Vol. I, ed. D. M. Palliser (Cambridge, 2000), pp. 105–26.

Broad, John. 'Parish Economies of Welfare, 1650–1834', *Historical Journal*, 42, 4 (1999), pp. 985–1006.

Brundage, Anthony. *The English Poor Laws, 1700–1930* (Basingstoke, 2002).

Bucer, Martin. *A Treatise, How Almose Ought to be Distributed* [1557?], *The English Experience*, No. 779 (Amsterdam, 1976).

Buckatzsch, E. J. 'The Geographical Distribution of Wealth in England, 1086–1843', *Economic History Review*, 2nd ser. III (1950), pp. 180–202.

Burke, Edmund. *Thoughts on Scarcity* (London, 1800).

Burn, Richard. *The History of the Poor Laws: With Observations* (London, 1764).

Bushaway, R. W. *By Rite: Custom, Ceremony and Community in England, 1700–1880* (London, 1982).

—— 'Rite, Legitimation and Community in Southern England, 1700–1850: The Ideology of Custom', in Barry Stapleton, ed., *Conflict and Community in Southern England* (Stroud, 1992), pp. 110–34.

Calvin, John. 'On Civil Government' [*The Institutes of the Christian Religion*, Bk. IV, ch. xx], in *John Calvin on God and Political Duty*, F. T. McNeill, ed. (New York, 1950).

—— *The Institutes of the Christian Religion*, ed. J. T. McNeill, trans. F. L. Battles, 2 vols (Philadelphia, 1960).

Capkova, Dagmar. 'Comenius and his Ideals: Escape from the Labyrinth', in Mark Greengrass, Michael Leslie and Timothy Raylor, eds, *Samuel Hartlib and Universal Reformation* (Cambridge, 1994), pp. 75–91.

Carnworth, Julia. 'The Churchwardens' Accounts of Thames, Oxford-shire, *c*.1443–1524', in Dorothy L. Clayton, Richard G. Davies and Peter McNiven, eds, *Trade, Devotion and Governance: Papers in Later Medieval History* (Stroud, 1994), pp. 177–97.

Cary, John. *A Discourse on Trade, and other Matters Relative to it Wrote at the Request of Several Members of Parliament* (London, 1745).

Caspari, Fritz. *Humanism and the Social Order in England* (Chicago, 1954).

Chamberlen, Peter. *The Poore Mans Advocate, or, England's Samaritan* ... (London, 1649).

Chaucer, Geoffrey. *The Canterbury Tales*, ed. Arthur Burrell (London, 1908).

Cheke, Sir John. *The Hurt of Sedicion* ... *to a Commune Welth* (London, 1549) *STC* 5109.

Christianson, Paul. 'Royal and Parliamentary Voices on the Ancient Constitution, *c*.1604–21', in Linda Levy Peck, ed., *The Mental World of the Jacobean Court* (Cambridge, 1991), pp. 71–95.

Cicero. *The Three Books of Tullius Offyce*, trans. R. Whittinton (London, 1534) *STC* 5278.

Clark, Peter. 'The Migrant in the Kentish Towns 1580–1640', in Clark and Paul Slack, eds, *Crisis and Order in English Towns, 1500–1700* (London, 1972), pp. 117–63.

—— and Paul Slack, eds *Crisis and Order in English Towns* (London, 1972).

—— —— eds, *English Towns in Transition, 1500–1700* (New York, 1976).

Clebsch, W. A. *England's Earliest Protestants* (New Haven, CT, 1964).

Coates, Ben. 'Poor Relief in London During the English Revolution Revisited', *The London Journal*, 25, 2 (2000), pp. 39–58.

Coleman, D. C. *The Economy of England, 1450–1750* (London, 1977).

Collinson, Patrick. *The Religion of Protestants: The Church in English Society, 1559–1625* (Oxford, 1982).

—— *The Birthpangs of Protestant England: Religious and Cultural Change in the Sixteenth and Seventeenth Centuries* (Basingstoke, 1988).

—— *Puritan Character, Polemics and Polarities in Early Seventeenth-Century English Culture* (Los Angeles, 1989).

—— 'England', in B. Scribner, Roy Porter and Mikulás Teich, eds, *The Reformation in National Context* (Cambridge, 1994), pp. 80–94.

Colquhoun, Patrick. *A Treatise on Indigence* ... *for Ameliorating the Conditions of the Poor* ... *Particularly the Rising Generation* (London, 1806).

Cooper, Tim. *The Last Generation of English Catholic Clergy: Parish Priests in the Diocese of Coventry and Lichfield in the Early Sixteenth Century* (Woodbridge, 1999).

Copland, Robert. *Hyeway to the Spittal House* (London, 1535–36).

Crowley, Robert. *The Way to Wealth* (1550), *Selected Works*, EETS, extra ser., No. 15.

Crowther, Anne. 'Health Care and Poor Relief in Provincial England', in Ole Peter Grell, Andrew Cunningham and Robert Jutte, eds, *Health Care and Poor Relief in 18th and 19th Century Northern Europe* (Aldershot, 2001), pp. 203–19.

Cruickshanks, Evaline. *Political Untouchables: The Tories and the '45* (London, 1979).

Coulton, G. C. *Social Life in Britain From the Conquest to the Reformation* (Cambridge, 1919).

Cullum, Patricia H. '"For Pore People Harberles": What was the Function of the Maisonsdieu?', in Dorothy J. Clayton, Richard G. Davies and Peter McNiven, eds, *Trade, Devotion and Governance* (Stroud, 1994), pp. 36–54.

Davies, C. S. L. 'Popular Religion and the Pilgrimage of Grace', in Anthony Fletcher and John Stevenson, eds, *Order and Disorder in Early Modern England* (Cambridge, 1985), pp. 58–91.

Davis, Natalie Z. 'Poor Relief, Humanism and Heresy: The Case of Lyon', *Studies in Medieval and Renaissance History*, 5 (1968), pp. 217–75.

Dean, David. *Law-Making and Society in Late Elizabethan England: The Parliament of England, 1584–1601* (Cambridge, 1996).

Defoe, Daniel. *Giving Alms No Charity* (London, 1704).

Dewar, Mary. *Sir Thomas Smith: A Tudor Intellectual in Office* (London, 1964).

D'ewes, Sir Simonds. *The Journals of All the Parliaments during the Reign of Queen Elizabeth* (London, 1973 [1682]).

De Vries, J. 'Purchasing Power and the World of Goods', in John Brewer and Roy Porter, eds, *Consumption and the World of Goods* (London, 1993), pp. 85–132.

Dickens, Arthur G. *The English Reformation* (London, 1964).

Disney, John. *A View of Ancient Laws . . .* (London, 1729).

Douglas, Richard M. 'Talent and Vocation in Humanist and Protestant Thought', in Theodore K. Rabb and Jerrold E. Seigel, eds, *Action and Contemplation in Early Modern Europe* (Princeton, NJ, 1969), pp. 261–98.

Douie, D. L. *The Nature and the Effect of the Heresy of the Fraticelli* (Manchester, 1932).

Dowling, M. 'Anne Boleyn and Reform', *Journal of Ecclesiastical History*, XXXV (1984), pp. 30–46.

Dudley, Edmund. *The Tree of Commonwealth* [*c*.1510], ed. D. M. Brodie (Cambridge, 1948).

Duffy, Eamon. *The Stripping of the Altars: Traditional Religion in England, c.1400–c.1580* (New Haven, CT, 1992).

Duncan, J. S. *Collections Relative to the Systematic Relief of the Poor* (Bath, 1815).

Dyer, Alan. *Decline and Growth in English Towns, 1400–1640* (London, 1991).

Dyer, Christopher. '"The Retreat from Marginal Land": The Growth and Decline of Medieval Rural Settlements', in Michael Aston, David Austin and Christopher Dyer, eds, *The Rural Settlements of Medieval England: Studies Dedicated to Maurice Beresford and John Hurst* (Oxford, 1989), pp. 45–57.

——*Standards of Living in the Later Middle Ages* (Cambridge, 1989).

——*Everyday Life in Medieval England* (London, 1994).

Eden, Sir Frederic Morton. *The State of the Poor; Or, An History of the Laboring Classes in England*, 3 vols (London, 1797).

——*Catalogue* (1806).

Elton, G. R. 'An Early Tudor Poor Law', *Economic History Review*, 2nd ser., VI (1953), pp. 55–67.

——*The Tudor Revolution in Government* (Cambridge, 1953).

——*Policy and Police* (Cambridge, 1972).

——*Reform and Renewal* (Cambridge, 1973).

Elyot, Thomas. *The Boke Named the Governor* [1531], ed. Henry H. S. Croft, 2 vols (London, 1883).

Erasmus, *Education of a Christian Prince* (New York, 1936 [1516]).

Erickson, Carolly. *The Medieval Vision* (New York, 1976).

Evans, Connie S. '"An Echo of the Multitude": The Intersection of Governmental and Private Poverty Initiatives in Early Modern Exeter', *Albion*, 32, 3 (Autumn 2000), pp. 408–28.

Ferguson, Arthur B. *The Indian Summer of English Chivalry* (Durham, NC, 1960).

——*The Articulate Citizen and the English Renaissance* (Durham, NC, 1965).

——*Clio Unbound* (Durham, NC, 1979).

Fideler, Paul A. 'Christian Humanism and Poor Law Reform in Early Tudor England', *Societas*, IV, 4 (1974), pp. 269–85.

——'Poverty, Policy and Providence: The Tudors and the Poor', in Fideler and T. F. Mayer, eds, *Political Thought and the Tudor Commonwealth* (London and New York, 1992), ch. 7.

—— 'Societas, Civitas and Early Elizabethan Poverty Relief', in Charles Carleton et al., eds, State, Sovereigns and Society in Early Modern England: Essays in Honour of A. J. Slavin (Stroud, 1998), pp. 59–69.

—— 'Impressions of a Century of Historiography', Albion, 32, 3 (Fall 2000), pp. 381–407.

Fish, Simon. A Supplication for the Beggars [1529?], ed. Frederick J. Furnival, EETS, extra ser. No. 13 (London, 1871).

Fletcher, Anthony. Tudor Rebellions, 2nd edn (London, 1973).

Fortesque, Sir John. The Governance of England [1471], ed. Charles Plummer (Oxford, 1885).

Fox, Alistair. 'English Humanism and the Body Politic', in Fox and John Guy, eds, Reassessing the Henrician Age (Oxford, 1986), pp. 34–51.

Francis, W. Nelson, ed. The Book of Vices and Virtues, EETS, orig. ser. No. 217 (London, 1942).

French, H. R. 'Social Status, Localism and the "Middle Sort of People" in England, 1620–1750', Past and Present, 166 (February 2000), pp. 66–99.

—— 'The Search for the "Middle Sort of People" in England', Historical Journal, 43, 1 (March 2000) pp. 277–93.

Froissart, Jean. Chronicles of England, France and Adjoining Countries, trans. Thomas Jones, 4 vols (Havod, 1803–15).

George, Charles H., and Katherine George. The Protestant Mind of the English Reformation (Princeton, NJ, 1961).

Gerrish, B. A. Grace and Reason: A Study in the Theology of Luther (Oxford, 1962).

Getz, Faye. Medicine in the English Middle Ages (Princeton, NJ, 1998).

Gibbs, Gary. 'New Duties For the Parish Community in Tudor London', in Katherine L. French, Garry Gibbs and Beat A. Kumin, eds, The Parish in English Life, 1400–1600 (Manchester, 1997), pp. 163–77.

Given-Wilson, Chris. 'Service, Serfdom and English Labor Legislation, 1350–1500', in Anne Curry and Elizabeth Matthew, eds, Concepts and Patterns of Service in the Later Middle Ages (Woodbridge, 2000), pp. 21–37.

Goldberg, P. J. P. 'Coventry's "Lollard" Programme of 1492 and the Making of Utopia', in Rosemary Horrox and Sarah Rees Jones, eds, Pragmatic Utopias: Ideals and Communities, 1200–1630 (Cambridge, 2001), pp. 97–116.

Great Britain. PRO. Letters and Papers, Foreign and Domestic of the Reign of Henry VIII, catalogued by J. S. Brewer, 2nd rev. edn, 21 vols (Vaduz, 1965 [reprint of 1888 edn).

Greenblatt, Stephen. *Renaissance Self-Fashioning: More to Shakespeare* (Chicago, 1980).

—— *Hamlet in Purgatory* (Princeton, NJ, 2001).

Greengrass, Mark, Michael Leslie, and Timothy Raylor, eds, *Samuel Hartlib and Universal Reformation* (Cambridge, 1994), Introduction.

Gregory, Jeremy. 'The Making of a Protestant Nation: "Success" and "Failure" in England's Long Reformation', in Nicholas Tyacke, ed., *England's Long Reformation, 1500–1800* (London, 1998), pp. 307–33.

Grell, Ole Peter. 'The Protestant Imperative of Christian Care and Neighbourly Love', in Grell and Andrew Cunningham, eds, *Health Care and Poor Relief in Protestant Europe, 1500–1700* (London and New York, 1997), ch. 2.

—— and Andrew Cunningham. 'The Reformation and Changes in Welfare Provision in Early Modern Northern Europe', in Grell and Cunningham, eds, *Health Care and Poor Relief in Protestant Europe, 1500–1700* (London and New York, 1997), ch. 1.

Grimm, H. J. 'Luther's Contributions to Sixteenth-Century Organization of Poor Relief', *Archiv für Reformationsgeschichte*, 61 (1970), pp. 222–34.

Guy, John A. 'The Tudor Commonwealth: Revising Thomas Cromwell', *Historical Journal*, 23 (1980), pp. 681–8.

—— *Christopher St. German on Chancery and Statute*, Seldon Society, suppl. ser. (1985), Vol. 6.

Gwynn, Aubry. *The English Austin Friars in the Time of Wyclif* (Oxford, 1940).

Hadwin, F. W. 'Deflating Philanthropy', *Economic History Review*, 2nd ser., 31 (1978), pp. 105–17.

Halliday, Paul D. *Dismembering the Body Politic: Partisan Politics in England's Towns, 1650–1730* (Cambridge, 1998).

Hands, A. R. *Charities and Social Aid in Greece and Rome* (London, 1968).

Harman, Thomas. *A Caveat for Commen Cursetors Vulgarely called Vagabones* (London, 1567).

Harrison, Scott M. *The Pilgrimage of Grace in the Lake Counties, 1536–37* (London, 1981).

Harte, N. B. 'State Control of Dress and Social Change in Pre-Industrial England', in D. C. Coleman and A. H. John, eds, *Trade, Government and Economy in Pre-Industrial England* (London, 1976), pp. 132–65.

Hartlib, Samuel. *London's Charity inlarged, Stilling the Orphans Cry* (1650).

Hatcher, John. 'England in the Aftermath of the Black Death', *Past and Present*, 144 (1994), pp. 3–35.

—— 'Understanding the Population History of England, 1450–1750', *Past and Present*, 180 (August 2003), pp. 83–130.

Hay, William. *Remarks on the Laws Relating to the Poor with Proposals for their Better Relief and Employment* (London, 1735).

Hazlitt, W. C., ed. *Remains of the Early Popular Poetry of England* (London, 1866).

Heal, Felicity. *Hospitality in Early Modern England* (Oxford, 1990).

Herlan, Ronald. 'Poor Relief in London during the English Revolution', *Journal of British Studies*, 18, 2 (1979), pp. 30–51

Herrup, Cynthia B. 'The Counties and the Country: Some Thoughts on Seventeenth-Century Historiography', in G. Eley and William Hunt, eds, *Reviving the English Revolution: Reflections and Elaborations on the Work of Christopher Hill* (London, 1988), pp. 289–304

Hill, Christopher. *Society and Puritanism in Pre-Revolutionary England* (New York, 1964).

Hilton, Rodney. *Class Conflict and the Crisis of Feudalism* (London, 1990).

—— 'Status and Class in the Medieval Town', in T. R. Slater and Gervase Rosser, eds, *The Church in the Medieval Town* (Aldershot, 1998), pp. 9–19.

Himmelfarb, Gertrude. *The Idea of Poverty: England in the Early Industrial Age* (New York, 1984).

Hindle, Steve. 'Exclusion Crises: Poverty, Migration and Parochial Responsibility in English Rural Communities', *Rural History* (1996). pp. 125–49.

—— 'The Birthpangs of Welfare: Poor Relief and Parish Governance in Seventeenth-Century Warwickshire', *Dugdale Society Occasional Papers*, No. 40 (2000).

—— *The State and Social Change in Early Modern England, c.1550–1640* (Basingstoke, 2000).

—— 'Dearth, Fasting and Alms: The Campaign for General Hospitality in Late Elizabethan England', *Past and Present*, 172 (August 2001), pp. 44–86.

Hintermaier, John. 'The First Modern Refugees? Charity, Entitlement, and Persuasion in the Huguenot Immigration of the 1680s', *Albion*, 32, 3 (2000), pp. 429–49.

Hitchcock, Robert. *A Pollitique Platt for the Honour of the Prince, the Greate Profite of the Publique State, etc.* (London, 1580).

Holderness, B. A. *Pre-Industrial England: Economy and Society from 1500 to 1750* (London, 1976).

Horne, Thomas A. '"The Poor Have a Claim Founded in the Law of Nature"...', *Journal of the History of Philosophy*, XXIII, 1 (1985), pp. 51–70.

—— *Property Rights and Poverty: Political Argument in Britain, 1605–1834* (Chapel Hill, NC, 1990).

Hotson, Howard. 'Philosophical Pedagogy in Reformed Central Europe between Ramus and Comenius', in Mark Greengrass, Michael Leslie and Timothy Raylor, eds, *Samuel Hartlib and Universal Reformation* (Cambridge, 1994), pp. 29–50.

Hoyle, R. W. *The Pilgrimage of Grace and the Politics of the 1530s* (Oxford, 2001).

Hufton, Olwen H. *The Poor of Eighteenth-Century France, 1750–1789* (Oxford, 1974).

Hutton, Ronald. *The Rise and Fall of Merry England: The Ritual Year, 1400–1700* (Oxford, 1994).

—— *The Stations of the Sun: A History of the Ritual Year in Britain* (New York, 1996).

Ingram, Martin. 'Reformation of Manners in Early Modern England', in Paul Griffiths, Adam Fox and Steve Hindle, eds, *The Experience of Authority in Early Modern England* (Basingstoke, 1996), pp. 47–88.

James VI and I. *Political Writings*, ed. Johann P. Sommerville (Cambridge, 1994).

James, Margaret. *Social Problems and Policy during the Puritan Revolution* (London, 1966 [1930]).

Johnson, Samuel. *A Dictionary of the English Language* (London, 1755).

Jones, Norman. *The Birth of the Elizabethan Age* (Oxford, 1993).

Jones, Sarah Rees. 'Thomas More's *Utopia* and Medieval London', in Rosemary Horrox and Jones, eds, *Pragmatic Utopias: Ideals and Communities, 1200–1630* (Cambridge, 2001), pp. 117–35.

Jones, Whitney R. D. *The Tudor Commonwealth, 1529–1559* (London, 1970).

Jordan, W. K. *Philanthropy in England, 1480–1660* (London, 1959).

—— *The Charities of London, 1480–1660* (London, 1960).

—— *The Charities of Rural England, 1480–1660* (London, 1961).

—— *Edward VI: The Young King* (Cambridge, MA, 1968).

Katz, Michael B., and Christoph Sachze, eds. *The Mixed Economy of Social Welfare* (Baden-Baden, 1996).

Keen, Maurice H. *The Outlaws of Medieval Legend* (London, 1961).

King, Gregory. *Natural and Political Observations on the State and Condition of England* (London, 1688).

King, Peter. 'Pauper Inventories and the Material Lives of the Poor in the Eighteenth and Early Nineteenth Centuries', in Tim Hitchcock, King, and Pamela Sharpe, eds, *Chronicling Poverty: The Voices and Strategies of the English Poor, 1640–1840* (Basingstoke, 1997). pp. 155–91.

King, Steven. 'Reconstructing Lives: The Poor, the Poor Law and Welfare in Calverley, 1650–1820', *Social History*, 22, 3 (October 1997), pp. 318–38.

——*Poverty and Welfare in England, 1700–1850* (Manchester, 2000).

—— and Alannah Tomkins, Editors' Introduction, *The Poor in England, 1700–1850: An Economy of Makeshifts* (Manchester and New York, 2003).

Kingdon, Robert M. 'Social Welfare in Calvin's Geneva', *American Historical Review*, 76 (1971, pp. 50–69.

Kosminsky, E. A. *Studies in the Agrarian History of England in the Thirteenth Century*, trans. R. Kisch (Oxford, 1956).

Kowaleski, Maryanne. *Local Markets and Regional Trade in Medieval Exeter* (Cambridge, 1995).

Kramnick, I. F. *Bolingbrode and His Circle: The Politics of Nostaligia in the Age of Walpole* (Cambridge, MA, 1968).

Lake, Peter. 'Calvinism and the English Church, 1570–1636', in Margo Todd, ed., *Reformation and Revolution: Politics and Religion in Early Modern England* (London and New York, 1995), Ch. 10.

—— 'Periodization, Politics and "The Social"', *Journal of British Studies*, 37, 3 (July 1998), pp. 279–90.

Land, S. K. *The Norfolk Rising of 1549* (Ipswich, 1977).

Landau, Norma. 'The Laws of Settlement and the Surveillance of Immigration in Eighteenth-Century Kent', *Continuity and Change*, 3, 3 (1998), pp. 391–420.

—— 'The Eighteenth-Century Context of the Laws of Settlement', *Continuity and Change*, 6, 3 (1991), pp. 417–39.

Landes, David M. *The Wealth and Poverty of Nations* (New York, 1995).

Langland, William. *The Vision of Piers the Plowman*, Modern English by Henry Wells (New York, 1945).

Latimer, Hugh. 'Sermon of the Plough', *Works*, ed. G. E. Corrie, 2 vols (Cambridge, 1844–5), I.

Lawrence, Thomas. *Some pity on the poor: or, a way how poor people may be supplied with labor and relief without begging* ... (London, c.1650).

Lee, Leonard. *A Remonstrance Humbly Presented to the High and Honourable Court of Parliament* ... (London, 1644).

Lees, Lynn Hollen. *The Solidarities of Strangers: The English Poor Laws and the People, 1700–1948* (Cambridge, 1998).

Lieberman, David. *The Province of Legislation Determined* (Cambridge, 1989).

Leonard, E. M. *The Early History of English Poor Relief* (New York, 1965 [1900]).

Lever, Thomas. 'A fruitful sermon made in Poules Church', *Sermons*, ed. E. Arber (London, 1871).

Levine, David, and Keith Wrightson. *The Making of an Industrial Society: Whickham, 1560–1765* (Oxford, 1991).

————*Poverty and Piety in an English Village: Terling, 1525–1700* (Oxford, 1995 [1979]).

Levy, F. J. *Tudor Historical Thought* (San Marino, CA, 1967).

Logan, George. *The Meaning of More's Utopia* (Princeton, NJ, 1983).

Luther, Martin. 'Ordinance for a Common Chest [1523]', in F. R. Salter, ed., *Some Early Tracts on Poor Relief* (London, 1926), pp. 80–96.

———*The Freedom of a Christian* [1520], in *The Reformation Writings of Luther* trans. B. L. Woolf, (London, 1952).

MacCaffrey, Wallace. *Exeter, 1540–1640* (Cambridge, MA, 1975).

Malthus, Thomas Robert. *An Essay on the Principle of Population* (London, 1798); new edn (London, 1803).

Mantuan, Johannes Baptista. *The Cytezen and Uplondyshman*, trans. Alexander Barclay, ed. R. W. Fairholt, Percey Society; Early English Poetry, Vol. XXII (London, 1847).

Marshall, Dorothy. *The English Poor in the Eighteenth Century* (London, 1926).

Masschaele, James. *Peasants, Merchants, and Markets: Inland Trade in Medieval England, 1150–1350* (Basingstoke, 1997).

Mate, Mavis. 'The Economic and Social Roots of Medieval Popular Rebellion: Sussex in 1450–51', *Economic History Review*, XLV, 4 (Nov. 1992), pp. 661–76.

Mayhew, N. 'Modelling Medieval Monetisation', in R. H. Britnell and B. M. S. Campbell, eds, *A Commercialising Society* (Manchester, 1995), pp. 55–77.

Mayer, T. F. 'Thomas Starkey's Aristocratic Reform Programme', *History of Political Thought*, 7 (1986), pp. 439–61.

———*Thomas Starkey and the Commonweal* (Cambridge, 1989).

McIntosh, Marjorie K. 'Local Responses to the Poor in Late Medieval and Tudor England', *Continuity and Change*, 3, 2 (1988), pp. 209–45.

———*Controlling Misbehavior in England, 1370–1600* (Cambridge, 1998).

Mohl, Ruth. *The Three Estates in Medieval and Renaissance Literature* (New York, 1933).

Mokyr, Joel. 'The New Economic History and the Industrial Revolution', in Mokyr, ed., *The British Industrial Revolution: An Economic Perspective* (Boulder, CO, 1995), pp. 1–131.

Montainge, Michel de. *Essays Written in French by Michael Lord of Montaigne*, trans. John Florio (London, 1613).

Moore, John. *The Crying Sin of England, of not Caring for the Poor...* (London, 1653).

More, Thomas. *A Supplycacion of Soulys* (London, 1529).

——*Utopia* [1516], in *The Complete Works of St. Thomas More*, ed. J. H. Hexter and Edward Surtz, Vol. 4 (New Haven, CT, 1965).

Morison, Richard. *A Remedy for Sedition* [1536], ed. E. M. Cox (London, 1933).

Morrill, John. *The Revolt in the Provinces*, 2nd edn (London, 1998).

Muldrew, Craig. 'Interpreting the Market: The Ethics of Credit and Community Relations in Early Modern England', *Social History*, 18, 2 (May 1993), pp. 163–83.

Newell, Fiona. 'Social Mobility in the Population of Aldenham, Hertfordshire, 1600–1800', in Doris Jones-Baker, ed., *Hertfordshire in History: Papers Presented to Lionel Munby* (Hertford, 1991), pp. 109–24.

Norberg, Kathryn. *Rich and Poor in Grenoble, 1600–1814* (Berkeley, CA, 1985).

Orme, Nicholas, and Margaret Webster. *The English Hospital, 1070–1570* (New Haven, CT, 1995).

Ottaway, Susannah R. *The Decline of Life: Old Age in Eighteenth-Century England* (Cambridge, 2004).

Owst, G. R. *Literature and Pulpit in Medieval England*, 2nd edn (New York, 1961).

Paley, William. *Principles of Moral and Political Philosophy* (London, 1785).

Parker, Henry. *Dives and Pauper* (London, 1534).

Patch, Howard R. *The Goddess Fortuna in Mediaeval Literature* (New York, 1967 [1927]).

Patten, John. *English Towns, 1500–1700* (Hamden, CT, 1978).

Pearl, Valerie. 'Social Policy in Early Modern London', in Hugh Lloyd-Jones, Pearl and Blair Worden, eds, *History and Imagination: Essays in Honour of H. R. Trevor-Roper* (London, 1981), pp. 115–31.

Pelling, Margaret. *The Common Lot: Sickness, Medical Occupations and the Urban Poor in Early Modern England* (London, 1998).

Peltonen, Markku. *Classical Humanism and Republicanism in English Political Thought, 1570–1640* (Cambridge, 1995).

Perkins, William. *Cases of Conscience* [1606], *Works*, 3 vols (London, 1612–13), III.

Petty, William. *A Treatise of Taxes & Contributions* [1662], in *The Economic Writings of Sir William Petty*, ed., Charles Henry Hull, 2 vols (New York, 1963), I.

Phillipson, Nicholas. 'Adam Smith as Civic Moralist', in Istvan Hont and Michael Ignatieff, eds, *Wealth and Virtue: The Shaping of Political Economy in the Scottish Enlightenment* (Cambridge, 1983), pp. 179–202.

Platt, Colin. *The English Medieval Town* (London, 1976).

Pocock, J. G. A. 'The Origins of the Study of the Past: A Comparative Approach', *Comparative Studies in Society and History*, 4 (1962), pp. 209–46.
—— *Virtue, Commerce and History* (Cambridge, 1985).
Pollard, A. F. *England under Protector Somerset* (London, 1900).
Poos, L. R. 'The Social Context of Statute of Laborers Enforcement', *Law and History Review*, I, 1 (Spring 1983), pp. 27–52.
Poynter, J. R. *Society and Pauperism: English Ideas on Poor Relief, 1795–1834* (London, 1969).
Pullan, Brain. *Rich and Poor in Renaissance Venice* (Oxford, 1971).
Quintrell, B. W. 'The Making of Charles I's Book of Orders', *English Historical Review*, 95 (1980), pp. 553–72.
Rappaport, Steve. *Worlds Within Worlds: Structures of Life in Sixteenth-Century London* (Cambridge, 1989).
Rawcliffe, Carole. *Medicine for the Soul* (Stroud, 1999).
—— 'Curing Bodies and Healing Souls: Pilgrimage and Sick in Medieval East Anglia', in Colin Morris and Peter Roberts, eds, *Pilgrimage: The English Experience from Becket to Bunyan* (Cambridge, 2000), pp. 108–40.
Rein, Martin. 'Value-Critical Policy Analysis', in D. Callahan and B. Jennings, eds, *Ethics, the Social Sciences, and Policy Analysis* (New York, 1983), pp. 83–111.
Report of the Select Committee of the House of Commons on the Poor Laws (London, 1817).
Ribton-Turner, C. J. *A History of Vagrants and Vagrancy and Beggars and Begging* (London, 1887).
Richmond, Colin. 'Victorian Values in Fifteenth-Century England: The Ewelme Almshouse Statutes', in Rosemary Horrox and Sarah Rees Jones, eds, *Pragmatic Utopias: Ideals and Communities, 1200–1630* (Cambridge, 2001), pp. 224–41.
Robbins, Caroline. *The Eighteenth-Century Commonwealthmen* (Cambridge, MA, 1959).
Roberts, Peter. 'Elizabethan Players and Minstrels and the Legislation of 1572 Against Retainers and Vagabonds', in Anthony Fletcher and Peter Roberts, eds, *Religion, Culture and Society in Early Modern Britain* (Cambridge, 1994), pp. 29–55.
Rubin, Miri. *Charity and Community in Medieval Cambridge* (Cambridge, 1987).
—— 'The Poor', in Rosemary Horrox, ed., *Fifteenth-Century Attitudes: Perceptions of Society in Late Medieval England* (Cambridge, 1994), pp. 169–82.

Ruggles, Thomas. *The History of the Poor, Their Rights, Duties, and the Laws Respecting Them*, 2 vols (London, 1793–94); 2nd edn in 1 vol. (London, 1797).

Rushton, Peter. 'The Poor Law, The Parish and the Community in North-East England, 1600–1800', *Northern History*, XXV (1989), pp. 135–52.

Scarisbrick, J. J. 'Cardinal Wolsey and the Common Weal', in E. W. Ives, R. J. Knecht and Scarisbrick, eds, *Wealth and Power in Tudor England* (London, 1978), pp. 45–67.

Schen, Claire S. 'Constructing the Poor in Early Seventeenth Century London', *Albion*, 32, 3 (Fall 2000), pp. 450–63.

——*Charity and Lay Piety in Reformation London, 1500–1620* (Aldershot, 2002).

Schlatter, R. *Private Property* (New Brunswick, NJ, 1951).

Schofield, R. S. 'The Geographical Distribution of Wealth in England, 1334–1649', *Economic History Review*, 2nd ser., 18, 3 (December 1965), pp. 483–510.

Seneca, *The Works of Lucius Annaeus Seneca, Both Moral and Natural*, trans. Thomas Lodge (London, 1614).

Siena, Kevin P. *Venereal Disease, Hospitals and the Urban Poor* (Rochester, NY, 2004).

Skinner, Quentin. *The Foundations of Modern Political Thought*, 2 vols (Cambridge, 1978).

——'Sir Thomas More's *Utopia* and the Language of Renaissance Humanism', in Anthony Pagden, ed., *The Languages of Political Theory in Early-Modern Europe* (Cambridge, 1987), pp. 123–57.

Slack, Paul. 'Poverty and Politics in Salisbury', in Peter Clark and Slack, eds, *Crisis and Order in English Towns, 1500–1700* (London, 1972), pp. 164–203.

——'Vagrants and Vagrancy in England, 1598–1664', *Economic History Review*, 2nd ser., 27 (August 1974), pp. 360–78.

——'Social Policy and the Constraints of Government, 1547–58', in Jennifer Loach and Robert Tittler, eds, *The Mid-Tudor Polity, c.1540–1560* (London, 1980), pp. 94–115.

——'Books of Orders: The Making of English Social Policy, 1577–1631', *Transactions of the Royal Historical Society*, 30 (1980), pp. 1–22.

——*Poverty and Policy in Tudor and Stuart England* (London, 1988).

——*The English Poor Law 1531–1782* (Stroud, 1990).

——'Hospitals, Workhouses and the Relief of the Poor in Early Modern London', in Ole Peter Grell and Andrew Cunningham, eds, *Health*

Care and Poor Relief in Protestant Europe, 1500–1700 (London and New York, 1997), pp. 234–51.

——*From Reformation to Improvement: Public Welfare in Early Modern England* (Oxford, 1999).

Smail, John. *Merchants, Markets and Manufacturers* (Basingstoke, 1999).

Smith, Sir Thomas. *A Discourse of the Commonweal of this Realm of England* [1581], ed. Mary Dewar (Charlottsville, VA, 1969).

Snell, K. D. M. *Annals of the Laboring Poor: Social Change and Agrarian England, 1660–1900* (Cambridge, 1985).

——'Pauper Settlement and the Right to Poor Relief in England and Wales', *Continuity and Change*, 6, 3 (1991), pp. 375–415.

——'Settlement, Poor law and the Rural Historian: New Approaches and Opportunities', *Rural History*, 3, 2 (1992), pp. 145–72.

Sokoll, Thomas, ed., *Essex Pauper Letters, 1731–1837* (Oxford, 2001).

Solar, Peter M. 'Poor Relief and English Economic Development Before the Industrial Revolution', *Economic History Review*, 2nd ser., 48, 1 (1995), pp. 1–22.

Spufford, Margaret. *Contrasting Communities: English Villagers in the Sixteenth and Seventeenth Centuries* (Cambridge, 1974).

——'Puritanism and Social Control?', in A. Fletcher and J. Stevenson, eds, *Order and Disorder in Early Modern England* (Cambridge, 1985), pp. 41–57.

Starkey, David. 'Which Age of Reform?', in C. Coleman and Starkey, eds, *Revolution Reassessed* (Oxford, 1986), pp. 13–27.

Starkey, Thomas. *An exhortation . . . to unitie and obedience* (London, 1536).

——*A Dialogue Between Pole and Lupset* [1529–32?], ed. T. F. Mayer (London, 1989).

The Statutes of the Realm, 12 vols (London, 1963 [reprint of 1810–28 edn].

Stone, Lawrence. *The Crisis of the Aristocracy* (Oxford, 1976).

——*The Family, Sex and Marriage in England, 1500–1800* (New York, 1977).

Tawney, R. H. *Religion and the Rise of Capitalism: A Historical Study* (Gloucester, MA 1954 [1926]).

——*The Agrarian Problem in the Sixteenth Century* (New York, 1967 [1912]).

Taylor, James Stephen. 'The Impact of Pauper Settlement, 1691–1834', *Past and Present*, 73 (November 1976), pp. 42–74.

Thomas, Keith. *Religion and the Decline of Magic* (New York, 1971).

Thompson, E. P. *Customs in Common* (London, 1991).

Thomson, David. 'Welfare and the Historians', in Lloyd Bonfield, Richard M. Smith and Keith Wrightson, eds, *The World We Have Gained* (Oxford, 1986), pp. 355–78.

Thomson, J. A. F. 'Piety and Charity in Late Medieval London', *Journal of Ecclesiastical History*, 16 (1965), pp. 178–95.

Tierney, Brian. *Medieval Poor Law* (Berkeley, CA, 1959).

Tittler, Robert. 'Reformation, Resources and Authority in English Towns: An Overview', in Patrick Collinson and John Craig, eds, *The Reformation in English Towns, 1500–1640* (New York, 1998), pp. 190–201.

—— *The Reformation and the Towns in England* (Oxford, 1998).

Todd, Margo. 'Seneca and the Protestant Mind: The Influence of Stoicism on Puritan Ethics', *Archiv für Reformationsgeschichte* 74 (1983), pp. 182–200.

—— *Christian Humanism and the Puritan Social Order* (Cambridge, 1987).

Townsend, Joseph. *A Dissertation on the Poor Laws* (London, 1786; 1817).

Trevelyan, G. M. *English Social History* (London, 1946).

Trinkaus, Charles. 'Renaissance Problems in Calvin's Theology', *Studies in the Renaissance,* Vol. I (1954), pp. 59–80.

—— 'The religious foundations of Luther's social views', in J. H. Mundy, R. W. Emery and B. N. Nelson, eds, *Essays in Medieval Life and Thought* (New York, 1955), pp. 71–87.

Troeltsch, Ernst. *The Social Teachings of the Christian Churches*, trans. O. Wyon, 2 vols (New York, 1931).

Tuck, Richard. *Philosophy and Government, 1572–1651* (Cambridge, 1993).

Tyndale, William. 'The Prologue into the Fourth Booke of Moses called Numeri', in T. Russell, ed., *The Works of the English Reformers: William Tyndale and John Frith*, 3 vols (London, 1831), I.

—— 'Prologue upon the Gospel of St. Matthew [1523]', in H. Walter, ed., *Doctrinal Treatises and Introductions to Different Portions of the Holy Scriptures* (Cambridge, 1848).

—— 'An Exposition upon ... Matthew', in *The Work of William Tyndale*, ed. G. E. Duffield (Appleford, 1964).

Underdown, David. *Revel, Riot, and Rebellion: Popular Politics and Culture in England 1603–1660* (Oxford, 1985).

—— *Fire from Heaven* (London, 1992).

Valenze, Deborah. *The First Industrial Woman* (Oxford, 1995).

Vives, Juan. 'Concerning the Relief of the Poor [*De subventione pauperum,* 1526]', trans. Margaret M. Sherwood, *Studies in Social Work*, 11 (1917), pp. 1–47.

Wales, Tim. 'Poverty, Poor Relief and the Life-Cycle: Some Evidence from Seventeenth-Century Norfolk', in Richard M. Smith, ed., *Land, Kinship and Life-Cycle* (Cambridge, 1984), pp. 351–404.

Walter, John. 'The Social Economy of Dearth in Early Modern England', in Walter and Roger Schofield, eds, *Famine, Disease and the Social Order in Early Modern Society* (Cambridge, 1989).

—— 'Public Transcripts, Popular Agency and the Politics of Subsistence in Early Modern England', in M. J. Braddick and Walter, eds, *Negotiating Power in Early Modern Society* (Cambridge, 2001), pp. 123–48.

—— and Keith Wrightson. 'Dearth and the Social Order in Early Modern England', *Past and Present*, 71 (May 1976), pp. 22–42.

Wear, Andrew. 'Religious Beliefs and Medicine in Early Modern England', in Wear, ed., *Health and Healing in Early Modern England* (Aldershot, 1998), pp. 145–69.

Webb, Sidney, and Beatrice Webb. *English Local Government: English Poor Law History: Part I. The Old Poor Law* (London, 1927).

Webster, Charles. *The Great Instauration: Science, Medicine and Reform, 1626–1660* (London, 1975).

Wexler, V. G. 'David Hume's Discovery of a New Scene of Historical Thought', *Eighteenth Century Studies*, 10 (1976–77), pp. 185–202.

Weyland, John. *A Short Inquiry into the Policy, Humanity, and Past Effects for the Poor Laws . . .* (London, 1807).

Willard, J. 'Taxation Boroughs and Parliamentary Boroughs, 1294–1336', in J. G. Edwards, V. H. Galbraith and E. F. Jacob, eds, *Historical Essays in Honour of James Tait* (Manchester, 1933), pp. 417–35.

Wilson, Thomas. *The Rule of Reason Concerning the Arte of Logique* (London, 1552).

Wood, Andy. 'The Place of Custom in Plebeian Political Culture: England, 1550–1800', *Social History*, 22, 1 (January 1997), pp. 46–60.

—— *The Politics of Social Conflict: The Peak Country, 1520–1770* (Cambridge, 1999).

Wood, Neal. *Cicero's Social and Political Thought* (Berkeley, CA, 1988).

—— 'Cicero and the Political Thought of the Early English Renaissance', *Modern Language Quarterly*, 51, 2 (June 1990), pp. 185–207.

—— 'Foundations of Political Economy: The New Moral Philosophy of Sir Thomas Smith', in Paul A. Fideler and T. F. Mayer, eds, *Political Thought and the Tudor Commonwealth* (London and New York, 1992), ch. 5.

Woodward, D. 'The Background to the Statute of Artificers: The Genesis of Labor Policy', *Economic History Review*, 2nd ser., 1, 33 (1980), pp. 32–44.

Woodward, Richard. *An Argument in Support of the Right of the Poor in the Kingdom of Ireland, to a National Provision . . .* (London, 1775 [1768, 1772]).

—— *An Address to the Public, on the Expediency of a Regular Plan for the Maintenance and Government of the Poor* . . . (London, 1775).

Woolfson, Jonathan, ed. *Reassessing Tudor Humanism* (Basingstoke, 2000).

Workman, H. B. *John Wyclif*, 2 vols (Oxford, 1926).

Wrightson, Keith. *English Society, 1500–1680* (London, 1982).

—— ' "Sorts of People" in Tudor and Stuart England', in Jonathan Barry and Christopher Brooks, eds, The *Middling Sort of People* (Basingstoke, 1994), pp. 28–51.

—— 'The Politics of the Parish in Early Modern England', in Paul Griffiths, Adam Fox and Steve Hindle, eds, *The Experience of Authority in Early Modern England* (Basingstoke, 1996), pp. 10–46.

—— *Earthly Necessities: Economic Lives in Early Modern Britain* (New Haven, CT, and London, 2000).

Wrigley, E. A. 'The Growth of Population in Eighteenth-Century England: A Conundrum Resolved', *Past and Present*, 98 (February 1983), pp. 121–50.

—— *Continuity, Chance and Change* (Cambridge, 1988).

—— and R. S. Schofield, R. *The Population History of England, 1541–1871: A Reconstruction* (Cambridge, 1989 [London, 1981]).

Ziemke, D. C. *Love for the Neighbor in Luther's Theology* (Minneapolis, 1963).

Zook, Melinda S. *Radical Whigs and Conspiratorial Politics in Late Stuart England* (University Park, PE, 1999).

Index